MW00771985

Colloquial

Persian

The Colloquial Series

Series adviser: Gary King

The following languages are available in the Colloquial series:

Afrikaans
Albanian
Amharic
Arabic (Levantine)
Arabic of Egypt
Arabic of the Gulf and Saudi Arabia
Basque
Bulgarian
* Cambodian
* Cantonese
* Chinese
Croatian and Serbian
Czech
Danish
Dutch
Estonian
Finnish
French
German
Greek
Gujarati
Hindi
Hungarian
Icelandic
Indonesian
Italian
Japanese
Korean
Latvian
Lithuanian
Malay
Mongolian
Norwegian
Panjabi
Persian
Polish
Portuguese
Portuguese of Brazil
Romanian
* Russian
Scottish Gaelic
Slovak
Slovene
Somali
* Spanish
Spanish of Latin America
Swedish
* Thai
Turkish
Urdu
Ukrainian
* Vietnamese
Welsh

Accompanying cassette(s) (*and CDs) are available for all the above titles. They can be ordered through your bookseller, or send payment with order to Taylor & Francis/Routledge Ltd, ITPS, Cheriton House, North Way, Andover, Hants SP10 5BE, UK, or to Routledge Inc, 29 West 35th Street, New York NY 10001, USA.

COLLOQUIAL CD-ROMs: Multimedia Language Courses
Available in: Chinese, French, Portuguese and Spanish

Colloquial
Persian

The Complete Course for Beginners

Abdi Rafiee

London and New York

First published 2001
by Routledge
11 New Fetter Lane, London EC4P 4EE

Simultaneously published in the USA and Canada
by Routledge
29 West 35th Street, New York, NY 10001

Reprinted 2002, 2003

Routledge is an imprint of the Taylor & Francis Group

© 2001 Abdi Rafiee

Typeset in Times by Network Languages Limited, UK.
Printed and bound in Great Britain by Biddles Ltd, Guildford and King's Lynn

All rights reserved. No part of this book may be reprinted or reproduced or utilised in any form or by any electronic, mechanical, or other means, now known or hereafter invented, including photocopying and recording, or in any information storage or retrieval system, without permission in writing from the publishers.

British Library Cataloguing in Publication Data
A catalogue record for this book is available from the British Library

Library of Congress Cataloguing in Publication Data
Rafiee, Abdi, 1947–
Colloquial Persian: the complete course for beginners / Abdi Rafiee.
p. cm. — (Colloquials)
1. Persian language – Textbooks for foreign speakers – English. I. Title.
PK6239.5E5 R34 2001
491.55′82421 – dc21 00-062752

ISBN 0–415–15749–8 (book)
ISBN 0–415–15750–1 (cassettes)
ISBN 0–415–28907–6 (CDs)
ISBN 0–415–15751–X (book, CD and cassettes course)

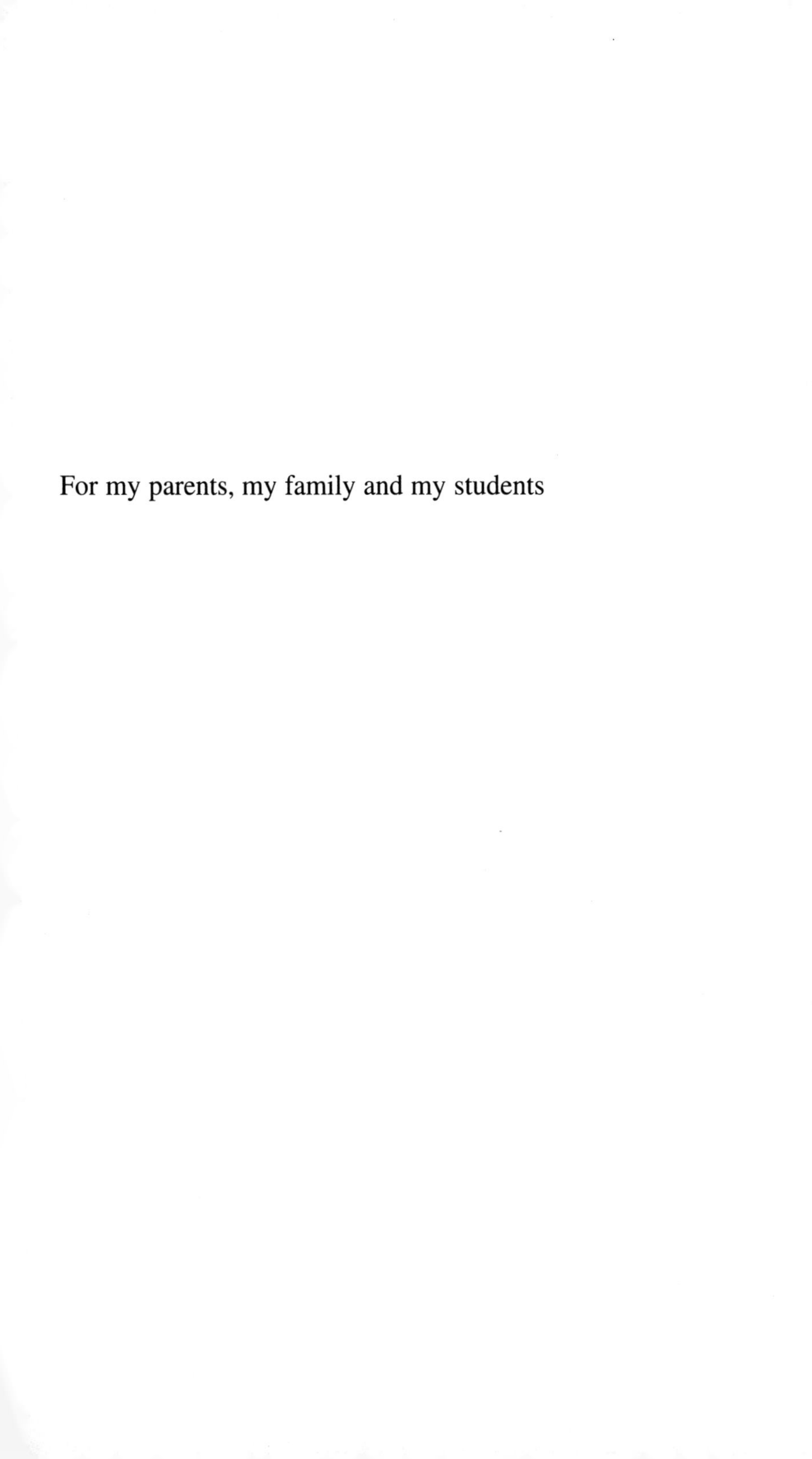

For my parents, my family and my students

Contents

Acknowledgements

I would like to record my sincere gratitude to my sons, Hameed and Siam, for putting up with a part-time father while this course was being prepared, and to my wife, Sima, for filling the gap, as well as for reading the manuscript and making valuable suggestions. My thanks also go to the editorial team at Routledge for their comments and support.

Introduction

Congratulations on taking the first step towards learning the language of Hafez, Sa`di, Ferdowsi and Khayyam, to name but a few of the literary giants Iran has proudly produced over the centuries as part of its contribution to the wealth of the world's cultural heritage.

On a practical level, I hope you will agree with the notion that a European learning another European language is one thing; a European learning a non-European language is quite another. We cannot separate a language from the cultural factors (beliefs, assumptions, etc.) that have influenced and shaped it over the years. The cultural gap is significantly narrower and shallower between language communities within Europe, than between Europe and the East. This means that a European attempting to learn an Eastern language, will need to bridge a much wider and deeper cultural gap, than if he or she were learning another European language.

In this course, I have tried to present a holistic picture of the Persian language, which includes not only the grammar of the word, the phrase and the sentence (i.e. the traditional view of grammar) but also the 'grammar' of what to say to whom and how to say or not to say it (i.e. the grammar of communication). So, we will be concerned not just with 'grammatical accuracy', but also with social and cultural appropriateness of what we say in Persian.

Learning a foreign language without bothering about the (often) culture-specific norms governing the use of that language would be like learning how to drive a car without bothering about the Highway Code!

Who is the course intended for?

This course is intended for two types of learner:

(a) Those who wish to learn to speak, read and write in Persian.

(b) Those who wish to be able to communicate in Persian, without learning the script.

Type of Persian used

The type of Persian used in this course is educated colloquial Tehrani, which is understood throughout Iran, thanks to the media. Although the principal objective of this course is to introduce spoken Persian, sufficient guidance is given for those who wish to go on to study literary Persian.

Use of jargon

I have tried to keep grammatical jargon to a minimum. Where a technical word is used, it is often backed up by a clarifying example. For instance, under **Demonstratives**, you are told: How to say 'this'/'these'; 'that'/those'.

Layout of the book

The book is divided into two parts. The first part introduces the Persian sound system and the script supported by a comprehensive exercise at the end. The second part comprises sixteen lessons. Each lesson contains two dialogues in which everyday language is introduced in its appropriate social and cultural setting. Each dialogue is supported by **Vocabulary**, **Language points** and **Exercises**. Each lesson ends with a **Comprehension test**, which brings together the main language points introduced in the lesson.

Sound change in casual speech

Some sounds tend to influence the quality or length of their neighbours. Sound changes familiar to English speakers are not reflected in the transcription. Examples: **n** followed by **b**, **p**, **m** is pronounced **m**. For example, **šanbe** 'Saturday' is pronounced **šambe**. In the transcription, however, the original form **šanbe** has been used to prevent a clash with the Persian spelling.

The consonant cluster **nd** is normally reduced to **n** as in **raftand** 'they went', which is often reduced to **raftan**. Again, the original form **raftand** is reflected in the transcription.

Using the course

Listening

Listening to Persian spoken by native speakers helps you to gain mastery of the sound system, improve your pronunciation and develop a good Persian accent. Dialogues and exercises involving listening are marked with a cassette icon ▪.

The dialogues

To understand each dialogue, you need to look not only at the vocabulary but also at the language points where linguistic and relevant cultural explanations are given. You may also need to refer to the glossaries at the end of the book.

The exercises

In most cases, the first question in each exercise has been answered as an example. The last exercise after each dialogue is intended to broaden the lens and use the grammar in a variety of other contexts. For these exercises and the comprehension test at the end of each lesson, you will need to refer to the glossaries at the end of the book. All the answers are given in **Key to the exercises**.

Role plays

This is a very important part of the course. Each lesson is supplemented with a series of role-play exercises. These are fully explained on the accompanying cassettes. Follow the instructions and make the most of your free time (e.g. in the car; in the kitchen; or at bed time).

A bilingual dictionary – an essential tool

This course hopes to help you get to a stage where you can study the language independently. This is where a 'good' (English–Persian, Persian–English) dictionary will be an essential tool.

You can help improve the course

Everything is known by everyone. 'Everyone' has yet to be born!
(a famous Persian saying)

Your comments on the form and content of the course would be most welcome. If an aspect of the language has not been covered (sufficiently), please let us know.

On the English transcription

The English transcription of Persian words appears in **bold type**. Letters or symbols in round brackets represent sounds that are normally dropped in casual speech. All English transcription should be read according to the values given below.

Symbol	*Sounds like*	*In the (mostly English) word(s)*
ā	a	father
a	a	add
ai	i	ice
b	b	bad
c	ch	church
d	d	dad
e	e	egg
ei	ei	rein
f	f	fee
g	g	good
ĝ	g	regime
h	h	hand
i	i	ski
j	j	joke
k	k	kite
l	l	leek (*not* keel)
m	m	mad
n	n	noon
o	awe	awe (British; shorter)
oi	oi	coin
ou	ou	dough (American)
p	p	pad
q	–	French 'r' (harder)
r	r	road (Scottish)

Symbol	*Sounds like*	*In the (mostly English) word(s)*
s	s	sad
s̄	sh	she
t	t	tea
u	u	rude
ui	ooey	gooey (one syllable)
v	v	vest
w	w	west
x	ch	loch; Bach
y	y	yeast
z	z	zip
`	–	Cockney 't' in water

Note: Persian consonants and vowels are described on pp. 7–19.

Abbreviations used in the book

a	adjective	*op*	opposite
adv	adverb	*p*	preposition
col	colloquial	*pl*	plural
con	conjunction	*pol*	polite
dem	demonstrative	*ps*	present stem
f	formal	*SI*	structured infinitive
inf	informal	*sing*	singular
l	literary	*SO*	someone
lit	literally	*ST*	something
n	noun	*sub*	subjunctive

Cross-referencing style

Cross-references are made throughout the book to the particular page number(s).

Reading and writing in Persian

Introduction

Modern Persian uses the Arabic alphabet. The Persian sounds **c**, **g**, **ĝ** and **p** are not represented by any Arabic letters. Therefore, when the Arabic script was adopted, four of its letters were slightly modified to produce new letters representing the above sounds.

Persian is written and read from right to left. The first page of a Persian book is the page nearest to the right-hand side cover. Persian numbers, however, are written and read from left to right.

Initially it would be better to write on ruled paper to help you to develop a pleasant-looking handwriting. This is because letters are positioned in relation to a horizontal line.

Already, you will know a few hundred words commonly used in Persian! These are the words Persian has borrowed from other (mostly European) languages. Some of these words are pronounced in Persian more or less the same as they are in their language(s) of origin, e.g. 'soup', 'team', 'jet'. Others have been slightly modified to fit into the Persian sound system: **kelās** for 'class'. To minimize the 'unknown' area, some of these 'familiar' words will be used when introducing the Persian script. The purpose here is to use a familiar launching pad that would, I hope, help the learner land smoothly on the Persian writing pad, so to speak.

When we learn a new language with a writing system entirely different from that of our own, we are often concerned about (if not intimidated by) at least two things:

(a) having to learn a completely new set of symbols;
(b) having to cope with potential irregularities in the relationship between the symbols and the sounds they represent.

On (a), I cannot say much except to assure you that the comparatively 'phonetic' nature of the Persian alphabet greatly facilitates the learning of the writing system. In terms of the relation between what you see and how you pronounce it, Persian is much more consistent than English. Most sounds are represented by only one letter in Persian.

In Persian, the maximum number of letters representing the same sound is four. These are the letters that represent the sound **z**. Significantly, wherever you see any of these four letters, you can be absolutely certain that the sound represented is **z**.

The alphabet (including the consonants)

There are 32 letters in the alphabet. They help to represent 24 consonants and 11 vowels. English speakers will need to learn two new (consonant) sounds. The remaining consonants and vowels are more or less familiar to English speakers. The letter و **vāv** is mute in certain words.

Please do not be intimidated by what I am going to show you now – the entire alphabet! The purpose is to give you a bird's-eye view of all the Persian letters, and their various shapes, in their natural (alphabetical) order. This is the order in which you will need to remember the letters if you wish to make good use of your Persian–English dictionary. Furthermore, it will be used as a reference later when individual letters are introduced.

Chart 1 The alphabet (including the consonants)

Persian letters showing their various shapes in a word

Sound	*Shapes*				*Name*
	Final separate	*Final joined*	*Medial*	*Initial*	
(see vowels)	ا	ا	ا	(see vowels)	**alef**
b	ب	ب	بـ	بـ	**be**
p	پ	پ	پـ	پـ	**pe**
t	ت	ت	تـ	تـ	**te**
s	ث	ث	ثـ	ثـ	**se**
j	ج	ج	جـ	جـ	**jim**
c	چ	چ	چـ	چـ	**ce**
h	ح	ح	حـ	حـ	**he-jimi**
x	خ	خ	خـ	خـ	**xe**
d	د	د	د	د	**dāl**

Sound	*Shapes*				*Name*
	Final separate	*Final joined*	*Medial*	*Initial*	
z	ذ	ذ	ذ	ذ	**zāl**
r	ر	ر	ر	ر	**re**
z	ز	ز	ز	ز	**ze**
ĝ	ژ	ژ	ژ	ژ	**ĝe**
s	س	س	سـ	سـ	**sin**
s̄	ش	ش	شـ	شـ	**s̄in**
s	ص	ص	صـ	صـ	**sād**
z	ض	ض	ضـ	ضـ	**zād**
t	ط	ط	ط	ط	**tā**
z	ظ	ظ	ظ	ظ	**zā**
ʽ	ع	ـع	ـعـ	عـ	**ein**
q	غ	ـغ	ـغـ	غـ	**qein**
f	ف	ف	فـ	فـ	**fe**
q	ق	ق	قـ	قـ	**qāf**
k	ک	ک	کـ	کـ	**kāf**
g	گ	گ	گـ	گـ	**gāf**
l	ل	ل	لـ	لـ	**lām**
m	م	م	مـ	مـ	**mim**
n	ن	ن	نـ	نـ	**nun**
v	و	و	و	و	**vāv**
h	ه	ه	ـهـ	هـ	**he-do-ces̄m**
y	ی	ـی	یـ	یـ	**ye**

A bird's-eye view of the alphabet reveals the following facts.

On sounds

Two consonant sounds are unfamiliar to English speakers: **x** (letter خ **xe**) and **q** (letters غ **qein** and ق **qāf**).

Persian **x** is very similar to the sound represented by 'ch' in (Scottish) 'loch' and in German 'Bach'. Persian **q** is very close to French 'r', only a bit harder.

Most Persian sounds are represented by one letter each.

t is represented by 2 letters: ت **te** and ط **tā**
q is represented by 2 letters: غ **qein** and ق **qāf**
h is represented by 2 letters: ح **he-jimi** and ه **he-do-cešm**
s is represented by 3 letters: ث **se**, س **sin** and ص **sād**
z is represented by 4 letters: ذ **zāl**, ز **ze**, ض **zād** and ظ **zā**
` is represented by letter ع **ein** and ***hamze*** (see **glottal stop**, pp. 17–18).

On shapes

Each letter may have one, two, three or four shapes for various positions in a word. Nine letters have more or less the same shape for all positions in a word. These are:

ا **alef**, د **dāl**, ذ **zāl**, ر **re**, ز **ze**, ژ **ĝe**, ط **tā**, ظ **zā**, و **vāv**

Twenty letters have two shapes: small (for the beginning or middle of a word) and large (for the end of a word):

بـ ب **be**, پـ پ **pe**, تـ ت **te**, ثـ ث **se**, جـ ج **jim**, چـ چ **ce**, حـ ح **he-jimi**, خـ خ **xe**,
سـ س **sin**, شـ ش **šin**, صـ ص **sād**, ضـ ض **zād**, فـ ف **fe**, قـ ق **qāf**,
کـ ک **kāf**, گـ گ **gāf**, لـ ل **lām**, مـ م **mim**, نـ ن **nun**, یـ ی **ye**

Letter ه **he-do-cešm** has three shapes: initial, medial and final. Letters ع **ein** and غ **qein** have four shapes: initial, medial, final joined and final separate. Within the same word, all but 7 letters can be connected to the letters on either side – in handwriting and in print. These 7 letters can only be connected to the preceding (not the following) letter. These are:

ا **alef**, د **dāl**, ذ **zāl**, ر **re**, ز **ze**, ژ **ĝe**, و **vāv**

Note: As we go through the examples, you will note that the final shapes of some letters (when occurring after a connectable letter) are very slightly modified to make the 'connection' easier (and nicer). In the introduction to Persian letters, some of the most common European loanwords and names will be used. However, please bear in mind that these non-Persian words are not always pronounced by Iranians exactly as they are pronounced in their language of origin.

Word stress normally falls on the last syllable of a word. Underlining indicates stress. Stressed or unstressed, a Persian vowel is normally pronounced in full.

The vowels

Persian vowels are fairly similar to their English counterparts.

Chart 2 Persian vowels showing their various shapes

	Vowel shapes		*Vowel symbol*
Final	*Medial*	*Initial*	
ا	ا	آ	**ā**
و	و	او	**u**
ی	یـ	ایـ	**i**
ه	ـَ	اَ	**a**
ه	ـِ	اِ	**e**
و	ـُ	اُ	**o**
ای	ایـ	آیـ	**ai**
ـِ ی	ـِ یـ	اِیـ	**ei**
ـُ وْ	ـُ وْ	اُوْ	**ou**
وی	ویـ	اُیـ	**oi**
وی	ویـ	اویـ	**ui**

In addition to their roles as consonants, letters و **vāv**, هـ **he-do-cešm** and ی **ye** (see **Chart 1**, pp. 7–8) are used to represent vowels in the medial and final positions. Thus, the shape of a vowel may slightly change depending on where it occurs in a word: beginning, middle or end. When the word begins with a vowel, the first letter, ا **alef**, is used as a prop: اَ = **a**, اِ = **e**, اُ = **o**. Sometimes, depending on the spelling of the word, letter ع **ein** acts as a prop. The first six are called pure vowels. The remaining five are compound vowels (diphthongs).

Vowels **ā**, **u** and **i** are long. Vowels **a**, **e** and **o** are short. Vowels **ai**, **ei**, **ou** and **oi** are more or less similar to their English counterparts. Vowel **ui** is similar to the sound represented by '-ooey' in the English word 'gooey' but pronounced as one syllable – **gui** rather than **gu** + **i**.

Most vowels are represented by letters and are therefore incorporated into the word. Other vowels use add-on symbols that are placed above or below the letters they follow. A stroke placed above a letter (ـَ) represents the sound **a**; below it, represents **e**. The symbol (ُ) placed above a letter (ـُ) represents the vowel **o**. These symbols are placed above, or below, the consonant they follow, e.g. بَ = **ba**, بِ = **be**, بُ = **bo**.

In the middle column, the horizontal line (ـــ) has been used as a dummy consonant to show the position of the Persian vowel symbols (ـَـِـُ) in relation to the consonant they follow – i.e. above or below it. Unlike the long vowels, these short-vowel symbols are not incorporated into the main body of the word. The final version of these vowels, however, make use of proper letters and are therefore incorporated into the word.

The final shape of letter ـه **he-do-cešm** (i.e. ه) is used as the final shape of both vowels **a** and **e**. You may be relieved to know that there is only one word in Persian that ends in the vowel **a** and uses (ه) to represent it. That word is **na** meaning 'no' (a negative reply). Now, with the help of the two charts in this section (see pp. 7–8, 10) let us do some reading and writing.

Unjoinable letters

We begin with the seven unjoinable letters referred to earlier. These are consonant letters: د **dāl**, ذ **zāl**, ر **re**, ز **ze**, ژ **ĝe**, و **vāv** and the first letter in the alphabet, ا **alef**, which is used in vowels. Some of the vowels are also introduced in this section. You are reminded that these seven letters cannot be connected to the *following* letter, but can be connected to a preceding letter, if it is a joinable one. To write the word **dād** 'she'/'he gave', we need:

d = letter **dāl** = د
ā = medial shape of vowel **ā** = ا
d = letter **dāl** = د
Here is the result: داد

To write the word **āzād** 'free', we need:

ā = initial shape of vowel **ā** = آ
z = letter **ze** = ز
ā = medial shape of vowel **ā** = ا
d = letter **dāl** = د
The result is: آزاد

To write the word **dud** 'smoke', we need:

d = letter **dāl** = د
u = medial shape of vowel **u** = و
d = letter **dāl** = د
Here is the result: دود

To write the word **did** 'he'/'she saw', we need:

d = letter **dāl** = د
i = medial shape of vowel **i** = ـيـ
d = letter **dāl** = د
Here is the result: ديد

Note: The medial shape of vowel **i** uses letter **ye** which is a joinable letter. This is why ـيـ and د are connected.

To write the word **dad** 'beast', we need:

d = letter **dāl** = د
a = medial shape of vowel **a** = ـَـ
d = letter **dāl** = د
Here is the result: دَد

To write the word **reĝe** 'parade', we need:

r = letter **re** = ر
e = medial shape of vowel **e** = ـِـ
ĝ = letter **ĝe** = ژ
e = final shape of vowel **e** = ه
Here is the result: رِژه

To write the word **roz** 'rose' (flower), we need:

r = letter **re** = ر
o = medial shape of vowel **o** = ـُـ
z = letter **ze** = ز
Here is the result: رُز

To write the word **daiv** 'diving board', we need:

d = letter **dāl** = د
ai = medial shape of vowel **ai** = ایـ
v = letter **vāv** = و
Here is the result: دایو

To write the word **dei** (the tenth month in the Iranian calendar), we need:

d = letter **dāl** = د
ei = final shape of vowel **ei** = ـِ ی
Here is the result: دِی

To write the word **dou** 'running', we need:

d = letter **dāl** = د
ou = final shape of vowel **ou** = ـُ وْ
Here is the result: دُوْ

The short vowel symbols (ـَـِـُـ) which are placed above or below the line are normally dropped. This should not cause much difficulty once the skeleton of the word has become familiar to us.

Joinable letters

So far, we have been introduced to the unjoinable letters together with the various shapes of some of the more common vowels. In this section, we will see joinable letters and their various shapes, as well as the remaining vowels, in action. An attempt has been made to include all possible shapes of letters, beginning with smaller words.

Letters ب **be**, پ **pe**, ت **te**, ث **se** use the same skeleton. Their difference is in the number and position of dots. Letter ن **nun** may also be included here, although its final shape is deeper and rounded. To write **bād** 'wind', we need:

b = initial shape of letter **be** = بـ
ā = medial shape of vowel **ā** = ا
d = letter **dāl** = د
The result looks like this: باد

To write **tip** 'brigade', we need:

t = initial shape of letter **te** = تـ
i = medial shape of vowel **i** = یـ
p = final shape of letter **pe** = پ
The result looks like this: تیپ

To write **na** 'no', we need:

n = initial shape of letter **nun** = نـ
a = final shape of vowel **a** = ه
The result looks like this: نه

To write **bad** 'bad', we need:

b = initial shape of letter **be** = بـ
a = medial shape of vowel **a** = ـَ
d = letter **dāl** = د
The result looks like this: بَد

Note: The medial shape of vowel **a** is not a letter and therefore not included in the skeleton of the word. This is why بـ and د are connected. This rule applies to all instances where a vowel is represented by a sign placed above or below a preceding letter.

Letters ج **jim**, چ **ce**, ح **he-jimi**, خ **xe** use the same skeleton. Their difference is in the number and position of dots. To write **cāp** 'printing', we need:

c = initial shape of letter **ce** = چـ
ā = medial shape of vowel **ā** = ـا
p = final shape of letter **pe** = ـپ
The result is: چاپ

To write **jip** 'jeep', we need:

j = initial shape of letter **jim** = جـ
i = medial shape of vowel **i** = ـیـ
p = final shape of letter **pe** = ـپ
The result is: جیپ

To write **jet** 'jet', we need:

j = initial shape of letter **jim** = جـ
e = medial shape of vowel **e** = ـِـ
t = final shape of letter **te** = ـت
The result is: جِت

To write **pic** 'screw', we need:

p = initial shape of letter **pe** = پـ
i = medial shape of vowel **i** = ـیـ
c = final shape of letter **ce** = ـچ
The result is: پیچ

Letters س **sin** and ش **s̄in** use the same skeleton. Their difference is in dots.

To write the English loanword **saiz** 'size', we need:

s = initial shape of letter **sin** = سـ
ai = medial shape of vowel **ai** = ـایـ
z = letter **ze** = ز
The result is: سایز

To write **ris̄** 'beard', we need:

r = letter **re** = ر
i = medial shape of vowel **i** = ـیـ
s̄ = final shape of letter **s̄in** = ـش
The result is: ریش

Letters ف **fe** and ق **qāf** use a more or less similar skeleton. The final shape of ق **qāf** is deeper and rounded. To write **fis̄** 'fiche', 'docket', we need:

f = initial shape of letter **fe** = فـ
i = medial shape of vowel **i** = ـیـ
s̄ = final shape of letter **s̄in** = ـش
The result is: فیش

To write **faqir** 'beggar', we need:

f = initial shape of letter **fe** = فـ
a = medial shape of vowel **a** = ـَـ
q = medial shape of letter **qāf** = قـ
i = medial shape of vowel **i** = يـ
r = letter **re** = ر
The result is: فَقير

To write **rafiq** 'friend', we need:

r = letter **re** = ر
a = medial shape of vowel **a** = ـَـ
f = medial shape of letter **fe** = فـ
i = medial shape of vowel **i** = يـ
q = final shape of letter **qāf** = ق
The result is: رَفيق

Letters ک **kāf** and گ **gāf** use the same skeleton – the latter has an additional stroke close to, and parallel with the original. To write **jak** 'jack', we need:

j = initial shape of letter **jim** = جـ
a = medial shape of vowel **a** = ـَـ
k = final shape of letter **kāf** = ک
The result is: جَک

To write **kaj** 'tilted', we need:

k = initial shape of letter **kāf** = کـ
a = medial shape of vowel **a** = ـَـ
j = final shape of letter **jim** = ج
The result is: کَج

Note the two shapes of letter ل **lām** in the following words:

elephant **fil** فيل kilo **kilu** کيلو Lee **li** لی Eileen **ailin** آيلين

Note: A combination of letter ل **lām** and the first letter (ا **alef**) used in the vowel **ā** often looks like this: لا when standing alone; and like this: ـلا when joined up to a preceding letter, e.g.

class **kelās** کِلاس a town **lār** لار

Note the two shapes of letter م **mim** in these words:

timer **taimer** تايمِر
team **tim** تيم
atom **atom** اَتُم
omelette **omlet** اُملِت
mode, fashion **mod** مُد
zoom **zum** زوم
family, relatives **fāmil** فاميل

Note the three shapes of letter هـ **he-do-česm** in these words:

hotel **hotel** هُتِل spring (season) **bahār** بَهار hall **hāl** هال
Fahrenheit **fārenhait** فارِنهایت shah **šāh** شاه

The vowel **oi** is very rare in Persian. The only example normally given is **xoi**, the name of a town in Iran. To write this word in Persian, we need:

x = initial shape of letter **xe** = خـ
oi = final shape of vowel **oi** = وی
Here is the result: خوی

Vowel **ui** occurs mostly in literary Persian, as in گوی **gui** 'ball' and بوی **bui** 'smell'. A more common example is رویداد **ruidād** 'event'.

Letters ص **sād** and ض **zād** use the same skeleton. The latter has one dot over it. Note their two shapes:

hundred **sad** صَد
destination **maqsad** مَقصَد
special **maxsus** مَخصوص
multiplication **zarb** ضَرب
ill **mariz** مَریض

Letters ط **tā** and ظ **zā** use the same skeleton but the latter has a dot over it. They have only one shape.

Letters ع **ein** and غ **qein** use the same skeleton. The latter has a dot over it. They have four shapes.

To write **`id** 'festival', we need:

` = initial shape of letter **ein** = عـ
i = medial shape of vowel **i** = ـیـ
d = letter **dāl** = د
The result is: عید

To write **ba`d** 'then', we need:

b = initial shape of letter **be** = بـ
a = medial shape of vowel **a** = ـَـ
` = medial shape of letter **ein** = ـعـ
d = letter **dāl** = د
The result is: بَعد

To write **rob`** 'quarter', we need:

r = letter **re** = ر
o = medial shape of vowel **o** = ـُـ
b = medial shape of letter **be** = ـبـ
` = final joined shape of letter **ein** = ـع
The result is: رُبع

To write **šar`** 'divine law', we need:

š = initial shape of letter **šin** = شـ
a = medial shape of vowel **a** = ـَ
r = letter **re** = ر
` = final separate shape of letter **ein** = ع
The result is: شَرع

Note: The final separate shape of ع **ein** and غ **qein** is used when the preceding letter is unjoinable.

The glottal stop

The glottal stop (`) is the sound of 't' in words like 'water' when pronounced with a Cockney accent. The glottal stop can occur in all three positions: beginning, middle or end of a word. At the beginning of a word, it may be represented by:

- the initial form of any of the vowels described above – using the first letter in the alphabet: ا (see **Chart 2** above, p. 10); or by:
- the initial form of letter **ein** عـ (see above).

Occurring in the medial or final position, the glottal stop may be represented by:

- An appropriate shape of letter ع **ein** (e.g. بَعد **ba`d**; رَعد **ra`d**); or by:
- A feature called ***hamze***, which will be explained below.

The generic shape of ***hamze*** is (ء). In Persian, the ***hamze*** sign occurs in the middle or at the end of a word. Depending on the spelling of the word, it is placed over one of these letters:

أ ئـ ؤ

Examples:

boss **ra`is** رئیس
head, apex **ra`s** رَأس
faithful, a believer **mo`men** مُؤمِن

In the final position, the ***hamze*** sign may also occur on its own. Examples:

badness, evil **su`** سوء an essay **enšā`** اِنشاء object, thing **šei`** شِیء

The glottal stop is often replaced by a softer sound, or omitted altogether, when it occurs in the middle or at the end of a word – particularly in casual speech. Consider the word بَعد **ba`d** 'then', 'afterwards', which is pronounced **ba:d** in casual speech. To compensate for the loss of the glottal stop, the preceding vowel **a** is prolonged. (Note: The spelling is not affected.) It is this increased length of the vowel that distinguishes this word from: بَد **bad** 'bad'. The *hamze* occurring between vowels may be replaced by **y**,

asset **dārāyi** دارایی asset **dārā`i** دارائی

or simply ignored resulting in a soft glide from the first vowel to the second: اِرائه **erāe** 'presentation'. In the final position, it is completely ignored: اِمضاء **emzā** 'signature'.

Note: Since all vowels occurring initially normally begin with a glottal stop, the use of the symbol (`) in the initial position was considered unnecessary and therefore omitted from the English transcription.

Other signs used in the Persian script

tašdid (gemination) = (ّ)

Gemination is the double pronunciation of a sound (normally a consonant) within a word. The letter representing that sound is written only once, but with a *tašdid* sign over it to show that the sound of that letter should be pronounced long. Examples:

foreign exchange bureau **sarrāfi** صَرّافی child **bacce** بچّه

Sometimes the presence of *tašdid* creates a difference in meaning, as in:

a builder **bannā** بَنّا a building **banā** بَنا
substance, matter **mādde** مادّه female (animal) **māde** ماده

tanvin = (ً)

This sign normally appears over an **alef** (اً). The combination is pronounced **an**. Examples:

about (in the region of) **hodudan** حُدوداً
approximately **taqriban** تقریباً

sokun = (ْ)

Normally placed over a consonant, this sign shows that the consonant is not followed by a vowel. It is used to prevent confusion. For instance, to ensure that the English loanword 'mask' is pronounced correctly in Persian, i.e. as one syllable **māsk** (rather than **māsek**, etc.), a *sokun* may be placed over the (ســ), thus: ماسْک **māsk** 'mask'. This sign has been used with the letter **vāv** وْ to represent a **w** sound in the vowel **ou**, e.g. شُوْ **šou** 'show'.

The short alef = (ٰ)

Used in words of Arabic origin, this sign represents an **ā** sound. Its most common position is over letter **ye** (یٰ). The combination is pronounced **ā**. Examples:

Jesus **isā** عیسیٰ   Moses **musā** موسیٰ   even **hattā** حَتّیٰ

We have now covered all the various shapes of Persian vowels and consonants, as well as the other signs used in the script. The exercise below is to help us to revise all the above. **Charts 1** and **2** may be used as a reference in the future and, if needed, when attempting the following exercise. (The answers are given at the end of **Key to the exercises**, pp. 207–36.)

Match the English–Persian equivalents

1 hard **saxt**
2 e.g. **masalan**
3 nail **mix**
4 essence **zāt**
5 sauce **sos**
6 good **xub**
7 guarantor **zāmen**
8 five **panj**
9 mask **māsk**
10 yard **yārd**
11 under **zir**
12 posing **ĝest**
13 a minor **saqir**
14 service **servis**
15 parrot **tuti**
16 protection **hefz**
17 tasty **laziz**
18 then **ba`d**
19 beard **riš**
20 oppression **zolm**
21 signature **emzā`**
22 builder **bannā**
23 one third **sols**
24 asset **dārāyi**
25 boss **ra`is**
26 photograph **aks**
27 asphalt **āsfālt**
28 poor **faqir**
29 Tehran **tehrān**
30 nine **noh**
31 gas **gāz**
32 rival **harif**
33 furniture **mobl**
34 lamp **lāmp**
35 shah **šāh**
36 size **saiz**
37 pilgrim **hāji**
38 greedy **haris**
39 ill **mariz**
40 citizen **tābe`**
41 a blade **tiq**
42 nearly **taqriban**
43 hundred **sad**
44 a fly **magas**
45 believer **mo`men**
46 visa **vizā**
47 kilo **kilu**
48 absorption **jazb**
49 Pope **pāp**
50 AIDS **eidz**
51 bottle **botri**
52 decision **tasmim**
53 question **so`āl**
54 responsible **mas`ul**
55 hall **hāl**
56 spoon **qāšoq**
57 cheque **cek**
58 passport **pāsport**
59 atom **atom**
60 often **aqlab**
61 building **banā**
62 asset **dārā`i**
63 apex, head **ra`s**
64 no **na**
65 oppressed **mazlum**
66 fuse **fiuz**
67 morning **sobh**
68 badness **su`**
69 child **bacce**
70 agent **ma`mur**

اَتُم ...	پاپ ...	حاجی ...	سوء ...
اَغلَب ...	پاسپورت ...	حِفظ ...	سُؤال ...
اِمضاء ...	تابع ...	دارائی ...	سِرویس ...
اِیدز ...	تقریباً ...	دارایی ...	شاه ...
بَچّه ...	تیغ ...	ذات ...	صُبح ...
بُطری ...	تَصمیم ...	رَأس ...	صَد ...
بَعد ...	ثُلث ...	رَئیس ...	صَغیر ...
بَنا ...	جَذب ...	سایز ...	فیوز ...
بَنّا ...	چِک ...	سُس ...	فَقیر ...

قاشُق ...	عَکس ...	پَنج ...
کیلو ...	لامپ ...	ضامِن ...
گاز ...	مُبل ...	ظُلم ...
ماسْک ...	مَگَس ...	طوطی ...
مَأمور ...	حَریص ...	ژِست ...
مُؤمِن ...	مَریض ...	زیر ...
مَسئول ...	حَریف ...	
مَظلوم ...	ریش ...	
نه ...	آسفالت ...	
ویزا ...	لَذیذ ...	
هال ...	میخ ...	
یارد ...	سَخت ...	
تِهران ...	مَثَلاً ...	
نُه ...	خوب ...	

1 سلام salām

Greetings

By the end of this lesson, you should be able to:

- exchange greeting at various times of the day and say 'goodbye'
- introduce yourself
- say 'thank you'
- use the polite form for 'you', 'he', 'she'

Dialogue 1 Greeting and leave-taking

It's 8 a.m. at the office. Members of staff greet each other briefly and go into their offices. Later in the evening, they say goodbye.

A: سلام. صبح بخیر.
B: سلام. صبح بخیر.

A: خدا حافظ. شب بخیر.
B: خدا حافظ. شب بخیر.

A: **salām. sob(h) bexeir.**
B: **salām. sob(h) bexeir.**

A: **xodā (h)āfez. šab bexeir.**
B: **xodā (h)āfez. šab bexeir.**

A: *Hello. Good morning.*
B: *Hello. Good morning.*

A: *Goodbye. Goodnight.*
B: *Goodbye. Goodnight.*

Vocabulary

سلام	**salām**	hello	خدا	**xodā**	God
صبح	**sob(h)**	morning	حافظ	**hāfez**	protector
بخیر	**bexeir**	may it be good	شب	**šab**	night

Language points

How to say 'good morning'

Here is the formula:

صبح	**sob(h)**	morning +
بخیر	**bexeir**	may it be good
صبح بخیر	**sob(h) bexeir**	Good morning

The same formula can be used to say:

شب بخیر	**šab bexeir**	Good night
عصر بخیر	**asr bexeir**	Good (late) afternoon
روز بخیر	**ruz bexeir**	Good day
ظهر بخیر	**zohr bexeir**	Good mid-day/noon
سفر بخیر	**safar bexeir**	(Have a) good journey

NB: Younger people are expected to say سلام **salām** 'hello' first.

Exercise 1

Match a letter with a number. Follow the example.

1	صبح	**sobh**	[b]	(a) night
2	سلام	**salām**	[ ]	(b) morning
3	شب	**šab**	[ ]	(c) hello
4	خدا حافظ	**xodā hāfez**	[ ]	(d) good morning
5	صبح بخیر	**sob(h) bexeir**	[ ]	(e) goodnight
6	شب بخیر	**šab bexeir**	[ ]	(f) goodbye

Exercise 2

Can you say these in Persian?

1 Good day.
2 Good afternoon.
3 (Have a) good journey.
4 Good mid-day/noon.

Dialogue 2 Introducing yourself

Mr Reza Farzad (F) has just been called by the information desk officer (O) at the airport in Tehran.

F: سلام خانم. من فرزاد هستم. رضا فرزاد.
O: آها بله، این تلفن برای شماست.
F: مرسی خانم. الو؟ ...

F: **salām xānom. man farzād hastam. rezā farzād.**
O: **āhā bale, in telefon barāye šomāst.**
F: **mersi xānom. alou? . . .**

F: *Hello madam. I'm Farzad. Reza Farzad.*
O: *Ah yes, this telephone call is for you.*
F: *Thank you madam. Hello? . . .*

Vocabulary

خانم	**xānom**	madam	تلفن	**telefon**	telephone
من	**man**	I	برای	**barāye**	for
رضا	**Rezā**	male name	شما	**šomā**	you (*f*)
هستم	**hastam**	(I) am	برای	**barāye**	
آها	**āhā**	Ah, Aha, Oh	شماست	**šomāst**	(it)'s for you
بله	**bale**	yes	مرسی	**mersi**	thanks
این	**in**	this	الو	**alou**	hello (telephone)

Language points

Personal pronouns

من **man** I
تو **to** you *(inf)*
او **u** he, she
آن **ān** it, that

ما **mā** we
شما **šomā** you *(f, pl)*
آنها **ānhā** they

Verb 'to be' in the present simple tense

How to say 'I am fine'; 'you are fine'; etc.

من خوب هستم.	**man xub hastam.**	I am fine.
تو خوب هستی.	**to xub hasti.**	You (*inf*) are fine.
او خوب است.	**u xub ast.**	He/She is fine.
آن خوب است.	**ān xub ast.**	It/That is fine.
ما خوب هستیم.	**mā xub hastim.**	We are fine.
شما خوب هستید.	**šomā xub hastid.**	You are fine.
آنها خوب هستند.	**ānhā xub hastand.**	They are fine.

The verb normally comes at the end of the sentence. After some vowels (such as **ā**) است **ast** 'is' often loses its vowel. Thus, شما **šomā** 'you' followed by است **ast** becomes شماست **šomāst**, as in this sentence from Dialogue 2:

این تلفن برای شماست. **in telefon barāye šomāst.**
This telephone call is for you.

In colloquial Persian, the sequence of sounds **ān** is often pronounced **un**. Thus, آن **ān** 'that'/'it' and آنها **ānhā** 'they' will be written as اون **un** and

اونها **unhā** in this book to reflect their colloquial pronunciation. Similarly, the sound combination **ām** is often pronounced **um** in some words, e.g. کدام **kodām** 'which' and آرام **ārām** 'calm' which are pronounced کدوم **kodum** and آروم **ārum** respectively.

Polite forms of 'you', 'he', 'she'

تو **to** 'you' and its verb forms are generally used among children and between close friends and relatives of similar age or social status (spouses, siblings). شما **šomā** 'you' and its verb forms are used between strangers and those who have a formal relationship, such as business people in formal meetings. A senior in age or status may use تو **to**, and receive شما **šomā**, when talking with a junior (compare with French *tu* and *vous*). If unsure, use شما **šomā**.

A more polite form for او **u** 'he'/'she', would be ایشون **išun** used with a plural verb form, e.g.

ایشون خانم جانسون هستند.
išun xānom-e jānson hastand.
She is Ms Johnson. (This is Ms Johnson – when introducing)

Exercise 3

Using the information given above (see p. 25), replace the word خوب **xub** 'fine' with خوشحال **xošhāl** 'happy', to produce the Persian equivalents of 'I am happy'; 'you are', and so on.

Exercise 4

Can you say these in Persian?

1 Hello, sir. I am Peter Brown. Oh yes, this message is for you.
2 This parcel is for Ms Ahmadi.
3 This present is for you.
4 This present/gift is for Mr Ahmadi.
5 This is Ms Ahmadi. (introducing)

Comprehension

A has just called into a travel agency. B is the travel agent.

A: سلام.
B: سلام. عصر بخیر.
A: عصر بخیر. من احمدی هستم.
B: آها بله، این بلیت برای شماست. این پیغام هم برای شماست.
A: خیلی ممنون.
B: سفر بخیر.
A: مرسی. خدا حافظ.
B: خدا حافظ.

A: **salām.**
B: **salām. asr bexeir.**
A: **asr bexeir. man ahmadi hastam.**
B: **āhā bale, in belit barāye šomāst. in peiqām ham barāye šomāst.**
A: **xeili mamnun.**
B: **safar bexeir.**
A: **mersi. xodā hāfez.**
B: **xodā hāfez.**

1 What time of the day is it?
2 Who is A? (What's his name?)
3 What is B offering A?
4 What is B wishing?

2 احوالپرسی
ahvālporsi
Enquiring about health

By the end of this lesson, you should be able to:

- say 'How are you?' and respond to a similar question
- introduce yourself, say 'Pleased to meet you,' and reciprocate
- enquire about other people
- express possession

Dialogue 1 How're you?

Bahman (B) is ringing his close friend Ali (A). Here are their opening and closing words.

A: الو؟
B: علی جان، سلام.
A: سلام، چطوری؟
B: خوبم، مرسی. تو چطوری؟
A: بد نیستم، مرسی.

[a few minutes later]

B: خب، فعلاً خدا حافظ.
A: خدا حافظ.

A: **alou?**
B: **ali jān, salām.**
A: **salām, ceto(u)ri?**
B: **xubam, mersi. to ceto(u)ri?**
A: **bad nistam, mersi.**

[a few minutes later]

B: **xob, fe(`)lan xodā (h)āfez.**
A: **xodā (h)āfez.**

A: *Hello?*
B: (lit) *Dear Ali, hello.*
A: *Hello, how're you?*
B: *I'm fine, thank you. How're you?*
A: *I'm not bad, thanks.*

[a few minutes later]

B: *OK, goodbye for now.*
A: *Goodbye.*

Vocabulary

علی	**ali**	male name	خوبم	**xubam**	I'm fine
جان	**jān**	dear	بد	**bad**	bad
چطور	**ceto(u)r**	how	نیستم	**nistam**	I'm not
چطوری	**ceto(u)ri**	how're you	خبٍ	**xob**	OK (then)
خوب	**xub**	good, fine	فعلاً	**fe(`)lan**	for now

Language points

Contraction

How to say 'I'm fine', 'you're fine', etc.

This is the shortened form of the verb 'to be' introduced at p. 25.

(من) خوبم.	**(man) xubam.**	I'm fine.
(تو) خوبی.	**(to) xubi.**	(*inf*) You're fine.
(او) خوبه.	**(u) xube.**	He/She's fine.
(اون) خوبه.	**(un) xube.**	It/That's fine.
(ما) خوبیم.	**(mā) xubim.**	We're fine.
(شما) خوبید.	**(šomā) xubid.**	You're fine.
(اونها) خوبند.	**(unhā) xuband.**	They're fine.

In the above sentences, what comes after the word خوب **xub** 'fine' are the reduced forms of the verb بودن **budan** 'to be'. They also act as **personal endings** for other verbs. Since these endings indicate 'person', the personal pronouns are often omitted as redundant – hence the brackets. These unstressed endings are very important and must be learned at an early stage.

Note: In casual speech, the second- and third-person plural endings ید **-id** and ند **-and** are replaced by ین **-in** and ن **-an**, respectively.

Exercise 1

Using the above information, replace the word خوب **xub** 'fine' with خوشحال **xošhāl** 'happy', to produce the Persian equivalents of 'I'm happy'; 'you're happy', and so on.

Negative form of verb 'to be' in the present tense

How to say 'I'm not', 'you're not', and so on.

من ... نیستم.	**man . . . nistam.**	I'm not . . .
تو ... نیستی.	**to . . . nisti.**	(*inf*) You're not . . .
او ... نیست.	**u . . . nist.**	He/She's not . . .
اون ... نیست.	**un . . . nist.**	It/That's not . . .
ما ... نیستیم.	**mā . . . nistim.**	We're not . . .

شما ... نیستید.	**šomā . . . nistid.**	You're not . . .
اونها ... نیستند.	**un(h)ā . . . nistand.**	They're not . . .

Exercise 2

We all had lunch an hour ago. None of us are hungry now. Complete the following sentences to express this.

1 **.______ من گرسنه man gorosne ______.** I am not hungry.
Example: **.من گرسنه نیستم man gorosne nistam.**
2 **.______ ما گرسنه mā gorosne ______.** We are not hungry.
3 **.______ تو گرسنه to gorosne ______.** You are not hungry.
4 **.______ اونها گرسنه unhā gorosne ______.** They are not hungry.
5 **.______ شما گرسنه šomā gorosne ______.** You are not hungry.
6 **.______ او گرسنه u gorosne ______.** S/he is not hungry.

Exercise 3

Can you say these in Persian?

1 How's Ahmad?	He's fine, thanks.
2 How's Mum/Dad?	S/he's fine, thanks.
3 How're you? (*inf*)	I'm not bad, thank you.

Dialogue 2 Pleased to meet you!

Ahmadi (A) *is mingling among his guests. He's just met a new face* (B).

A: سلام. من احمدی هستم. اسم شما چیه؟
B: سلام. من بهزادی هستم.
A: خوشوقتم.
B: من هم همینطور.
A: خب، حالتون چطوره؟
B: خوبم، مرسی. شما چطورید؟
A: بد نیستم، مرسی.

[pointing to some pictures on the wall, B *asks]*

B: این آقا کیه؟
A: اون پدرمه.
B: این خانم کیه؟
A: اون مادرمه.

A: **salām. man ahmadi hastam. esm-e šomā cie?**
B: **salām. man behzādi hastam.**
A: **xošvaqtam.**
B: **man (h)am haminto(u)r.**
A: **xob, hāletun ceto(u)re?**
B: **xubam, mersi. šomā ceto(u)rid?**
A: **bad nistam, mersi.**

[pointing to some pictures on the wall, B *asks]*

B: **in āqā kie?**
A: **un pedarame.**
B: **in xānom kie?**
A: **un mādarame.**

A: *Hello. I am Ahmadi. What's your name?*
B: *Hello. I am Behzadi.*
A: *I'm pleased (to meet you).*
B: *Same here. (or: Me too.)*
A: *So, how're you? (*lit *How's your health?)*
B: *I'm fine, thank you. How're you?*
A: *I'm not bad, thank you.*

[pointing to some pictures on the wall, B *asks]*

B: *Who's this gentleman?*
A: *That's my father.*
B: *Who's this lady?*
A: *That's my mother.*

Vocabulary

اسم	**esm**	name	چطور	**ceto(u)r**	how
چی	**ci**	what	این	**in**	this
چیه	**cie**	what's	آقا	**āqā**	gentleman
خوشوقت	**xošvaqt**	pleased	کی	**ki**	who
خوشوقتم	**xošvaqtam**	I'm pleased	اون	**un**	that
هم	**ham**	also, too	پدر	**pedar**	father
همینطور	**haminto(u)r**	same way	پدرم	**pedaram**	my father
حال	**hāl**	health	مادر	**mādar**	mother
حالتون	**hāletun**	your health			

Language points

Expressing possession

How to say 'your name'

One common way to show possession is to use the linking sound **e** (called **ezāfe**) as shown in this formula:

Belonging + **e** + owner

Examples:

تلفن جک	**telefon-e jak**	Jack's telephone
تلفن شما	**telefon-e šomā**	your telephone
اسم شما	**esm-e šomā**	your name

Exercise 4

Can you give the Persian equivalents of these phrases using the **ezāfe**? Follow the example.

1 His/her car ماشین او **māšin-e u**
2 Our car ________
3 His/her telephone ________
4 Your flat ________
5 Their home ________
6 Your car ________

*Other 'linking' functions of the **ezāfe***

Linking a forename to a surname:

حسن احمدی **hasan-e ahmadi** (Mr) Hassan Ahmadi

With foreign names, no linking sound is normally added:

جرج نیکسون **jorj nikson** George Nixon

Linking two nouns:

خیابان آکسفورد **xiābān-e āksford** Oxford Street
میدان ونک **meidān-e vanak** Vanak Square

Linking a noun and an adjective:

فیلم بد **film-e bad** bad film
تلفن عمومی **telefon-e omumi** public telephone
آپارتمان قشنگ **āpārtemān-e qašang** nice flat

After a vowel, the **ezāfe** is slightly modified as **ye**:

بابا	**bābā**	dad
بابایِ خوب	**bābā-ye xub**	good dad

Exercise 5

Make pairs by following the example.

Set (a)	*Set (b)*
بو **bu** smell	بلند **boland** long
مو **mu** hair	بد **bad** bad
بابا **bābā** dad	خوب **xub** good
فیلم **film** film	بور **bur** blond(e)
	مشکی **meški** black

1 Good smell = بوی خوب **bu-ye xub**
2 Long hair = ______
3 Good hair = ______
4 Bad film = ______
5 Blond hair = ______
6 Black hair = ______
7 Good dad = ______

How to say 'mine', 'yours', and so on

The **ezāfe** is also used to produce possessive pronouns, e.g.

مال من	**māl-e man**	mine (*lit* property of me)
مال شما	**māl-e šomā**	yours

We can also show possession by using the following (unstressed) **possessive endings**. Here, they are used with the word سوپ **sup** 'soup'.

سوپم	**supam**	my soup
سوپت	**supet**	your soup (*inf*)
سوپش	**supeš**	his/her/its soup
سوپمون	**supemun**	our soup
سوپتون	**supetun**	your soup
سوپشون	**supešun**	their soup

In literary Persian, some of the above are written and pronounced slightly differently:

سوپت	**supat**	your soup (*inf*)
سوپش	**supaš**	his/her/its soup
سوپمان	**supemān**	our soup
سوپتان	**supetān**	your soup
سوپشان	**supešān**	their soup

The pattern حالتون چطوره؟ **hāletun ceto(u)re?** 'how're you?' in the above dialogue (p. 31) literally means 'how's your health?' The word for 'health' is حال **hāl**.

Exercise 6

Repeat Exercise 4 using appropriate possessive endings. Follow the example.

1 ماشینش **māšineš**
2 ______
3 ______
4 ______
5 ______
6 ______

How to say 'so am I'; 'so do I'; 'so have I', and so on

For all the above, and other similar ones, Persian uses:

من هم همینطور. **man (h)am haminto(u)r.**
Same here. (*lit* I also in the same way.)

Exercise 7

Respond to the statements in Persian. Follow the example.

I'm hungry.
1 So am I. من هم همینطور. **man ham haminto(u)r.**
2 So are we. ______
3 So is Peter. ______
I live in London.
4 So do I. ______
5 So does s/he. ______
I've seen *Titanic*.
6 So have I. ______

Questions

While a statement has a falling tone, a 'yes'/'no' question uses a rising tone, as in English. Unlike English, no change in word order is necessary.

شما خوبید. **šomā xubid.** You're good/fine/OK. (falling)
شما خوبید؟ **šomā xubid?** Are you good/fine/OK? (rising)
شما دکترید؟ **šomā doktorid?** Are you a doctor? (rising)
خسته‌اید؟ **xasteid?** Are you tired? (rising)

As in English, questions beginning with the following question words have a falling tone.

کی **ki** who　　کی **kei** when
چرا **cerā** why　　کدوم **kodum** which
چه **ce** what; چی **ci** what (more *col*)
چطور **ceto(u)r** how; چه جور **ce jur** how (*col*)
کجا **kojā** where; کو Where is it? (*col*)
چند **cand** how many; چند تا **cand tā** how many (more *col*)

Note: The above question words normally carry the sentence stress. After چند/چند تا **cand tā/cand** 'how many?', the noun takes a singular form.

چیه؟	**cie?**	What is it?
کیه؟	**kie?**	Who is it?
چطوره؟	**ceto(u)re?**	How is it?
کجایید؟	**kojāyid?**	Where are you?
چند تا ماشین؟	**cand tā māšin?**	How many cars?

Demonstratives

How to say 'this'/'these'; 'that'/'those'

این **in** this　　اینها **inhā** these
اون **un** that　　اونها **unhā** those

Examples:

این چیه؟ **in cie?** What's this?
اون تلفنه. **un telefone.** That's/it's (a) telephone.
این تلفن مال کیه؟ **in telefon māl-e kie?** Whose telephone is this? (*lit* Whose property is this telephone?)
اون تلفن مال منه. **un telefon māl-e mane**. That telephone is mine.

Note how we say 'these'/'those' 'telephones' in Persian:

این/اون تلفن‌ها **in/un telefonhā** these/those telephones (*lit* this/that telephones)

(For plural markers, see pp. 42–3.)

Exercise 8

Complete these sentences with the help of the English translations.

1 ____ چیه؟ — ____ **cie?** What's your name?
Example: اسمتون چیه؟ **esmetun cie?** What's your name?
2 ____ چیه؟ — ____ **cie?** What's your address?
3 ____ چیه؟ — ____ **cie?** What's your nationality?
4 ____ چیه؟ — ____ **cie?** What's your phone number?
5 ____ چیه؟ — ____ **cie?** What's your date of birth?

Exercise 9

Can you say these in Persian?

1 How's your mother? — She's fine, thanks.
2 Where's your car? — It's here.
3 What's your job? — I'm a doctor.
4 Who's this? — That's my brother.
5 What's that? — It's my lunch.
6 Whose car is this? — It's mine.
7 Your flat is pretty/nice. — Thank you.

Comprehension

This morning, B, a Londoner, received a phone call from an Iranian colleague, Ahmad Kazemi (A).

A: سلام. احمد کاظمی هستم.
B: سلام، حالتون چطوره؟
A: خوبم، مرسی. حال شما چطوره؟
B: بد نیستم، مرسی. کجایید؟
A: لندن.
B: کدوم هتل؟
A: هتل تهران.
B: تنهایید؟

A: نه، پدر، مادر، خواهر و برادرم هم اینجا هستند.
B: هتلتون کجاست؟
A: خیابان ریجنت. نزدیک میدان آکسفورد.
B: هتل چطوره؟
A: بد نیست. کوچکه اما قشنگه.

A: **salām. ahmad-e kāzemi hastam.**
B: **salām, hāletun ceto(u)re?**
A: **xubam, mersi. hāl-e šomā ceto(u)re?**
B: **bad nistam, mersi. kojāyid?**
A: **landan.**
B: **kodum hotel?**
A: **hotel(-e) tehrān**
B: **tanhāyid?**
A: **na, pedar, mādar, xāhar va barādaram ham injā hastand.**
B: **hoteletun kojāst?**
A: **xiābān-e rijent. nazdik-e meidān-e āksford.**
B: **hotel ceto(u)re?**
A: **bad nist. kuceke ammā qašange.**

1 From which city is A phoning?
2 Who is he with?
3 Where is he staying?
4 How does he feel about the accommodation?

3 کجایی هستید؟
kojāyi hastid?

Where are you from?

By the end of this lesson, you should be able to:

- seek and give personal details: gender, nationality, marital status, place of birth, hobbies, occupation, place of work
- introduce B to C
- pay, and respond to, compliments
- talk about age
- use numbers

Dialogue 1 Party game: Who am I?

At an Iranian party held in London, each guest is given the picture of a well-known figure. The winner will be the first person to identify another guest by merely asking questions.

A: شما زن هستید؟
B: نه.
A: ملّیتتون چیه؟
B: انگلیسی هستم.
A: شما متأهّلید؟
B: بله.
A: خانمتون کجایی هستند؟
B: اون هم انگلیسیه.
A: محلّ تولّدتون کجاست؟
B: لندن.
A: سرگرمی‌هاتون چیه؟
B: موسیقی، ورزش، مطالعه.
A: کارتون چیه؟
B: کارمند هستم.
A: محلّ کارتون کجاست؟
B: خیابان داونینگ، پلاک ۱۰

A: شما تونی بلر هستید؟
B: بله، مرسی.

A: **šomā zan hastid?**
B: **na.**
A: **melliyatetun cie?**
B: **engelisi hastam.**
A: **šomā mota`ahhelid?**
B: **bale.**
A: **xānometun kojāyi hastand?**
B: **un (h)am engelisie.**
A: **mahall-e tavallodetun kojāst?**
B: **landan.**
A: **sargarmihātun cie?**
B: **musiqi, varzeš, motāle`e.**
A: **kāretun cie?**
B: **kārmand hastam.**
A: **mahall-e kāretun kojāst?**
B: **xiābān-e dāwning, pelāk-e dah.**
A: **šomā toni beler hastid?**
B: **bale, mersi.**

A: *Are you a woman?*
B: *No.*
A: *What's your nationality?*
B: *I'm English.*
A: *Are you married?*
B: *Yes.*
A: *Where does your wife come from?*
B: *She too is English.*
A: *Where's your place of birth?*
B: *London.*
A: *What are your hobbies?*
B: *Music, sport, reading.*
A: *What's your job?*
B: *I'm a (civil) servant.*
A: *Where's your place of work?*
B: *Downing Street, No. 10.*
A: *Are you Tony Blair?*
B: *Yes, thank you.*

Vocabulary

زن	**zan**	woman
ملّیت	**melliyat**	nationality
انگلیسی	**engelisi**	English, British
متأهّل	**mota`ahhel**	married
خانم	**xānom**	wife, madam
کجا	**kojā**	where
کجایی	**kojāyi**	where from
سرگرمی	**sargarmi**	hobby
سرگرمی‌ها	**sargarmihā**	hobbies
موسیقی	**musiqi**	music
مطالعه	**motāle`e**	reading
ورزش	**varzeš**	sport
محلّ	**mahall**	place
تولّد	**tavallod**	birth
کجاست	**kojāst**	where's
لندن	**landan**	London
کار	**kār**	job, work
کارمند	**kārmand**	(civil) servant
خیابان	**xiābān**	street
خیابان داونینگ	**xiābān-e dāwning**	Downing Street
پلاک	**pelāk**	(house) number

Language points

How to describe nationality

Here is the formula:

Place name + ی **i** → *Native of that place*
ایران **irān** Iran → ایرانی **irāni** Iranian
ژاپن **ĝāpon** Japan → ژاپنی **ĝāponi** Japanese
انگلیس **engelis** England → انگلیسی **engelisi** English
اسکاتلند **eskātland** Scotland → اسکاتلندی **eskātlandi** Scottish

When a name ends in a vowel, the ending یی **-yi** is used:

آمریکا **āmrikā** America → آمریکایی **āmrikāyi** American
کانادا **kānādā** Canada → کانادایی **kānādāyi** Canadian
استرالیا **osterāliā** Australia → استرالیایی **osterāliāyi** Australian

If a place name ends in **i**, the following forms may be used:

لیبی **libi** Libya →
(a) لیبیایی **libiāyi** Libyan (person)
(b) اهل لیبی **ahl-e libi** a native of Libya
(c) ساخت لیبی **sāxt-e libi** made in Libya

Word stress is shifted over to the suffix in all the above cases.

Exercise 1

Fill in the right column. Follow the example.

	Place name	*Native*
1	تهران **tehrān** Tehran	تهرانی **tehrāni** From Tehran
2	لندن **landan** London	______ Londoner
3	ایتالیا **itāliā** Italy	______ Italian
4	پاریس **pāris** Paris	______ Parisian
5	مشهد **mas̄had** Mashad	______ From Mashad
6	اصفهان **esfahān** Esfahan	______ From Esfahan

Exercise 2

You have met a Persian speaker at a social gathering. Find out:

1 If he/she is Iranian.
2 If he/she is married.
3 Where he/she was born.
4 Where he/she works.
5 Where his wife/her husband comes from.
6 What his/her hobbies are.

Plural of nouns

The most common way to make a noun plural is by adding the suffix ها **-hā**:

تلفن **telefon** telephone → تلفن‌ها **telefonhā** telephones
سرگرمی **sargarmi** hobby → سرگرمی‌ها **sargarmihā** hobbies

With inanimate nouns, the verb often takes a singular form:

بچّه‌ها کجاند؟ **baccehā kojānd?** Where are the children?
کتاب‌ها کجاست؟ **ketābhā kojāst?** Where are (*lit* is) the books?

The هـ **h** of the plural marker is often dropped in speech.

For animate nouns, the suffix ان **-ān** is normally used in more formal contexts.

مرد **mard** man — مردان **mardān** men
دوست **dust** friend — دوستان **dustān** friends

Adjectives can also be pluralised in Persian:

خوب **xub** good خوبان **xubān** the good (i.e. good people)
تپلی **topoli** plump تپلی‌ها **topolihā** plump ones

The plural endings introduced above carry the word stress.

Exercise 3

Write the plural of these nouns, and then write their English equivalents. Follow the example.

1	آپارتمان	**āpārtemān**	→	آپارتمان‌ها **āpārtemānhā** flats
2	ماشین	**māšin**	→	______
3	روزنامه	**ruznāme**	→	______
4	ایرانی	**irāni**	→	______
5	دوست	**dust**	→	______

Exercise 4

Can you say these in Persian?

1 Where are you from?
2 I'm French/Italian/German/Spanish.
3 I'm from London/Manchester.
4 My place of birth is London/Paris/New York.

Dialogue 2 Introducing B to C

A has invited his colleague, Mr Morris (B), for dinner. A introduces Mr Morris to his wife (C).

A: آقای موریس همکارم (هستند)، و ایشون خانمم هستند.
C: خوشوقتم.
B: من هم همینطور. آپارتمان قشنگی دارید.
C: متشکّرم. لطف دارید.

A: **āqā-ye moris hamkāram (hastand), va išun xānomam hastand.**
C: **xošvaqtam.**
B: **man (h)am haminto(u)r. āpārtemān-e qašangi dārid.**
C: **mot(a)šakkeram. lotf dārid.**

A: *Mr Morris (is) my colleague, and this (* lit *she) is my wife.*
C: *I'm pleased (to meet you).*
B: *So am I. You have a nice flat.*
C: *Thank you. That's very kind of you (* lit *You have kindness).*

Vocabulary

آقای	**āqā-ye**	Mr	قشنگ	**qašang**	nice, pretty
همکار	**hamkār**	colleague	دارید	**dārid**	you have
ایشون	**išun**	he, she (*pol*)	داشتن (دار)	**dāštan (dār)**	to have
خوشوقت	**xošvaqt**	pleased	متشکّر	**mot(a)šakker**	grateful
آپارتمان	**āpārtemān**	apartment	لطف	**lotf**	kindness

Language points

The verb 'to have'

All Persian verbs (infinitives) end with these two sounds **-an**, e.g. بودن **budan** 'to be', داشتن **dāštan** 'to have'. Persian verbs have two stems (or roots): *present stem* and *past stem*, used for present and past tenses, respectively. The past stem is regularly obtainable from the infinitive by omitting the last two sounds **-an**. The present stem of most verbs is irregular. Therefore, with every new verb introduced, its present stem is placed in round brackets after it. (**Note:** Where applicable, the literary form of a present stem will appear in square brackets.)

بودن (هست) **budan (hast)** to be

داشتن (دار) **dāštan (dār)** to have

(For the verb 'to be', see p. 25.)

To say 'I have', 'you have', etc., in Persian, follow this formula:

present stem + personal ending

(For personal endings, see p. 30.)

من ماشین دارم. **man māšin dāram.** I have (a) car.
تو ماشین داری. **to māšin dāri.** You (*inf*) have (a) car.
او ماشین داره. **u māšin dāre.** He/she (*inf*) has (a) car.
ما ماشین داریم. **mā māšin dārim.** We have (a) car.
شما ماشین دارید. **šomā māšin dārid.** You have (a) car.
اونها ماشین دارند. **unhā māšin dārand.** They have (a) car.

To make this verb negative, add نـ **na-** to the beginning:

من ماشین ندارم. **man māšin nadāram.** I don't have a car.

Note: The stress is shifted over to نـ **na-**.

As will be seen below, we do not need the Persian equivalent of 'a' (indefinite article) for this pattern. Hence, the word 'a' appears in brackets in the English translations.

The verb داشتن **dāštan** 'to have' is used to talk about age, for example:

من ۲۰ سال دارم. **man bist sāl dāram.** I am 20 years old.
(*lit* I have twenty year(s).) **Note:** Noun comes in the singular.
شما چند سال دارید؟ **šomā cand sāl dārid?** How old are you?
(*lit* How many year(s) do you have?) **Note:** Noun in the singular.

Note: Nouns following numbers come in the singular.

Exercise 5

Match a letter with a number to produce the equivalents of 'I have', 'you have', etc. Follow the example.

1	من **man**	[c]	(a) داری **dāri**
2	تو **to**	[ ]	(b) داریم **dārim**
3	او **u**	[ ]	(c) دارم **dāram**
4	ما **mā**	[ ]	(d) دارید **dārid**
5	شما **šomā**	[ ]	(e) دارند **dārand**
6	اونها **unhā**	[ ]	(f) داره **dāre**

Exercise 6

Make these sentences negative, by following the example.

1 .من پول دارم **man pul dāram.** I have money.
.من پول ندارم **man pul nadāram.** I don't have money.
2 .تو بلیت داری **to belit dāri.** You have a ticket.
3 .او ۲۵ سال داره **u bist o panj sāl dāre.** He/she is 25 years old.
4 .ما اتاق خالی داریم **mā otāq-e xāli dārim.** We have vacant rooms.
5 .شما وقت دارید **šomā vaqt dārid.** You have time.
6 .اونها تلفن دارند **unhā telefon dārand.** They have a telephone.

Numbers

Cardinal

You will note that from 21 onwards we add و **o** 'and' between numbers.

0	۰	صفر	**sefr**
1	۱	یک	**yek**
2	۲	دو	**do**
3	۳	سه	**se**
4	۴	چهار	**cahār** (*col* **cār**)
5	۵	پنج	**panj**
6	۶	شش	**šeš** (*col* **šiš**)
7	۷	هفت	**haft**
8	۸	هشت	**hašt**
9	۹	نه	**noh**
10	۱۰	ده	**dah**
11	۱۱	یازده	**yāzdah**
12	۱۲	دوازده	**davāzdah**
13	۱۳	سیزده	**sizdah**
14	۱۴	چهارده	**cahārdah** (*col* **cārdah**)
15	۱۵	پانزده	**pānzdah** (*col* **punzdah**)
16	۱۶	شانزده	**šānzdah** (*col* **šunzdah**)
17	۱۷	هفده	**hefdah** (*col* **hivdah**)
18	۱۸	هجده	**hejdah** (*col* **hiĝdah**)
19	۱۹	نوزده	**nuzdah**
20	۲۰	بیست	**bist**
21	۲۱	بیست و یک	**bist o yek**
22	۲۲	بیست و دو	**bist o do**
29	۲۹	بیست و نه	**bist o noh**

30	۳۰	سی	**si**
31	۳۱	سی و یک	**si o yek**
40	۴۰	چهل	**cehel** (*col* **cel**)
50	۵۰	پنجاه	**panjāh**
60	۶۰	شصت	**šast**
70	۷۰	هفتاد	**haftād**
80	۸۰	هشتاد	**haštād**
90	۹۰	نود	**navad**
100	۱۰۰	صد	**sad**
101	۱۰۱	صد و یک	**sad o yek**
110	۱۱۰	صد و ده	**sad o dah**
199	۱۹۹	صد و نود و نه	**sad o navad o noh**
200	۲۰۰	دویست	**devist** (*col* **divist**)
300	۳۰۰	سیصد	**sisad**
400	۴۰۰	چهارصد	**cahārsad** (*col* **cārsad**)
500	۵۰۰	پانصد	**pānsad** (*col* **punsad**)
600	۶۰۰	ششصد	**šešsad**
700	۷۰۰	هفتصد	**haftsad** (*col* **hafsad**)
800	۸۰۰	هشتصد	**haštsad** (*col* **haššad**)
900	۹۰۰	نهصد	**nohsad**
1,000	۱۰۰۰	هزار	**hezār**
1,001	۱۰۰۱	هزار و یک	**hezār o yek**
1,962	۱۹۶۲	هزار و نهصد و شصت و دو	**hezār o nohsad o šast o do**
2,786	۲۷۸۶	دو هزار و هفتصد و هشتاد و شش	**do hezār o haftsad o haštād o šeš**
10,524	۱۰۵۲۴	ده هزار و پانصد و بیست و چهار	**dah hezār o pānsad o bist o c(ah)ār**
100,000	۱۰۰۰۰۰	صد هزار	**sad hezār**
1,000,000	۱۰۰۰۰۰۰	یک میلیون	**yek milyun**
1,365,497	۱۳۶۵۴۹۷		

یک میلیون و سیصد و شصت و پنج هزار و چهارصد و نود و هفت
yek milyun o sisad o šast o panj hezār o c(ah)ārsad o navad o haft

After a number or چند تا **cand tā** 'how many?', the noun comes in the singular.

چند تا ماشین؟ **cand tā māšin?** How many cars (*lit* car)?
پنج ماشین **panj māšin** five cars (*lit* car)

Indefinite and definite articles

Generally, Persian does not distinguish between 'a car' and 'the car', as in:

ماشین خرابه.	**māšin xarābe.**	The car is broken.
ماشین دارید؟	**māšin dārid?**	Do you have a car?

Here is another example:

آپارتمان قشنگه.	**āpārtemān qašange.**	The flat is nice.
آپارتمان دارید؟	**āpārtemān dārid?**	Do you have a flat?

To indicate the indefinite, we use یک **ye(k)** 'one' before the noun:

یک آپارتمان در تهران داره و یک خونه در مشهد.
ye(k) āpārtemān dar tehrān dāre va ye(k) xune dar mašhad.
He has a flat in Tehran and a house in Mashad.

A less colloquial form uses the unstressed suffix ـی **i** (or یی **-yi** if the noun ends in a vowel):

آپارتمانی	**āpārtemāni**	a flat, an apartment
بابا	**bābā**	dad
بابایی	**bābāyi**	a dad

When the noun is qualified by an adjective, the ending goes after the adjective:

آپارتمان قشنگی دارید.
āpārtemān-e qašangi dārid. You have a nice flat.

Exercise 7

Can you say these in Persian?

1 You have a nice car/garden/house!
2 I'm sorry, I don't have time.
3 How old is he? He's 30 years old.
4 This is my friend Peter. He's English. This is my mother.
5 Pleased to meet you. So am I.
6 How many Iranian friends do you have?
7 I have five Iranian friends.

Comprehension

You have received a taped message from your Iranian penfriend.

سلام، من پرویز علیزاده هستم. من متأهل هستم. خانمم معلم انگلیسیه. ما مسلمان هستیم. محل تولد من مشهده. من کارمند هستم. ۳۵ سال دارم. خانمم ۳۱ سال داره. محلّ تولّدش آمریکاست اما ملّیّتش ایرانیه. سرگرمی من سینما و سرگرمی خانمم نقّاشیه. ما یک آپارتمان کوچک ولی قشنگ در تهران داریم.

salām, man parviz-e alizāde hastam. man mota`ahhel hastam. xānomam mo`allem-e engelisie. mā mosalmān hastim. mahall-e tavallod-e man mašhade. man kārmand hastam. si o panj sāl dāram. xānomam si o yek sāl dāre. mahall-e tavallodeš āmrikāst ammā melliyateš irānie. sargarmi-e man sinemā va sargarmi-e xānomam naqqāšie. mā yek āpārtemān-e kucek vali qašang dar tehrān dārim.

1 What is your friend's name?
2 What does he do for a living?
3 What is his wife's job?
4 What is his wife's nationality?
5 Where was she born?
6 What type of home do they have, and in which town?
7 Identify a word that shows he is happy with his home.
8 What do they do in their spare time?
9 What religion do they follow?

4 منزلتون کجاست؟ manzeletun kojāst?

Where's your home?

By the end of this lesson, you should be able to:

- seek and give home address
- ask about the availability of facilities
- express regret
- use ordinal numbers (first, second, etc.)
- ask and answer questions about family
- make comparisons
- express an opinion

Dialogue 1 Giving your details

Mrs Rezaee (R) is phoning for an ambulance for her husband, who has just fallen down the stairs. Here's an extract from her conversation with the hospital telephonist (T).

T: اسم بیمار چیه؟
R: حسن احمدی.
T: آدرستون چیه؟
R: تهران، خیابان مهر، پلاک ۸، طبقهٔ ششم، آپارتمان ۱۲.
T: کجای خیابان مهر هستید؟
R: سینما حافظ میدونید کجاست؟
T: بله.
R: درست روبروی سینما هستیم، پهلوی سوپرمارکت.
T: آسانسور دارید؟
R: داریم، امّا خرابه، متأسّفانه.
T: ای وای! خب، عیب نداره. شماره تلفنتون چنده؟
R: ۳۵۱۷۴۲

T: **esm-e bimār cie?**
R: **hasan-e ahmadi.**
T: **ādresetun cie?**
R: **tehrān, xiābān-e mehr, pelāk-e hašt, tabaqe-ye šešom, āpārtemān-e davāzdah.**
T: **kojā-ye xiābān-e mehr hastid?**
R: **sinemā hāfez midunid kojāst?**
T: **bale.**
R: **dorost ruberu-ye sinemā hastim, pahlu-ye supermārket.**
T: **āsānsor dārid?**
R: **dārim, ammā xarāb-e, mota(`)assefāne.**
T: **ei vai! xob, eib nadāre. šomāre telefonetun cande?**
R: **si o panj, hefdah, cel o do.**

T: *What's the name of the patient?*
R: *Hassan Ahmadi.*
T: *What's your address?*
R: *Tehran, Mehr Street, No. 8, 6th floor, Flat 12.*
T: *Where in Mehr Street are you (located)?*
R: *Do you know where Hafez cinema is?*
T: *Yes.*
R: *We're just opposite the cinema, next to the supermarket.*
T: *Do you have a lift?*
R: *We do, but it's broken, I'm afraid.*
T: *Oh dear! OK, never mind. What's your phone number?*
R: *35–17–42.*

Vocabulary

بیمار **bimār**	patient
آدرس **ādres**	address
طبقه **tabaqe**	floor
ششم **šešom**	sixth
میدونید **midunid**	you know
دونستن **dunestan**	
(دون) **(dun)**	to know
درست **dorost**	just, exactly
آسانسور **āsānsor**	lift
امّا **ammā**	but
خراب **xarāb**	broken
متأسّفانه **mota`assefāne**	unfortunately
ای وای **ei vai**	oh dear!
عیب **eib**	problem
شماره **šomāre**	number
تلفن **telefon**	telephone
چند **cand**	what?; how much?

Language points

Prepositions

Here are some common prepositions and prepositional phrases.
Note: In casual speech, the ی **-ye** is often dropped.

روبروی **ruberu-ye** opposite
پهلوی **pahlu-ye** next to
روی **ru-ye** on
زیر **zir-e** under
جلوی **jelo-ye** in front of
پشت **pošt-e** behind
در **dar** in (literary)
توی **tu-ye** in (*col*)
بیرون **birun-e** out/outside of
بالای **bālā-ye** above, over
پایین **pāyin-e** below, beneath
(در) طرف چپ **(dar) taraf-e cap-e** (on) the left side of
(در) طرف راست **(dar) taraf-e rāst-e** (on) the right side of

Exercise 1

Fill in the blanks with the appropriate preposition.

۱ – آپارتمان من ______ سینماست.
1 **āpārtemān-e man ______ sinemāst.**
My flat is opposite the cinema.

۲ – سینما ______ یک پمپ بنزین است.
2 **sinemā ______ yek pomp-e benzin ast.**
The cinema is next to a petrol station.

۳ – ساندویچ شما ______ میز است.
3 **sāndevic-e šomā ______ miz ast.**
Your sandwich is on the table.

۴ – مداد ______ میز است.
4 **medād ______ miz ast.**
The pencil is under the table.

۵ – تلفن همگانی ______ منزل ماست.
5 **telefon-e hamegāni ______ manzel-e māst.**
The public telephone is in front of our house.

۶ – خانهٔ احمد ______ سینماست.
6 **xāne-ye ahmad ______ sinemāst.**
Ahmad's house is behind the cinema.

۷ – آپارتمان علی ______ آپارتمان ماست.
7 **āpārtemān-e ali ______ āpārtemān-e māst.**
Ali's flat is above our flat.

From cardinal to ordinal

Let us look at how to convert cardinal numbers ('one', 'two', etc.) to ordinal numbers ('first', 'second', etc.).

For the first three, we say:

Cardinal numbers	*Ordinal numbers*
یک **yek** one	اوّل **avval** first
دو **do** two	دوّم **dovvom** second
سه **se** three	سوّم **sevvom** third

For all the other numbers, we add the (stressed) suffix **-om** to the end of the cardinal number to get an ordinal number.

چهار **c(ah)ār** four — چهارم **c(ah)ārom** fourth
پنج **panj** five — پنجم **panjom** fifth
بیست و یک **bist o yek** twenty one
بیست و یکم **bist o yekom** twenty first

Exercise 2

Can you give the Persian equivalents of these ordinal numbers?

(a) first = ______
(b) second = ______
(c) third = ______
(d) ninth = ______
(e) twenty first = ______
(f) seventieth = ______

Postal address

A postal address normally begins with the largest unit, i.e. name of the country, city/town, and ends with the smallest, i.e. house/flat number, followed by the name of the recipient, e.g.

ایران، تهران، کد پستی ۲۱۸۶۰۳، خیابان آبان، پلاک ۹،
منزل آقای احمدی

irān, tehrān, kod-e posti-e 218603, xiābān-e ābān, pelāk-e 9, manzel-e āqā-ye ahmadi

Iran, Tehran, Postcode 218603, Aban Street, No. 9, home of Mr Ahmadi

Exercise 3

Imagine you are the British Premier. You are inviting some Iranian friends to your home at No. 10 Downing Street, London SW1, England. Give your address in Persian.

Present simple tense

How to say 'I know', 'you know', etc.

Here is the formula:

Prefix میـ **mi-** + present stem of verb + personal ending

The colloquial form of the verb 'to know' is دونستن **dunestan**. Its present stem is دون **dun**. (For personal endings, see p. 30.)

من میدونم. **man midunam.** I know.
تو میدونی. **to miduni.** You (*inf*) know.
او میدونه. **u midune.** He/she knows.
ما میدونیم. **mā midunim.** We know.
شما میدونید. **šomā midunid.** You know.
اونها میدونند. **unhā midunand.** They know.

To make the verb negative, we add the prefix نـ **ne-**, e.g.

من نمیدونم. **man nemidunam.** I don't know.
شما نمیدونید. **šomā nemidunid.** You don't know.

Notes:

1 The negative prefix normally carries the word stress.
2 In literary Persian, the personal ending for او **u** 'he'/'she' and آن **ān** 'it'/'that' is د **-ad**. Compare:

او میخوره. **u mixore.** 'he/she eats' (*col*)
او میخورد. **u mixorad**. 'he/she eats' (*lit*)

The verb used is خوردن (خور) **xordan (xor)** 'to eat'.

Days of the week

شنبه **šanbe** Saturday (first day of the week)
یکشنبه **yekšanbe** Sunday
دوشنبه **došanbe** Monday
سه‌شنبه **sešanbe** Tuesday
چهارشنبه **c(ah)āršanbe** Wednesday
پنجشنبه **panjšanbe** Thursday
جمعه **jom`e** Friday (weekend)

Examples:

(روز) جمعه **(ruz-e) jom`e** on Friday
جمعه‌ها **jom`ehā** on Fridays
روزهای جمعه **ruzhā-ye jom`e** on Fridays

Exercise 4

Here's part of Ahmad's weekly timetable. Can you describe it in Persian? Follow the example.

1 Saturday, Monday, Wednesday: He goes to university.
2 Sunday: He plays the piano.
3 Tuesday: He reads books in the library.
4 Thursday evening: He has dinner with his friends. Then they go to the cinema.
5 Friday morning: He goes to a swimming pool.

۱ – احمد روزهای شنبه، دوشنبه و چهارشنبه به دانشگاه میره.
1 **ahmad ruzhā-ye šanbe, došanbe va c(ah)āršanbe be dānešgāh mire.** Ahmad goes to university on Saturdays, Mondays and Wednesdays.

How to say 'I come', 'you come', etc.

Verbs whose present stem ends with a vowel need a little more attention. This is because the personal endings which are added to it begin with a vowel. As two vowels do not normally follow each other within the same word, some adjustment is needed. The present stem of اومدن **umadan** 'to come' is a single vowel ا **ā**. Here is the result:

من میام. **man miām.** I come.
تو میای. **to miai.** You (*inf*) come.

او میاد.* **u miād.** He/she comes.
ما میایم. **mā miaim.** We come.
شما میاید. **šomā miaid.** You come.
اونها میاند. **un(h)ā miānd.** They come.

*For 'he', 'she' or 'it comes', colloquial Persian uses the literary ending د **-ad** with the initial vowel dropped.

Exercise 5

Match a letter with a number.

۱ – من هر روز به این کتابخونه میام.
1 **man har ruz be in ketābxune miām.**
۲ – شما هر روز به این رستوران میاید.
2 **šomā har ruz be in resturān miaid.**
۳ – اونها روزهای جمعه به منزل ما میاند.
3 **unhā ruzhā-ye jom`e be manzel-e mā miānd.**
۴ – احمد همیشه با من به سوپرمارکت میاد.
4 **ahmad hamiše bā man be supermārket miād.**
۵ – ما شب‌ها دیر به منزل میایم.
5 **mā šabhā dir be manzel miaim.**

(a) Ahmad always comes to the supermarket with me.
(b) I come to this library every day.
(c) We come home late at night.
(d) They come to our home on Fridays.
(e) You come to this restaurant every day.

Reading a telephone number

Telephone numbers are normally read in twos or threes:

۲۸۶۰۵۳ 286053	**devist o haštād o šeš, sefr, panjāh o se** two hundred and eighty six, zero, fifty three
۰۵۱ – ۷۴۱۹۰۰۷ 051-7419007	**sefr, panjāh o yek – haftād o cār, nuzdah, do sefr, haft** zero, fifty one – seventy-four, nineteen, double zero, seven

Exercise 6

Can you give these phone numbers to your Iranian friend?

(a) 7102683 (b) 3413509 (c) 445500
(d) 7853412 (e) 7890635 (f) 5036797

Exercise 7

Can you say these in Persian?

1 What's Ahmad's address? No. 24, Hafez Street, Tehran 16372.
2 Do you have a lighter? Yes, but it's broken, I'm afraid.
3 Which floor is your flat on? Fourth floor.
4 Where's my sandwich? It's on the table, in the kitchen.
5 The post office is opposite the petrol station, next to the cinema.
6 Your pen is under the chair.
7 Do you come here every day?
8 He doesn't know where we are.
9 Do they know we are here?
10 Do you know who she is?
11 Do you know what this is?

Dialogue 2 Asking about family 

An Iranian (I) and a British tourist (T) met a while ago when they took their seats on an Iran Air flight from London to Tehran. Here is an extract from their conversation.

I: کارتون چیه؟
T: اپراتور کامپیوتر هستم.
I: کجا کار میکنید؟
T: تو یک شرکت آمریکایی کار میکنم. شما چکار میکنید؟
I: معلّم هستم.
T: چی درس میدید؟
I: ریاضی درس میدم. . . .
T: این آقا پسرتونند؟
I: نه، برادرمه. خیلی از من کوچکتره. کوچکترین عضو خانواده است. شما خواهر و برادر دارید؟
T: نه، ندارم.
I: بچّه چطور؟
T: نه هنوز.

I: **kāretun cie?**
T: **operātor-e kāmpiuter hastam.**
I: **kojā kār mikonid?**
T: **tu ye(k) šerkat-e āmrikāyi kār mikonam. šomā cekār mikonid?**
I: **mo`allem hastam.**
T: **ci dars midid?**
I: **riāzi dars midam . . .**
T: **in āqā pesaretunand?**
I: **na, barādarame. xeili az man kucektare. kucektarin ozv-e xānevādast. šomā xāhar o barādar dārid?**
T: **na, nadāram.**
I: **bacce ceto(u)r?**
T: **na hanuz.**

I: *What's your job?*
T: *I'm a computer operator.*
I: *Where do you work?*
T: *I work for an American company. What do you do?*
I: *I'm a teacher.*
T: *What do you teach?*
I: *I teach maths . . .*
T: *Is this gentleman your son?*
I: *No, he's my brother. He's much younger than me. He's the youngest member of the family. Do you have brothers and sisters?*
T: *No, I haven't.*
I: *How about children?*
T: *Not yet.*

Vocabulary

اپراتور	**operātor**	operator
کامپیوتر	**kāmpiuter**	computer
کار میکنید	**kār mikonid**	you work
کار کردن	**kār kardan**	
(کن)	**(kon)**	to work
تو	**tu**	in, at
شرکت	**šerkat**	company
کار	**kār**	
میکنم	**mikonam**	I work
چکار	**cekār**	(*lit*) what work
میکنید	**mikonid**	you do
معلّم	**mo`allem**	teacher
درس	**dars**	lesson
میدید	**midid**	you give
درس دادن	**dars dādan**	
(د)	**(d)**	to teach
ریاضی	**riāzi**	maths
میدم	**midam**	I give
پسر	**pesar**	son, boy
برادر	**barādar**	brother
خیلی	**xeili**	very much

از	**az**	than	خانواده	**xānevāde**	family
کوچک	**kucek**	young, small	خواهر	**xāhar**	sister
			بچه	**bacce**	child
کوچکتر	**kucektar**	younger	چطور	**ceto(u)r**	how about
کوچکترین	**kucektarin**	youngest	نه	**na**	no
عضو	**ozv**	member	هنوز	**hanuz**	yet, still

Language points

Compound verbs

So far we have used simple one-word verbs, such as خوردن **xordan** 'to eat', دیدن **didan** 'to see', etc. A compound verb normally consists of two words: a verb and another word from any of the following categories: noun, adjective, adverb or preposition. For example, the word کار **kār** 'job', 'work' is put together with the verb کردن **kardan** 'to do' to produce the verb کار کردن **kār kardan** 'to work'. The verb کردن **kardan**, 'to do', helps to produce a very large number of compound verbs. It is therefore crucial to learn its present stem کن **kon** at an early stage – that is, now!

کار کردن (کن) **kār kardan (kon)** to work
من کار میکنم. **man kār mikonam.** I work.
تو کار میکنی. **to kār mikoni.** You (*inf*) work.
او کار میکنه. **u kār mikone.** He/she works.
ما کار میکنیم. **mā kār mikonim.** We work.
شما کار میکنید. **šomā kār mikonid.** You work.
اونها کار میکنند. **un(h)ā kār mikonand.** They work.

The other compound verb used in the above dialogue is:

درس دادن (د) **dars dādan (d)** to teach (*lit* to give lesson)

Comparative adjective

How to say 'younger'

We add the suffix تر **-tar** to the adjective. Example:

کوچک **kucek** small/young

کوچکتر **kucektar** smaller/younger

Note: Word stress is shifted over to the ending.

How to say 'X is younger than Y'

X از Y کوچکتر است.	**X az Y kucektar ast.**
X از Y کوچکتره.	**X az Y kucektare.** (*col*)

Exercise 8

Provide the missing word. Follow the example.

۱- رولزرویس ______ (than) فورد گرونتره.

1 **rolz-rois** ______ (than) **ford geruntare.**
A Rolls-Royce (car) is more expensive than a Ford.
Example:

rolz-rois az ford geruntare. رولزرویس از فورد گرونتره.

۲- فورد از رولزرویس ______ (smaller) ه.

2 **ford az rolz-rois** ______ (smaller) **e.**
A Ford is smaller than a Rolls-Royce.

۳- ایران از انگستان ______ (larger) ه.

3 **irān az engelestān** ______ (larger) **e.**
Iran is larger than England.

Superlative adjective

How to say 'youngest'

We add the suffix ترین **-tarin** to the adjective. Example:

کوچک **kucek** small, young
کوچکترین **kucektarin** smallest, youngest

Note the word order, which is similar to English:

کوچکترین عضو **kucektarin ozv** youngest member
بزرگترین شهر **bozorgtarin šahr** largest city
گرونترین اتومبیل **geruntarin otomobil** most expensive car
به نظر من، زیباترین شهر ایران اصفهان است.
be nazar-e man, zibātarin šahr-e irān esfahān ast.
In my opinion, the most beautiful city in Iran is Esfahan.

Exercise 9

Fill the blanks by following the example.

1 بدترین فیلم ← فیلم بد **film-e bad → badtarin film**
bad film → worst film
2 ____ ← اتومبیل گرون **otomobil-e gerun →** ____
expensive car → most expensive car
3 ____ ← آپارتمان ارزون **āpārtemān-e arzun →** ____
cheap flat → cheapest flat
4 ____ ← شهر بزرگ **šahr-e bozorg →** ____
big city → biggest city
5 ____ ← زن جوون **zan-e javun →** ____
young woman → youngest woman
6 ____ ← مرد مسنّ **mard-e mosenn →** ____
old man → oldest man

Extended family

Compared to English, Persian uses more descriptive words to refer to members of the extended family. Perhaps the most notorious example concerns the word 'cousin' with no fewer than eight equivalents in Persian:

عمو **amu** paternal uncle
عمّه **amme** paternal aunt
دایی **dāyi** maternal uncle
خاله **xāle** maternal aunt

To each of the above we add پسر **pesar** 'son', or دختر **doxtar** 'daughter', to produce the various meanings of 'cousin', e.g.

دختر عمو **doxtar amu** paternal uncle's daughter (cousin)
پسر خاله **pesar xāle** maternal aunt's son (cousin)

The linking sound **e** (**ezāfe**) is omitted for convenience.

Exercise 10

Can you say these in Persian?

1 Do you have a younger sister?
2 I'm three years older than my sister.
3 Are you the eldest member of the family?
4 My father is two years older than my aunt (his sister).
5 In my opinion, the best Iranian food is *chelo-kabab*.

6 Where is the nearest supermarket?
7 Where is the best restaurant?
8 I don't watch television.
9 I listen to the radio.

Comprehension

The following is what your Iranian penfriend wrote about her home in a recent letter.

ما یک خانه در غرب شیراز داریم. آدرس ما این است: شیراز، کد پستی ۱۸۲۴۸، خیابان سعدی، کوچه نرگس، پلاک ۱۵، منزل حسینی.
روبروی کوچهٔ ما یک پمپ بنزین است. در طرف راست کوچه یک پیتزا فروشی است. در طرف چپ کوچه نانوایی است. جلوی خانهٔ ما یک صندوق پست است. داخل کوچه، درب چهارم دست چپ منزل ما است.
خانهٔ ما زیاد بزرگ نیست امّا اتاق من بزرگترین اتاق در منزل ماست. اتاق خواهرم از اتاق من کوچکتر، ولی قشنگتر است. او در اتاقش عکس و پوستر زیاد دارد. من در اتاقم فقط یک پوستر بزرگ از شجریان دارم. به نظر من او بهترین خواننده ایران است.

mā yek xāne dar qarb-e širāz dārim. ādres-e mā in ast: širāz, kod-e posti-e 18248, xiābān-e sa`di, kuce-ye narges, pelāk-e 15, manzel-e hoseini. ruberu-ye kuce-ye mā yek pomp-e benzin ast. dar taraf-e rāst-e kuce yek pitzā forusi ast. dar taraf-e cap-e kuce nānvāyi ast. jelo-ye xāne-ye mā yek sanduq-e post ast. dāxel-e kuce, darb-e cahārom dast-e cap manzel-e mā ast. xāne-ye mā ziād bozorg nist ammā otāq-e man bozorgtarin otāq dar manzel-e māst. otāq-e xāharam az otāq-e man kucektar, vali qašangtar ast. u dar otāqaš aks va poster ziād dārad. man dar otāqam faqat yek poster-e bozorg az šajariān dāram. be nazar-e man u behtarin xānande-ye irān ast.

1 What is her address?
2 What landmarks does she give for her home address?
3 What comparisons does she make?
4 What opinion does she express?

5 ورود به تهران vorud be tehrān

Arriving in Tehran

By the end of this lesson, you should be able to:

- answer routine questions asked by immigration and customs officers
- wish someone a nice time and reciprocate
- suggest that you and others do something together
- talk about something you are doing now
- talk about something you will do in the future
- ask someone (not) to do something
- offer to do something for someone

Dialogue 1 How long will you stay in Iran?

An Australian tourist (T), *has just arrived at Tehran airport. The passport officer* (O) *begins the conversation.*

O: گذرنامه، لطفاً.
T: بفرمایید.
O: متشکّرم. چند وقت تو ایران میمونید؟
T: حدود ده روز.
O: آدرس مشخّصی دارید تو ایران؟
T: نه، میرم هتل.
O: بفرمایید.
T: مرسی، خداحافظ.
O: خداحافظ.

O: **gozarnāme, lotfan.**
T: **befarmāyid.**
O: **mot(a)šakkeram. cand vaqt tu irān mimunid?**
T: **hodud-e dah ruz.**
O: **ādres-e mošaxxasi dārid tu irān?**
T: **na, miram hotel.**
O: **befarmāyid.**
T: **mersi, xodā hāfez.**
O: **xodā hāfez.**

O: *Your passport, please.*
T: *Here you are.*
O: *Thank you. How long will you stay in Iran?*
T: *About ten days.*
O: *Do you have a known address in Iran?*
T: *No, I'll go to a hotel.*
O: *Here you are.*
T: *Thank you, goodbye.*
O: *Goodbye.*

Vocabulary

گذرنامه	**gozarnāme**	passport	متشکّر	**mot(a)šakker**	grateful
لطفا	**lotfan**	please	وقت	**vaqt**	time
بفرمایید	**befarmāyid**	Here you are	میمونید	**mimunid**	you (will) stay

موندن	**mundan**		مشخّص	**mosaxxas**	particular
(مون)	**(mun)**	to stay	میرم	**miram**	I'll go
حدود	**hodud-e**	about, approximately	رفتن (ر)	**raftan (r)**	to go
			هتل	**hotel**	hotel
روز	**ruz**	day			

Language points

Future simple tense

In colloquial Persian, the present simple tense (see p. 54) is also used to refer to a future act or fact. Therefore, the sentence:

به هتل میرم **be hotel miram**

can have either of these meanings:

'I go to a hotel', or 'I'll go to a hotel'.

Here is another sentence from the dialogue using the same structure:

چند وقت تو ایران میمونید؟
cand vaqt tu irān mimunid?
How long will you stay (or: will you be staying) in Iran?

Exercise 1

Fill the blanks with the appropriate form of the verb اومدن (ا) **umadan (ā)** 'to come'.

1 من با تو ____. **man bā to ____.** I'll come with you.
Answer من با تو میام. **man bā to miām.**
2 با من ____؟ **bā man ____?** Will you come with me?
3 او با ما ____. **u bā mā ____.** She'll come with us.
4 ما با شما ____. **mā bā šomā ____.** We'll come with you.
5 اونها با من ____. **unhā bā man ____.** They'll come with me.

Reduction

In casual speech, the sentence به هتل میرم **be hotel miram**, 'I'll go to a hotel' is often reduced to:

میرم هتل. **miram hotel.**

In this reduction, two things happen:

(a) The preposition به **be** 'to' is omitted.
(b) The verb میرم **miram** is placed before هتل **hotel**.

This sort of reduction normally occurs when verbs of motion (such as 'to go' and 'to come') are involved. Here is an example with the verb اومدن **umadan** 'to come':

هفته‌یی یک بار میاد اینجا.
hafteyi yek bār miād injā.
He/she comes here once a week.

Exercise 2

Can you tell an Iranian friend:

1 I'll come to your house tomorrow.
2 I'll go to Iran next year.
3 Will you come to my party next weekend?

Exercise 3

Provide the reduced forms of these sentences:

1 جمعه‌ها به سینما میریم.
jom`ehā be sinemā mirim.
We go to the cinema on Fridays.
Example: جمعه‌ها میریم سینما.
jom`ehā mirim sinemā.

2 ماهی دو بار به منزل ما میاد.
māhi do bār be manzel-e mā miād.
He/she comes to our house twice a month.

3 سالی یک بار به ایران میرم.
sāli yek bār be irān miram.
I go to Iran once a year.

4 هر روز دیر به اداره میاد.
har ruz dir be edāre miād.
He/she comes late to the office every day.

Present continuous

How to say 'I'm eating lunch'

Colloquial Persian uses the same structure (i.e. the present simple tense, introduced on p. 54) to express all these forms:

I eat = present simple
I'll eat = future simple
I'm eating = present continuous

The verb we need is خوردن (خور) **xordan (xor)** 'to eat'.
Persian for 'I'm eating lunch' is:

ناهار میخورم. **nāhār mixoram.**

To emphasise the fact that we are in the middle of doing something, we add the verb داشتن **dāštan** 'to have' (see pp. 44–5) as an auxiliary verb:

دارم ناهار میخورم. **dāram nāhār mixoram.**
I am (in the middle of) eating lunch.

To say: 'What are you doing right now?' in Persian is:

الآن داری چکار میکنی؟ **al`ān dāri cekār mikoni?**

Exercise 4

Match a letter with a number.

1 دارم شام میخورم. **dāram šām mixoram.**
2 دارم قهوه میخورم. **dāram qahve mixoram.**
3 دارند بازی میکنند. **dārand bāzi mikonand.**
4 دارم میرم خونه. **dāram miram xune.**

(a) I'm drinking coffee. [ ]
(b) They're playing. [ ]
(c) I'm going home. [ ]
(d) I'm eating/having dinner. [ ]

Exercise 5

Can you put these jumbled sentences in order?

1 من – میخورم – سوپ – دارم.
man – mixoram – sup – dāram.
2 ما – بازی میکنیم – داریم – تنیس.
mā – bāzi mikonim – dārim – tenis.

3 . داری - تو - تماشا میکنی - تلویزیون
dāri – to – tamāšā mikoni – televizion.
4 . نامه - او - مینویسه - داره
nāme – u – minevise – dāre.
5 . گوش میکنید - دارید - شما - رادیو - به
guš mikonid – dārid – šomā – rādio – be.

Exercise 6

Can you say these in Persian?

1 How long will you stay here? I'll stay here for a month.
2 Where will you stay? (or: Where will you be staying?) I'll rent a flat.
3 What are you doing right now?
I'm listening to the news.
I'm reading a newspaper.
4 What are you (will you be) doing this weekend?
Nothing. I'll stay at home.

Dialogue 2 Going through customs

Participants: customs officer (O) + passenger (P).

O: چمدونتونو بذارید رو میز، لطفاً.
P: بفرمایید.
O: چند نفرید؟
P: دو نفر. من و خانمم.
O: چی دارید؟
P: چیز خاصّی نداریم.
O: لوازم برقی دارید؟
P: فقط یک ریش‌تراش دارم.
O: مرسی. بفرمایید. خوش اومدید.

O: **camedunetun-o bezārid ru miz, lotfan.**
P: **befarmāyid.**
O: **cand nafarid?**
P: **do nafar. man o xānomam.**
O: **ci dārid?**
P: **ciz-e xassi nadārim.**
O: **lavāzem-e barqi dārid?**
P: **faqat ye(k) riš-tarāš dāram.**
O: **mersi. befarmāyid. xoš umadid.**

O: *Put your suitcase on the table, please.*
P: *Here you are.*
O: *How many of you are there (together)?*
P: *Two people. My wife and I.*
O: *What have you got (to declare)?*
P: *We haven't got anything special.*
O: *Do you have any electric appliances?*
P: *I only have a shaver.*
O: *Thanks. Go ahead. Welcome.*

Vocabulary

چمدون	**camedun**	suitcase	لوازم	**lavāzem**	appliances
چمدونتون	**camedunetun**	your suitcase	برقی	**barqi**	electric(al)
چند نفر	**cand nafar**	how many people	فقط	**faqat**	only
			ریش‌تراش	**riš-tarāš**	shaver
چیز	**ciz**	thing	خوش اومدید	**xoš umadid**	welcome (to a place)
خاصّ	**xāss**	special			

Language points

Definite article for a direct object

A direct object is one that is affected directly by the verb. So when you say 'I bought him a book', the word 'book' is the direct object because it was the book that was bought, not him! ('him' is the indirect object.) When you say 'I bought him the book', the word 'book' is now a definite direct object. In Persian, such an object is normally followed by the word را **rā**. In other words, when the object is known to both the speaker and the listener the speaker uses the word را **rā** after the object. For ease of reference, the word را **rā** will be called the 'object marker'.

(a) معمولاً برای ناهار یک ساندویچ میخورم.
ma`mulan barāye nāhār yek sāndevic mixoram.
I usually eat a sandwich for lunch.

(b) معمولاً ساندویچ را از سوپرمارکت میخرم.
ma`mulan sāndevic rā az supermārket mixaram.
I usually buy the sandwich from/at the supermarket.

You will note that no را **rā** is used after ساندویچ **sāndevic** 'sandwich' in (a) because it is 'a sandwich' (indefinite) while in (b) the word را **rā** is used to show that it is 'the sandwich' (definite).

Also note the following pair:

(c) معمولاً ساعت ۱۲ ناهار میخورم.
ma`mulan sā`at-e davāzdah nāhār mixoram.
I normally eat lunch at 12 o'clock.

(d) معمولاً ساعت ۱۲ ناهارم را میخورم.
ma`mulan sā`at-e davāzdah nāhāram rā mixoram.
I normally eat my lunch at 12 o'clock.

The object marker is not used in (c) because the speaker is talking about 'lunch' in general; while it is used in (d) because he is referring specifically to 'his lunch'. In casual speech, را **rā** is reduced to رو **ro** after vowels, and و **o** after consonants. In the English transcription, these will be shown as **-ro** and **-o** respectively. Here are examples (b) and (d) again showing را **rā** in its colloquial form و **-o**:

(b) معمولاً ساندویچو از سوپرمارکت میخرم.
ma`mulan sāndevic-o az supermārket mixaram.
I usually buy the sandwich from/at the supermarket.

(d) معمولاً ساعت ۱۲ ناهارمو میخورم.
ma`mulan sā`at-e davāzdah nāhāram-o mixoram.
I normally eat my lunch at 12 o'clock.

Note: The colloquial pronunciation of وَ **va** 'and' is also **o**. To prevent confusion between this and **-o** (as the colloquial form of را **rā**) a hyphen is placed before the object marker. Furthermore, in the Persian script, the و- **-o** (object marker) is connected to the object, while the و **o** meaning 'and' is preceded by a space.

فردا احمدو میبینم.
fardā ahmad-o mibinam. I'll see Ahmad tomorrow.

فردا احمد و پروینو میبینم.
fardā ahmad o parvin-o mibinam.
I'll see Ahmad and Parvin tomorrow.

You will also note that the direct object marker goes after the last object. Where the colloquial forms و **-o** and رو **-ro** are likely to cause confusion in the Persian script, the full form را **rā** will be used.

Note that را **rā** is not used where there is a preposition before the object:

به حرف پدرش گوش نمیکنه.
be harf-e pedareš guš nemikone.
He doesn't listen to his father's word/advice.

حرف پدرشو گوش نمیکنه.
harf-e pedareš-o guš nemikone.
He doesn't listen to his father's word/advice.

Exercise 7

With the help of the English translations, put the object marker را **rā** in the blanks where needed.

۱- من آب ___ زیاد میخورم.
1 **man āb ____ ziād mixoram.** I drink a lot of water.
۲- این آب ___ نمیخورم؛ خیلی سرده.
2 **in āb ____ nemixoram; xeili sarde.**
I won't drink this water; it's too cold.
۳- برای دسر معمولاً بستنی ___ میخورم.
3 **barāye deser ma`mulan bastani mixoram.**
I usually eat/have ice cream for dessert.
۴- کیک ___ میخورم اما بستنی ___ نمیخورم چون حالم خوب نیست.
4 **keik ____ mixoram ammā bastani ____ nemixoram con hālam xub nist.**
I'll eat the cake but I won't eat the ice cream because I'm not feeling well.
۵- هر روز او ___ میبینم.
5 **har ruz u ____ mibinam.** I see him every day.

Imperative

How to say 'Put it on the table, please'

The verb we need is گذاشتن (ذار) **gozāštan (zār)** 'to put'. To form the imperative, we add the prefix بـ **be-** to the present stem.

Note: The **be-** prefix carries the word stress.

بذار **bezār** Put . . .

This form is used when asking a close friend to do something. For a more formal request, we add the suffix ید **-id**:

بذارید **bezārid** Put . . .

Now a more complete picture of the sentence:

بذارید رو میز، لطفاً.
bezārid ru miz, lotfan. Put (it) on the table, please.

Now the sentence we met in the dialogue:

چمدونتونو بذارید رو میز، لطفاً.
camedunetun-o bezārid ru miz, lotfan.
Put your suitcase on the table, please.

To make the verb negative, we replace the بـ **be**- prefix with نـ **na**-:

چمدونتونو نذارید رو میز، لطفاً.
camedunetun-o nazārid ru miz, lotfan.
Don't put your suitcase on the table, please.

اونجا نشینید، لطفاً.
unjā našinid, lotfan. Don't sit there, please.

به من نگید چی شد.
be man nagid ci šod. Don't tell me what happened.

Note these special cases:

Formal	*Informal*	*Meaning*
برید **berid**	برو **boro(u)**	go
بگید **begid**	بگو **begu**	say/tell
بخورید **boxorid**	بخور **boxor**	eat
باشید **bāšid**	باش **bāš**	be
بدید **bedid**	بده **bede(h)**	give
بلند شید **boland šid**	بلند شو **boland šo(u)**	get up
صبر داشته باشید **sabr dāšte bāšid**	صبر داشته باش **sabr dāšte bāš**	Have patience

The verbs used are:

رفتن (ر) [رو] **raftan (r)[rav/rou]** to go
گفتن (گـ) [گو] **goftan (g)[gu]** to say, to tell
خوردن (خور) **xordan (xor)** to eat
بودن (هستـ/ باشـ) **budan (hast/bāš)** to be
دادن (د) [دهـ] **dādan (d)[dah/deh]** to give
داشتن (دار/ داشته باشـ) **dāštan (dār/dāšte bāš)** to have
بلند شدن (شـ) [شو] **boland šodan (š)[šav/šou]** to get up

Note the negative forms:

نرو **naro(u)** don't go (*inf*)
نخور **naxor** don't eat (*inf*)
نخورید **naxorid** don't eat (*f*)

نباش **nabāš** don't be (*inf*)
نباشید **nabāšid** don't be (*f*)
نده **nade(h)** don't give (*inf*)
بلند نشو **boland našo(u)** don't get up

Note what happens to the بـ **be-** prefix when the present stem of the verb begins with the vowel ا **ā**

اومدن (ا) **umadan (ā)** to come
آوردن (ار) **āvordan (ār)** to bring
بیا. **biā.** Come. (*inf*) بیارید. **biārid.** Bring. (*f*)

Also note the negative forms:

نیا. **nayā.** Don't come. (*inf*) نیارید. **nayārid.** Don't bring. (*f*)

Some compound verbs find it more convenient to drop the بـ **be-** prefix. Among them are بر گشتن (گرد) **bar gaštan (gard)** 'to return', and those formed with the help of the verb کردن (کن) **kardan (kon)** 'to do':

زودِ بر گردید. **zud bar gardid.** Return quickly.
لطفاً صبر کنید. **lotfan sabr konid.** Please wait.

To make the sentence negative, we add the نـ **na-** prefix:

تلفن نکنید. **telefon nakonid.** Don't telephone.
بر نگردید. **bar nagardid.** Don't return.

Also note these interesting cases:

ناهارتو بخور. **nāhāret-o boxor.** (Intonation: low fall)
Eat your lunch. (Request/order)

ناهارتو بخوری! **nāhāret-o boxori!** (Intonation: high fall)
Eat your lunch. (Don't forget! Make sure you do!)

تلویزیونو خراب نکن.
televizion-o xarāb nakon. (Intonation: low fall)
Don't break the television. (Request/pleading)

تلویزیونو خراب نکنی!
televizion-o xarāb nakoni! (Intonation: high fall)
Don't break the television! (Warning! Be careful not to!)

As in English, when we are asking someone to do us a favour, we use a question form (rather than the imperative):

اون پنجره‌رو میبندید لطفاً؟ **un panjara-ro mibandid lotfan?**
Will you close that window please?

Exercise 8

Are these Persian sentences correct equivalents for their English counterparts? If not, make the necessary corrections.

۱– لطفاً بشینید.
1 **lotfan bešinid.** Please sit down.

۲– لطفاً بچه‌هاتونو نیارید.
2 **lotfan baccehātun-o nayārid.** Please bring your children.

۳– لطفاً ساکت باشید.
3 **lotfan sāket bāšid.** Please be quiet.

۴– لطفاً به اتاق ده نرید.
4 **lotfan be otāq-e dah narid.** Please go to Room 10.

A polite 'go ahead' signal

The verb used is فرمودن (فرما) **farmudan (farmā)** which literally means 'to make a command'. Put in the imperative form, this is how it looks: بفرمایید **befarmāyid** meaning 'please go ahead'. This 'go ahead' signal, which we have already met (above), is used in various situations including: when answering the phone, offering food to a guest, offering a seat, handing something to someone, asking someone to go in/out first, etc. Naturally, this is often accompanied by an appropriate gesture.

How to say 'Let's go'

We can extend the imperative to first and third persons by adding the appropriate personal ending:

بریم. **berim.** Let's go.
برند خونه. **berand xune.** Let them go home.

The same form can be used for consultation or suggestion:

بریم؟ **berim?** Shall we go?

امشب بریم سینما؟ **emšab berim sinemā?**
Shall we go to the cinema tonight?

چایی بریزم؟ **cāyi berizam?** Shall I pour (you some) tea?

یک چایی دیگه بریزم؟ **yek cāyi-e dige berizam?**
Shall I pour (you) another (cup of) tea?

Exercise 9

What proposals are being made?

1 امشب بریم رستوران. **emšab berim resturān.**
2 حالا شام بخوریم. **hālā šām boxorim.**
3 حالا بخوابیم. **hālā bexābim.**
4 حالا بشینیم و ببینیم بابا بزرگ چی میگند.
hālā bešinim o bebinim bābā bozorg ci migand.
5 خب، حالا یک کمی تلویزیون تماشا کنیم.
xob, hālā yek kami televizion tamāšā konim.

How to say 'Have a nice time'

The pattern:

خوش بگذره. **xoš begzare.**
Have a nice time. (*lit* Let (the time) pass pleasantly (to you).)

This can be used in various contexts such as:

تعطیلات خوش بگذره.
ta`tilāt xoš begzare. Have a nice holiday.

آخر هفته خوش بگذره.
āxar-e hafte xoš begzare. Have a nice weekend.

مهمونی/پارتی خوش بگذره.
mehmuni/pārti xoš begzare. Have a nice (time at the) party.

A common reply is:

شما هم همینطور. **šomā ham haminto(u)r.** You too.

Exercise 10

Can you ask an Iranian friend:

1 To close the window.
2 To open the door.
3 To bring you some water.
4 To make some tea.
5 To pass the salt.
6 To eat some fruit.
7 Not to sit there.
8 To sit next to you.
9 Not to close the window.
10 Not to open the door.
11 Not to turn off the light.
12 To turn on the light.
13 To turn off the television.
14 To return home soon.

Sequencing

Note this sequencing difference between English and Persian:

من و پیتر **man o piter** Peter and I (*lit* I and Peter)
من و دوستم **man o dustam** my friend and I (*lit* I and my friend)
من و خانمم **man o xānomam** my wife and I (*lit* I and my wife)

Exercise 11

Can you say these in Persian?

1 What shall we eat for dinner?
2 I'll eat a sandwich.
3 I'll eat the sandwich.
4 I'll eat nothing.
5 Don't tell Ahmad (about it).
6 Don't go to his party.
7 Don't listen to him.
8 Close/open your eyes.
9 Enjoy the party.
10 Have a nice weekend.
11 My father and I will go to Iran next summer.
12 Shall we go to the supermarket this afternoon?
13 How many of you are there? There are four of us: my wife and I and two children.
14 Please come to our house and bring your children, too.

Comprehension

Listen to the conversation between James (J) *and the taxi driver* (D) *and answer the questions in English.*

J: این چمدونو کجا بذارم؟
D: بذارید تو صندوقِ عقب ... خب، کجا میرید؟
J: هتل فردوسی، لطفاً. میدونید کجاست؟
D: بله. ... اهل کجایید؟
J: استرالیا.
D: چند وقت تو ایرانِ میمونید؟
J: دو هفته ... لطفاً همینجا نگه دارید.
D: چشم، بفرمایید.
J: چند شد؟
D: ۲۰۰ تومن.
J: بفرمایید.
D: مرسی. خوش بگذره.

J: **in camedun-o kojā bezāram?**
D: **bezārid tu sanduq aqab . . . xob, kojā mirid?**
J: **hotel ferdousi, lotfan. midunid kojāst?**
D: **bale . . . ahl-e kojāyid?**
J: **osterāliā.**
D: **cand vaqt tu irān mimunid?**
J: **do hafte . . . lotfan haminjā negah dārid.**
D: **cašm, befarmāyid.**
J: **cand šod?**
D: **devist toman.**
J: **befarmāyid.**
D: **mersi. xoš begzare.**

1 What advice does J seek and get?
2 Why doesn't J give D the address of his destination?
3 How long does J intend to stay in Iran?
4 Where is he from?
5 How much does he pay for his fare?
6 What does the driver say at the end of the dialogue?

6 در ایران dar irān

In Iran

By the end of this lesson, you should be able to:

- get a taxi to your destination
- talk about what might/may/can/should/must happen
- talk about what you did the previous weekend
- ask someone if he/she wants you to do something for him/her
- book and check into a hotel
- complain about the standard of a hotel

Dialogue 1 Getting a taxi

Getting (hunting for!) a taxi in Tehran is an art! In the unlikely event of finding a completely empty taxi, here is a potential conversation a passenger (P) may hold with the driver (D).

P: تا شمرون چند؟
D: دویست تومن.
P: صد تومن میبرید؟
D: صد و پنجاه آخرش.
P: باشه. این چمدون خیلی سنگینه. میتونید بذارید تو صندوق عقب، لطفاً؟
D: خواهش میکنم ...
P: همینجاها پیاده میشم، مرسی. بفرمایید، ۱۵۰ تومن.

P: **tā šemrun cand?**
D: **devist toman.**
P: **sad toman mibarid?**
D: **sad o panjāh āxareš.**
P: **bāše. in camedun xeili sangine. mitunid bezārid tu sanduq aqab, lotfan?**
D: **xāheš mikonam . . .**

P: **haminjāhā piāde mišam, mersi. befarmāyid, sad o panjāh toman.**

P: *How much to Shemrun (Shemran)?*
D: *200 tumans.*
P: *Will you take (me there for) 100 tumans?*
D: *150 (tumans is) the last (price).*
P: *OK. This suitcase is very heavy. Can you put (it) in the boot, please?*
D: *By all means . . .*
P: *I'll get out somewhere here, thank you. Here you are, 150 tumans.*

Vocabulary

تا	**tā**	up to	میتونید	**mitunid**	can you
شمرون	**šemrun**	*col* for Shemiran (a place)	تونستن (تونـ)	**tunestan (tun)**	to be able
تومن	**toman**	tuman, Iranian currency = 10 rials	بذارید	**bezārid**	(you) put
میبرید	**mibarid**	will you take	صندوق عقب	**sanduq(-e) aqab**	rear trunk, car boot
بردن (بر)	**bordan (bar)**	to take/ carry	خواهش میکنم	**xāheš mikonam**	by all means
آخرش	**āxareš**	the final (price)	همینجا	**haminjā**	right here
باشه	**bāše**	OK	همینجاها	**haminjāhā**	somewhere here
سنگین	**sangin**	heavy	پیاده میشم	**piāde mišam**	I'll get out
			پیاده شدن (شـ)	**piāde šodan (š)**	to get out

Language points

Simple subjunctive

How to say 'Can you put it . . . ?'

The میـ **mi-** prefix (introduced at p. 54) suggests that the act or fact expressed by the verb is definite, as in:

امشب میریم سینما. **emšab mirim sinemā.**
We'll go (or: we're going) to the cinema tonight.

When the 'definiteness' of the act or fact expressed by the verb is somehow affected by a preceding verb, the second verb takes a بـ **be-** prefix, as in:

امشب میتونیم بریم سینما. **emšab mitunim berim sinemā.**
We can go to the cinema tonight.

Thus, when two verbs follow each other, the second verb takes a بـ **be-** prefix.

Verb 1: تونستن (تونـ) **tunestan (tun)** to be able
Verb 2: گذاشتن (ذار) **gozāštan (zār)** to put
میتونید **mitunid** you can
میذارید **mizārid** you put
میتونید بذارید **mitunid bezārid** you can put
میتونید بذارید تو صندوق عقب؟
mitunid bezārid tu sanduq aqab? Can you put (it) in the boot?

For ease of reference, the form taken by the second verb will be referred to as the 'subjunctive'. (Compare with the imperative, pp. 71–3.)

NB: With some compound verbs, the بـ **be-** prefix is dropped:

میتونم به شما تلفن کنم؟
mitunam be šomā telefon konam? Can I phone you?

How to say 'I want to go'

Here, again, we have two verbs to deal with:

Verb 1: خواستن (خوا) **xāstan (xā)** to want
Verb 2: رفتن (ر) **raftan (r)** to go

The formula is similar to the above. However, since the behaviour of verbs whose present stem ends in a vowel requires more attention, here is a fuller picture.

من میخوام برم. **man mixām beram.** I want to go.
تو میخوای بری. **to mixai beri.** You (*inf*) want to go.
او میخواد بره. **u mixād bere.** He/she wants to go.
ما میخوایم بریم. **mā mixaim berim.** We want to go.
شما میخواید برید. **šomā mixaid berid.** You want to go.
اونها میخواند برند. **unhā mixānd berand.** They want to go.

To make the above sentences negative, we add نـ **ne-** before میـ **mi**:

من نمیخوام برم. **man nemixām beram.** I don't want to go.

The literary present stem for Verbs 1 and 2 above are: خواه **xāh** and رو **rav** respectively. For example:

من میخواهم بروم. **man mixāham beravam.** I want to go.
او میخواهد برود. **u mixāhad beravad.** He/she wants to go.

Note the following examples where the subject of the second verb is a different person:

میخواید برم؟ **mixaid beram?** Do you want me to go?
میخواید پنجره‌رو ببندم؟ **mixaid panjara-ro bebandam?**
Do you want me to close the window?

Note: The verbs بودن **budan** 'to be' and داشتن **dāštan** 'to have', have their own special subjunctive stems, باش **bāš** and داشته باش **dāšte bāš** respectively.

ساعت هفت باید اونجا باشم. **sā`at-e haft bāyad unjā bāšam.**
I must be there at 7 o'clock.

میخواد دو تا کار داشته باشه. **mixād do tā kār dāšte bāše.**
He wants to have two jobs.

A verb occurring after these special verbs and verb forms normally takes the subjunctive form. Also note their negative forms.

باید برم. **bāyad beram.** I must go.
نباید برم. **nabāyad beram.** I mustn't go.
شاید برم. **šāyad beram.** I might go.
شاید نرم. **šāyad naram.** I might not go.
ممکنه برم. **momkene beram.** I may go.
ممکنه نرم. **momkene naram.** I may not go.
بهتره برم. **behtare beram.** I'd better go.
بهتره نرم. **behtare naram.** I'd better not go.

Exercise 1

Write the correct form of the verb in the blanks.

۱- میتونم پنجره‌رو ______ ؟ بستن (بند)
1 **mitunam panjara-ro ______? bastan (band)**
May I close the window?
Example: میتونم پنجره‌رو ببندم؟
mitunam panjara-ro bebandam?

۲- شاید اسمشو ______. دونستن (دون)
2 **šāyad esmeš-o ______. dunestan (dun)**
He might know her name.

۳- میخوای یک فیلم ______؟ دیدن (بین)

3 **mixai yek film ______? didan (bin)**
Do you want to see a film?

۴- میتونید درو ______؟ باز کردن (کن)

4 **mitunid dar-o ______? bāz kardan (kon)**
Can you open the door?

۵- باید به دوستم ______. تلفن کردن (کن)

5 **bāyad be dustam ______. telefon kardan (kon)**
I must phone my friend.

۶- میتونید ساعت ۹ اونجا ______؟ بودن (باش)

6 **mitunid sā`at-e noh unjā ______? budan (bāš)**
Can you be there at 9 o'clock? (See page 94 for 'time'.)

۷- شاید شماره تلفنشو ______. داشتن (داشته باش)

7 **šāyad šomāre telefoneš-o ______. dāštan (dāšte bāš)**
I might have his phone number.

Exercise 2

Use one of these words in each sentence and make the necessary changes.

شاید **šāyad** might
ممکنه **momkene** may
باید **bāyad** must/should

۱- پول خرد دارم. ←شاید پول خرد داشته باشم.

1 **pul-e xord dāram. → šāyad pul-e xord dāšte bāšam.**
I have some small change. → I might have some small change.

۲- ماشین ندارند. ← ______

2 **māšin nadārand. →**
They don't have a car. → They may not have a car.

۳- تلفن داره. ← ______

3 **telefon dāre. →**
He has a telephone. → He must have a telephone.

۴- اونها در منزل نیستند. ← ______

4 **unhā dar manzel nistand. →**
They are not at home. → They may not be at home.

Exercise 3

Fill in the blanks with the appropriate form of اومدن (ا) **umadan** (ā) 'to come'. Follow the example.

1 **man mixām bā to ____.** ۱- من میخوام با تو ____.
I want to come with you.

Example:
man mixām bā to biām. — من میخوام با تو بیام.

2 **mixaid bā man ____?** — ۲- میخواید با من ____؟
Do you want to come with me?

3 **u mixād bā mā ____.** — ۳- او میخواد با ما ____.
She wants to come with us.

4 **mā mixaim bā šomā ____.** — ۴- ما میخوایم با شما ____.
We want to come with you.

5 **unhā mixānd bā man ____.** — ۵- اونها میخواند با من ____.
They want to come with me.

Exercise 4

Can you say these in Persian?

1 Can I see the news? By all means.
2 Must you see this film right now? No, I can see (it) tomorrow.
3 Had we not better sit here?
4 I might have his phone number/address.
5 You must/should have patience.
6 You must be very happy.

Dialogue 2 Checking into a hotel

Mr Gowhari (G) booked a room when he telephoned the hotel last week. He has just arrived at the hotel where he is greeted by the receptionist (R). The porter is Parviz (P).

G: سلام، من گوهری هستم. هفتهٔ پیش تلفن کردم و یک
اتاق برای پنج روز رزرو کردم.
R: اجازه بدید دفترو نگاه کنم. بله، درسته قربان. شمارهٔ
اتاقتون سی و هشته.
G: متشکّرم ... ببخشید، ممکنه لطفاً بگید این
چمدون‌هارو بیارند بالا؟
R: بله قربان. پرویز جان، لطفاً چمدون‌های آقارو ببر
اتاق ۳۸.
P: بفرمایید آقا، از این طرف لطفاً ... این هم شماره
۳۸. اتاق خوبیه. رو به پارکه. منظره‌اش قشنگه.
G: چمدون‌ها سنگین بود. دست شما درد نکنه.
P: سر شما درد نکنه.
G: بفرمایید این قابل شما نیست.
P: خیلی ممنون.

G: **salām, man gouhari hastam. hafte-ye piš telefon kardam va yek otāq barāye panj ruz rezerv kardam.**

R: **ejāze bedid daftar-o negā(h) konam. bale, doroste qorbān. šomāre-ye otāqetun si o hašte.**

G: **mot(a)šakkeram . . . bebaxšid, momkene lotfan begid in camedun(h)ā-ro biārand bālā?**

R: **bale qorbān. parviz jān, lotfan camedun(h)ā-ye āqā-ro bebar otāq-e si o hašt.**

P: **befarmāyid āqā, az in taraf lotfan . . . in ham šomāre-ye si o hašt. otāq-e xubie. ru be pārke. manzaraš qašange.**

G: **camedun(h)ā sangin bud. dast-e šomā dard nakone.**

P: **sar-e šomā dard nakone.**

G: **befarmāyid, in qābel-e šomā nist.**

P: **xeili mamnun.**

G: *Hello, I'm Gowhari. Last week I telephoned and booked a room for five days.*

R: *Allow me to have a look in the book. Yes, that's right sir. Your room number is 38.*

G: *Thank you . . . Excuse me, could you please ask someone to bring the suitcases upstairs?*

R: *Yes sir. Dear Parviz, please take the gentleman's suitcases to room 38.*

P: *Let's go sir, this way please . . . Here's number 38. It's a good room. It's facing the park. It has a nice view.*

G: *The suitcases were heavy. Thank you.*

P: *You're welcome.*

G: *Here you are, this (tip) is not worthy of you.*

P: *Much obliged.*

Vocabulary

هفته	**hafte**	week
پیش	**piš**	last, ago
تلفن کردن	**telefon kardan**	to telephone
اتاق	**otāq**	room
رزرو کردن	**rezerv kardan**	to reserve, to book
اجازه	**ejāze**	permission
دفتر	**daftar**	book
نگاه کردن	**negāh kardan**	to look
درست	**dorost**	correct
قربان	**qorbān**	sir
بگید	**begid**	(could you) tell
بیارند	**biārand**	(so they can) bring
بالا	**bālā**	up, upstairs
ببر	**bebar**	take
این هم	**in ham**	here's (*lit* this also)
رو به	**ru be**	facing
منظره	**manzare**	view
دست شما درد نکنه	**dast-e šomā dard nakone**	thank you
سر شما درد نکنه	**sar-e šomā dard nakone**	you're welcome
قابل	**qābel**	worthy
ممنون	**mamnun**	obliged, grateful

Language points

Past simple tense

How to say 'I telephoned'

Here is the formula:

Past stem of verb + personal ending

All Persian verbs (infinitives) end with the sounds **-an**. To get the past stem of a verb, we omit these two sounds. The verb 'to telephone' is تلفن کردن **telefon kardan**. The past stem for کردن **kardan** is کرد **kard**.

من تلفن کردم. **man telefon kardam.** I telephoned.
تو تلفن کردی. **to telefon kardi.** You (*inf*) telephoned.
او تلفن کرد.* **u telefon kard.** He/she telephoned.
ما تلفن کردیم. **mā telefon kardim.** We telephoned.
شما تلفن کردید. **šomā telefon kardid.** You telephoned.
اونها تلفن کردند. **un(h)ā telefon kardand.** They telephoned.

*In this tense, no personal ending is used for third-person singular (i.e. he, she, it, etc.)

For the negative, we add the (stressed) prefix نـ **na-**:

من تلفن نکردم. **man telefon nakardam.** I didn't telephone.
تو تلفن نکردی. **to telefon nakardi.** You didn't telephone.

Exercise 5

Tell an Iranian friend about what you did last weekend. e.g.

1 I went to my friend's home on Saturday.
2 We watched television.
3 Then we went to the cinema.
4 On Sunday, my parents came to my house.
5 We had lunch together.

Structured infinitive

How to say 'to telephone someone'

A structured infinitive (*SI* for short), is a verb pattern that gives all the structural elements needed for constructing a sentence, with each element shown in its appropriate place. For instance 'to telephone someone' is a structured infinitive in English, on which basis you can make a sentence like: 'I telephoned Peter yesterday'. If we have the Persian equivalent of this *SI*, we should be able to make a similar sentence in Persian, with equal ease! Here it is:

به 'someone' تلفن کردن (کن)

be 'someone' telefon kardan (kon)
to telephone 'someone'

Based on the above Persian *SI*, let us make a sentence.

دیروز به پیتر تلفن کردم. **diruz be piter telefon kardam.**
I telephoned Peter yesterday.

You will note that the above Persian *SI* needs a preposition, به **be** 'to', while its English equivalent does not. This is what makes the notion of *SI* all the more important, since bilingual dictionaries often provide little structural help on what other elements, if any, are needed, and where to put them. They may give an equivalent for the word 'happy' in Persian, but that is where the learner is 'abandoned'. If the learner wanted to say, e.g., 'I'm happy with my car/flat/job, etc.', he would have no idea as to what preposition is used in Persian, if any, and where to put it. However, if we have the Persian equivalent of 'to be happy with X', we should have little difficulty in producing the above sentence in Persian. This and two further examples are given below.

از X راضی بودن (هست)
az 'X' rāzi budan (hast) to be happy with X

از X عصبانی بودن (هست)
az 'X' asabāni budan (hast) to be angry with X

(یک سؤال) از X پرسیدن (پرس)
(yek so`āl) az 'X' porsidan (pors) to ask X (a question)

Examples:

من از ماشین راضی هستم.
man az māšin rāzi hastam. I'm happy with the car.

شما از من عصبانی هستید؟
šomā az man asabāni hastid? Are you angry with me?

من یک سؤال از احمد پرسیدم.
man yek so`āl az ahmad porsidam. I asked Ahmad a question.

You will note that in all the Persian examples above, the preposition از **az** is used, which is a dictionary equivalent for the English word 'from'. In the first two examples, English uses the preposition 'with', and in the third, none. A dictionary equivalent for 'with' in Persian is با **bā**. Here is another useful *SI*:

منتظر ... بودن (هست) **montazer-e . . . budan (hast)**
to be waiting for . . .

منتظر کی هستی؟ **montazer-e ki hasti?** Who are you waiting for?
منتظر احمدم. **montazer-e ahmadam.** I'm waiting for Ahmad.
منتظر چی هستی؟ **montazer-e ci hasti?** What are you waiting for?
منتظر اخبارم. **montazer-e axbāram.** I'm waiting for the news.

Exercise 6

Fill in each blank with a preposition from the list below.

از **az** from با **bā** with به **be** to

۱- امروز صبح ــــ دوستم تلفن کردم.

1 **emruz sobh ____ dustam telefon kardam.**
This morning I phoned my friend.

۲- شما ــــ کارتون راضی هستید؟

2 **šomā ____ kāretun rāzi hastid?**
Are you happy with your job?

۳- چند سؤال ــــ معلم پرسیدم.

3 **cand so`āl ____ mo`allem porsidam.**
I asked the teacher some questions.

۴- من ــــ خانمم ــــ سینما رفتم.

4 **man ____ xānomam ____ sinemā raftam.**
I went to the cinema with my wife.

An idiom for 'thank you'

The expression دست شما درد نکنه **dast-e šomā dard nakone** 'thank you' (*lit* May your hand not ache!) is used to thank someone for something they have done for us, particularly with the use of their hands – e.g. handing something to us, or cooking a delicious meal for us, etc. An echo reply is normally

سر شما درد نکنه **sar-e šomā dard nakone** 'you're welcome'
(*lit* May your head not ache!)

A more casual exchange would be:

دستتون درد نکنه. **dastetun dard nakone.** Thank you.
سرتون درد نکنه. **saretun dard nakone.** You're welcome.

Exercise 7

At the dinner table, an Iranian friend has passed you the salt.

1 How do you thank them?
2 How would they respond?

Expressions used to book a hotel

هتل درجهٔ یک / پنج ستاره **hotel-e daraje-ye yek/panj setāre**
first-class/five-star hotel

اتاق یک / دو نفره دارید؟ **otāq-e yek/do nafare dārid?**
Do you have a room for one person/two people?

شبی چنده؟ **šabi cande?**
How much is it for each night?

برای هر نفر **barāye har nafar**
for each person

چک / کارت اعتباری قبول میکنید؟
cek/kārt-e e`tebāri qabul mikonid?
Do you accept cheques/credit cards?

اتاق با دوش / حمّام / توالت / تلفن دارید؟
otāq bā duš/hammām/tuālet/telefon dārid?
Do you have a room with a shower/bathroom/toilet/telephone?

قیمت شامل صبحانه / ناهار / شام میشه؟
qeimat šāmel-e sobhāne/nāhār/šām miše?
Does the price include breakfast/lunch/dinner?

پنج نفریم: دو نفر بزرگسال و سه تا بچه.
panj nafarim: do nafar bozorgsāl va se tā bacce.
We're five: two adults and three children.

Exercise 8

Translate the following sentences into English.

۱- دوتا اتاق ۲ نفره با دوش میخوام، لطفاً.
1 **do tā otāq-e do-nafare bā duš mixām, lotfan.**

۲- هتل درجهٔ ۲ میخوام.
2 **hotel-e daraje-ye do mixām.**

۳- ترجیحاً تو مرکز شهر باشه.
3 **tarjihan tu markaz-e šahr bāše.**

۴- این اتاق شبی چنده؟
4 **in otāq šabi cande?**

۵- این قیمت شامل صبحونه هم میشه؟
5 **in qeimat šāmel-e sobhune ham miše?**

Expressions used to complain about a hotel

ببخشید، میتونم با مدیر هتل صحبت کنم؟
bebaxšid, mitunam bā modir-e hotel sohbat konam?
Excuse me, can I speak with the hotel manager?

ملافه‌ها کثیفه. **malāfehā kasife.** The sheets are dirty.

تلفن کار نمیکنه. **telefon kār nemikone.**
The telephone is not working.

تلویزیون/دوش/شیر آب/پریز ریش‌تراش خرابه.
televizion/duš/šir-e āb/periz-e riš-taraš xarābe.
The television/shower/water tap/shaver socket is out of order.

Exercise 9

Can you say these in Persian?

1 I want a single room with a shower for two weeks.
2 Does the price include dinner, too? No, that's separate.
3 I'd like to book two seats for Mashad.
4 May I ask you a question? Go ahead.
5 May I have a word with the manager?
6 The lights in the bathroom are not working/broken.
7 The shower has no water.
8 What/who are you waiting for?
9 I'm waiting for the news.
10 I'm waiting for my friend.
11 Are you angry with me?
12 Are you happy with your income?
13 Yes, but I'm not happy with my boss!
14 I'll phone you tomorrow.

Comprehension

Listen to this conversation between a guest (G) and the hotel manager (M).

G: آقا من از این هتل اصلاً راضی نیستم.
M: چی شده قربان؟
G: من یک اتاق دونفرهٔ بزرگ رزرو کردم اما شما یک اتاق یک نفره به ما دادید با یک تخت اضافه. من اتاق با حمّام و وان خواستم، شما اتاق با دوش دادید. تلفن اتاق هم کار نمیکنه.

M: جداً معذرت میخوام. واقعاً شرمنده‌ام. امشب یک اتاق دونفرهٔ بزرگ خالی میشه. میتونم اون اتاقو به شما بدم.

G: راستش قصد داشتیم سه هفته بمونیم، امّا با این وضع حتّی یک هفته هم شاید نمونیم. در ضمن ممکنه به این مهمون‌های اتاق پهلویی بگید شب‌ها یک کمی ساکت‌تر باشند؟

M: حتماً. میل دارید با من بیاید اتاقو ببینید؟

G: الآن منتظر تلفن از انگلستانم. یک ساعت دیگه میام دفترتون.

M: باشه، منتظرتونم.

G: **āqā man az in hotel aslan rāzi nistam.**

M: **ci šode qorbān?**

G: **man yek otāq-e do-nafare-ye bozorg rezerv kardam ammā šomā yek otāq-e yek-nafare be mā dādid bā yek taxt-e ezāfe. man otāq-e bā hammām o vān xāstam, šomā otāq-e bā duš dādid. telefon-e otāq ham kār nemikone.**

M: **jeddan ma`zerat mixām. vāqe`an šarmandam. emšab yek otāq-e donafare-ye bozorg xāli miše. mitunam un otāq-o be šomā bedam.**

G: **rāsteš qasd dāštim se hafte bemunim, ammā bā in vaz` hattā yek hafte ham šāyad namunim. dar zemn momkene be in mehmunhā-ye otāq-e pahluyi begid šabhā yek kami sākettar bāšand?**

M: **hatman. meil dārid bā man biaid otāq-o bebinid?**

G: **al(`)ān montazer-e telefon az engelestānam. yek sā`at-e dige miām daftaretun.**

M: **bāše, montazeretunam.**

1 What three complaints does G make in his initial outburst?
2 How does the manager respond to this?
3 What remedy does the manager propose?
4 What change of plan is the guest considering and why?
5 What is the guest's fourth complaint?
6 What does the manager offer towards the end?
7 Why does the guest decline the offer at the time?

7 گفتگوی خیابانی
goftogu-ye xiābāni

Street talk

By the end of this lesson, you should be able to:

- ask and tell the time
- ask for and give directions
- ask an Iranian to speak more slowly and clearly
- describe location with reference to the points of compass
- talk about journey time and distance
- enquire about the availability of facilities in the area

Dialogue 1 Asking directions

Julie (J) is looking for the home address of an Iranian friend in Tehran. She has difficulty reading the address. She asks a passer-by (P) for help.

J: آقا ببخشید، ساعت چنده؟

P: هشت و نیم.

J: مرسی. این آدرسو میتونید بخونید، لطفاً؟

P: خیابان سینا، پلاک هشتاد.

J: خیابون سینا میدونید کجاست؟

P: مستقیم برید تا یک چهار راه بزرگ. اونجا، بپیچید دست چپ. خیابون سوّم دست راست خیابون سیناست.

J: ببخشید، فارسیم زیاد خوب نیست. ممکنه لطفاً یک کم آهسته‌تر و شمرده‌تر صحبت کنید؟

P: یعنی از اوّل همه‌رو دوباره بگم؟

J: اگه ممکنه.

P: بله، مستقیم برید تا ...

J: **āqā bebaxšid, sā`at cande?**
P: **hašt o nim.**
J: **mersi. in ādres-o mitunid bexunid, lotfan?**
P: **xiābān-e sinā, pelāk-e haštād.**
J: **xiābun-e sinā midunid kojāst?**
P: **mostaqim berid tā yek c(ah)ār rāh-e bozorg. unjā, bepicid dast-e cap. xiābun-e sevvom dast-e rāst xiābun-e sināst.**
J: **bebaxšid, fārsim ziād xub nist. momkene lotfan yek kam āhestetar va šomordetar sohbat konid?**
P: **ya`ni az avval hama-ro dobāre begam?**
J: **age momkene.**
P: **bale, mostaqim berid tā . . .**

J: *Excuse me sir, what time is it?*
P: *Half-past eight.*
J: *Thank you. Can you read this address (for me), please?*
P: *Sina Street, no. 80.*
J: *Do you know where Sina Street is?*
P: *Go straight up to a big cross-roads. There, turn left. The third road on the right is Sina Street.*
J: *I'm sorry, my Persian isn't that good. Would you please speak a bit more slowly and clearly?*
P: *You mean I should say all that again?*
J: *If possible.*
P: *Yes, go straight up to . . .*

Vocabulary

ساعت	**sā`at**	time, hour, clock	چهار راه	**c(ah)ār rāh**	cross-roads
			بپیچید	**bepicid**	turn
ساعت چنده؟	**sā`at cande?**	What time is it?	پیچیدن (پیچ)	**picidan (pic)**	to turn
بخونید	**bexunid**	(you) read	دست	**dast**	hand
خوندن (خونـ)	**xundan (xun)**	to read	چپ	**cap**	left
			راست	**rāst**	right
خیابون	**xiābun** *col* for خیابان **xiābān**	street	زیاد	**ziād**	much
			آهسته	**āheste**	slow(ly)
			شمرده	**šomorde**	clear(ly)
مستقیم	**mostaqim**	straight	صحبت کردن (کنـ)	**sohbat kardan (kon)**	to speak
تا	**tā**	up to; until			

یعنی	**ya`ni**	i.e.; you mean	بگم	**begam**	(for me) to say
همه	**hame**	all	اگه	**age**	if
دوباره	**dobāre**	again			

Exercise 1

An Iranian relative (R) has received a faxed message from his Australian friend, but can't read the handwriting. Can you translate this dialogue into Persian?

R: Excuse me, can you read this fax for me, please.
YOU: Certainly. Who is it from?
R: From my Australian friend.

[after you have read the letter]

R: Thank you very much.
YOU: Pleasure.

Language points

Asking and telling the time

ساعت چنده؟ **sā`at cande?** What time is it? (*lit* How much is the hour?)
ساعت هشته. **sā`at haš̄te.** It's 8 o'clock. (*lit* The hour is eight.)

Here are some other expressions of time:

ساعت هشت **sā`at-e haš̄t** (at) 8 o'clock
هشت و نیم **haš̄t o nim** half past 8 (*lit* eight and half)
هشت و ربع **haš̄t o rob`** a quarter past 8 (*lit* eight and quarter)
هشت و پنج دقیقه **haš̄t o panj da(q)iqe** 5 past 8 (*lit* 8 and 5 minutes)
یک ربع به هشت **ye(k) rob` be haš̄t** a quarter to eight

More 'streetwise' expressions

ببخشید، ساعت دارید؟ **bebaxš̄id, sā`at dārid?**
Excuse me, have you got the time (*lit* a watch)?

ببخشید، فرودگاه از کدوم طرف باید برم؟
bebaxš̄id, forudgāh az kodum taraf bāyad beram?
Excuse me, which way do I go to the airport?

میدونید از اینجا تا فرودگاه چقدر راه است؟
midunid az injā tā forudgāh ceqadr rāh ast (*col* **rāst)?**
Do you know how far it is from here to the airport?

پیاده یک ساعت؛ با ماشین ده دقیقه.
piāde ye(k) sā`at; bā māšin dah da(q)iqe.
One hour on foot; ten minutes by car.

شمال **šomāl** north; جنوب **jonub** south; شرق **šarq** east;
غرب **qarb** west; شمال شرق **šomāl-e šarq** north-east;
جنوب غرب **jonub-e qarb** south-west

سر نبش شمال غرب چهار راه
sar-e nabš-e šomāl-e qarb-e c(ah)ār rāh
on the north-west corner of the cross-roads/intersection

Exercise 2

Look at the following local map. Can you give directions to:

[A] the post office; [B] the telecom centre; [C] the supermarket

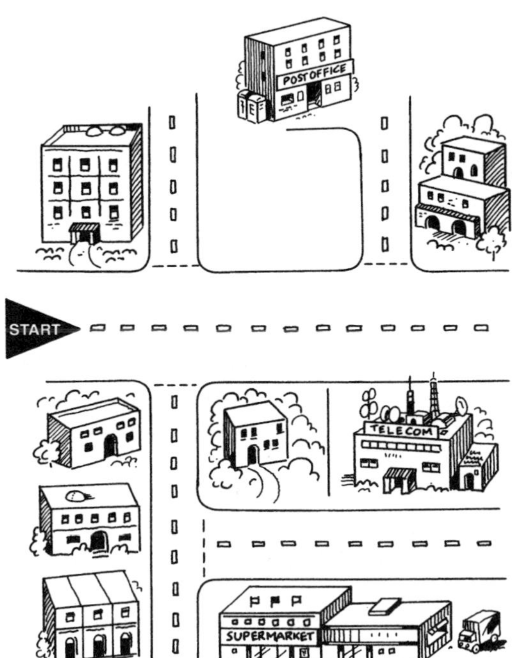

Exercise 3

Can you say these in Persian?

1 What time is it, please?
2 Half-past six.
3 A quarter to three.
4 A quarter past one.
5 Five minutes to twelve.
6 Five past eleven.
7 Sorry, I haven't got a watch.
8 Excuse me, where's the post office?
9 How far is it from here to the station?
10 It's half an hour's walk.
11 It's five minutes' drive.

Dialogue 2 Is there a public phone around here?

Julie (J) is now looking for a public telephone. She asks a passer-by (P) for help.

J: ببخشید، این اطراف تلفن عمومی هست؟
P: تو اون پستخونه چندتا هست.
J: ببخشید زحمت میدم، ۱۰ تومن پول خرد دارید، لطفاً؟ برای تلفن میخوام.
P: شاید داشته باشم. بفرمایید، یک پنج تومنی و پنج تا یک تومنی. خوبه؟
J: خوبه، یک دنیا ممنون. ببخشید، خیلی زحمت دادم.
P: چه زحمتی. شما خارجی هستید؟
J: بله، چطور مگه؟
P: فکر کردم شاید با تلفن‌های عمومی ایران آشنا نباشید.
J: درست حدس زدید.
P: فرق زیادی ندارند. فقط یادتون باشه بعد از اینکه پولو انداختید، بوق آزادو میشنوید.
J: از راهنماییتون خیلی متشکّرم.
P: خواهش میکنم. موفّق باشید.

J: **bebaxs̄id, in atrāf telefon-e omumi hast?**
P: **tu un postxune cand tā hast.**
J: **bebaxs̄id zahmat midam, dah toman pul-e xord dārid, lotfan? barāye telefon mixām.**
P: **s̄āyad dās̄te bās̄am. befarmāyid, yek panj-tomani o panj tā yek-tomani. xube?**

J: **xube, yek donyā mamnun. bebaxšid, xeili zahmat dādam.**
P: **ce zahmati. šomā xāreji hastid?**
J: **bale, ceto(u)r mage?**
P: **fekr kardam šāyad bā telefonhā-ye omumi-e irān āš(e)nā nabāšid.**
J: **dorost hads zadid.**
P: **farq-e ziādi nadārand. faqat yādetun bāše ba`d az inke pul-o andāxtid, buq-e āzād-o miš(e)navid.**
J: **az rāhnamāyitun xeili mot(a)šakkeram.**
P: **xāheš mikonam. mo(v)affaq bāšid.**

J: *Excuse me, is there a public telephone around here?*
P: *There are a few (of them) in that post office.*
J: *Sorry to bother you, can you change (this) 10-tuman note, please? I want (it) for the telephone.*
P: *I might have (some). Here you are, one five-tuman piece and five one-tuman pieces (coins). Is that (any) good?*
J: *That's fine, thanks a million. I'm sorry for troubling you.*
P: *No trouble. Are you from overseas?*
J: *Yes, but why?*
P: *I thought you might not be familiar with public telephones in Iran.*
J: *You're right. (* lit *You guessed correctly.)*
P: *They're not much different. Only remember (that) after you've put the money in, you'll hear the dialling tone.*
J: *Thank you very much for your advice.*
P: *You're welcome. Good luck.*

Vocabulary

این اطراف	**in atrāf**	around here (*lit* these quarters/ sides)
عمومی	**omumi**	public
پستخونه	**postxune**	post office
چند تا	**cand tā**	a few (of them)
زحمت دادن (د)	**zahmat dādan (d)**	to bother
پول	**pul**	money
خرد	**xord/xurd**	small
میخوام	**mixām**	I want
پنج تومنی	**panj tomani**	(a) five-tuman piece
دنیا	**donyā**	world
ممنون	**mamnun**	obliged, grateful
خارجی	**xāreji**	from overseas
آشنا	**āš(e)nā**	familiar
حدس زدن (زن)	**hads zadan (zan)**	to guess
فرق	**farq**	difference

یادتون باشه	**yādetun bāše**	remember	راهنمایی	**rāhnamāyi**	advice, guidance
انداختن (انداز)	**andāxtan (andāz)**	to put in	موفّق باشید	**mo(v)affaq bāšid**	good luck (*lit* be successful)
بوق آزاد	**buq-e āzād**	dialling tone			
شنیدن (شنو)	**šenidan (šenav)**	to hear			

Language points

How to say 'there is', 'there was', 'there were'

هست **hast** and بود **bud** (from the verb بودن **budan** 'to be') are used for the present and the past, respectively, regardless of number (singular or plural):

تو یخچال میوه هست؟ **tu yaxcāl mive hast?**
Is there (any) fruit in the fridge?

بله، چند تا سیب و پرتقال هست.
bale, cand tā sib o porteqāl hast.
Yes, there are a few apples and oranges.

تو کلاس شما چند تا پسر هست؟
tu kelās-e šomā cand tā pesar hast?
How many boys are there in your class?

تو کلاس من هشت تا پسر هست.
tu kelās-e man hašt tā pesar hast.
There are eight boys in my class.

پارسال، تو کلاسم فقط سه تا پسر بود.
pārsāl, tu kelāsam faqat se tā pesar bud.
Last year, there were only three boys in my class.

For the negative, نیست **nist** and نبود **nabud** are used for the present and the past, respectively:

تو یخچال میوه نیست.
tu yaxcāl mive nist. There is no fruit in the fridge.

پارسال، تو کلاسم دختر نبود.
pārsāl, tu kelāsam doxtar nabud.
Last year, there were no girls in my class.

Exercise 4

Can you translate these sentences into English?

۱- تو شهر شما ایرانی هست؟

1 **tu šahr-e šomā irāni hast?**

۲- تو محلهٔ شما رستوران ایرانی هست؟

2 **tu mahalle-ye šomā resturān-e irāni hast?**

۳- تو کلاستون تلویزیون هست؟

3 **tu kelāsetun televizion hast?**

۴- تو فریزر بستنی هست؟

4 **tu ferizer bastani hast?**

۵- بود ولی من خوردم.

5 **bud vali man xordam.**

More 'streetwise' expressions

ببخشید، این نزدیکی‌ها نانوایی هست؟
bebaxšid, in nazdikihā nānvāyi hast?
Excuse me, is there a baker's shop nearby?

ببخشید، ساعت خدمتتون هست؟
bebaxšid, sā`at xedmatetun hast?
Excuse me, have you got the time? (*pol/f*)

'After lunch' v. 'After I've had lunch'

(a) بعد از **ba`d az** after
(b) بعد از اینکه **ba`d az inke** after

As you can see, there are two ways of saying 'after' in Persian. We use (a) before a noun, and (b) before a sentence. Examples:

بعد از ناهار **ba`d az nāhār** after lunch

بعد از اینکه ناهار خوردم **ba`d az inke nāhār xordam**
after I've had lunch (*lit* after I ate lunch)

Note: The verb in the sentence following (b) is normally expressed in the past tense, regardless of the actual time of happening:

بعد از اینکه ناهار خوردم، میرم سینما.
ba`d az inke nāhār xordam, miram sinemā.
After I've had lunch, I'll go to the cinema. (future)

بعد از اینکه ناهار خوردم، رفتم سینما.
ba`d az inke nāhār xordam, raftam sinemā.
After I had lunch, I went to the cinema. (past)

Here is a sentence from Dialogue 2 (p. 96):

بعد از اینکه پولو انداختید، بوق آزادو میشنوید.
ba`d az inke pul-o andāxtid, buq-e āzād-o mis̄(e)navid.
After you've put the money in, you'll hear the dialling tone.

'Before lunch' v. 'Before I have lunch'

(a) قبل از **qabl az** before
(b) قبل از اینکه **qabl az inke** before

As you can see, there are two ways of saying 'before' in Persian. We use (a) before a noun, and (b) before a sentence. Examples:

قبل از ناهار
qabl az nāhār before lunch

قبل از اینکه ناهار بخورم
qabl az inke nāhār boxoram before I have lunch

Note: The verb in the sentence following (b) is normally expressed in the subjunctive (see p. 79) regardless of the actual time of happening:

قبل از اینکه ناهار بخورم، میرم سینما.
qabl az inke nāhār boxoram, miram sinemā.
Before I have lunch, I'll go to the cinema. (future)

قبل از اینکه ناهار بخورم، رفتم سینما.
qabl az inke nāhār boxoram, raftam sinemā.
Before I had lunch, I went to the cinema. (past)

Exercise 5

Write the longer version for each sentence using the appropriate form of the verb in brackets. Follow the example.

۱- بعد از کلاس میرم خونه. (تموم شدن (شـ))

1 **ba`d az kelās miram xune. (tamum s̄odan (s̄))**
After class I'll go home. (to finish)
Example: بعد از اینکه کلاس تموم شد، میرم خونه.
ba`d az inke kelās tamum s̄od, miram xune.
After the class is finished, I'll go home.

۲- بعد از کلاس رفتم خونه. (تموم شدن (شـ))
2 **ba`d az kelās raftam xune. (tamum šodan (š))**
After class I went home. (to finish)
۳- قبل از کلاس ناهار میخورم. (شروع شدن (شـ))
3 **qabl az kelās nāhār mixoram. (šoru` šodan (š))**
Before class I'll have lunch. (to begin)
۴- قبل از کلاس ناهار خوردم. (شروع شدن (شـ))
4 **qabl az kelās nāhār xordam. (šoru` šodan (š))**
Before class I had lunch. (to begin)
۵- دیشب قبل از خواب به ایران تلفن کردم. (خوابیدن (خواب))
5 **dišab qabl az xāb be irān telefon kardam. (xābidan (xāb))**
Last night before sleeping I telephoned Iran. (to sleep)

Exercise 6

Can you say these in Persian?

1 Excuse me, is there a post office/police station/library/supermarket around here?
2 Is there any milk in the fridge?
3 Are there any Iranians in your area?
4 Last year there were five Iranians in my class.
5 Before you go out, turn off the lights.
6 I phoned Ahmad before I left the office.
7 We'll have dinner after all the guests have come/arrived.

Comprehension

Yesterday you got this message on your answering machine.

سلام. جلال هستم. از هتل اطلس تلفن میکنم. از هتل راضی هستم، فقط صدای ترافیک یک کمی زیاده. راستی امشب من و خانمم، بعد از اینکه گردشمون تموم شد، میخوایم بریم سینما. دوست داریم تو هم با ما بیای. فیلم ساعت ۷ شب شروع میشه. پس بهتره ساعت ۶ همدیگه‌رو ببینیم تا وقت برای صحبت هم داشته باشیم. قبل از اینکه بریم سینما، با هم شام میخوریم. قراره بریم سینما حافظ. روبروی سینما یک رستوران هست. ساعت ۶ تو رستوران منتظرتیم. فعلاً خدا حافظ.

salām. jalāl hastam. az hotel atlas telefon mikonam. az hotel rāzi hastam, faqat sedā-ye terāfik yek kami ziāde. rāsti emšab man o

xānomam, ba`d az inke gardeš̄emun tamum šod, mixaim berim sinemā. dust dārim to ham bā mā biai. film sā`at-e haft-e šab šoru` miše. pas behtare sā`at-e šeš hamdiga-ro bebinim tā vaqt barāye sohbat ham dāšte bāšim. qabl az inke berim sinemā, bā ham šām mixorim. qarāre berim sinemā hāfez. ruberu-ye sinemā yek resturan hast. sā`at-e šeš tu resturān montazeretim. fe`lan xodā hāfez.

1 Who is calling?
2 Where is he phoning from?
3 How does he feel about the place?
4 Where is the caller going tonight and with whom?
5 What time does the event begin?
6 What does he intend to do before the event?
7 What has the caller been doing during the day?
8 What time does he want to see you and why?
9 Where will you be seeing him?

8 گرسنه‌اید؟ gorosneid?

Are you hungry?

By the end of this lesson, you should be able to:

- talk about food, drinks and your diet
- order a meal, complain about it, pay the bill
- enquire about various dishes
- seek and give permission to do something
- apologise for interrupting
- talk about how frequently you do things
- ask someone if he/she has ever done something

Dialogue 1 Are you on a diet?

Parviz (P) has difficulty sleeping at night. Here is part of his conversation with his doctor (D).

D: معمولاً شام چی میخورید؟
P: اغلب شام نمیخورم.
D: چرا؟ رژیم دارید؟
P: بله، امّا دیشب جوجه‌کباب خوردم.
D: وقتی هیچّی نمیخورید، خوابتون چطوره؟
P: باز هم نمیتونم بخوابم.

D: **ma`mulan šām ci mixorid?**
P: **aqlab šām nemixoram.**
D: **cerā? reĝim dārid?**
P: **bale, ammā dišab juje-kabāb xordam.**
D: **vaqti hicci nemixorid, xābetun ceto(u)re?**
P: **bāz (h)am nemitunam bexābam.**

D: *What do you normally eat for dinner?*
P: *I often don't eat dinner.*
D: *Why? Are you on a diet? (* lit *Do you have diet?)*

P: *Yes, but last night I ate chicken kebab.*
D: *How's your sleep when you don't eat anything?*
P: *Again, I can't sleep.*

Vocabulary

شام	**šām**	dinner	وقتی	**vaqti**	when
چرا	**cerā**	why	هیچی	**hicci**	nothing
رژیم	**reĝim**	diet	خواب	**xāb**	sleep
دیشب	**dišab**	last night	باز هم	**bāz ham**	again
جوجه	**juje**	chicken	خوابیدن	**xābidan**	
کباب	**kabāb**	kebab	(خوابـ)	**(xāb)**	to sleep

Language points

Adverbs of frequency

همیشه **hamiše** always
اغلب **aqlab** often
گاهی **gāhi** occasionally
هیچوقت **hic-vaqt** never
معمولاً **ma`mulan** usually, normally
بعضی وقتها **ba`zi vaqthā** sometimes
به ندرت **be nodrat** rarely

The above adverbs normally follow the subject, for example:

سیروس اغلب شام نمیخوره.
sirus aqlab šām nemixore. Sirus often doesn't eat dinner.

من به ندرت صبحونه میخورم.
man be nodrat sobhune mixoram. I rarely eat breakfast.

Double negative

How to say 'I never eat dinner'

هیچوقت **hic-vaqt** is a dictionary equivalent for 'ever' and 'never'.

شما هیچوقت شام میخورید؟
šomā hic-vaqt šām mixorid? Do you ever eat dinner?

من هیچوقت شام نمیخورم.
man hic-vaqt šām nemixoram. I never eat dinner. (*lit* I never don't eat dinner, *or* I don't ever eat dinner.)

Thus, when used in a positive question, هیچ‌وقت **hic-vaqt** means ‘ever’. When we use هیچ‌وقت **hic-vaqt** to mean ‘never’, we put the verb in the negative. All Persian words beginning with the negative prefix هیچ **hic-** (roughly meaning ‘not any’) fall in the same category. Here are some of the more common ones:

هیچ کس **hic-kas** nobody, not anyone
هیچ چیز **hic-ci(z)** nothing, anything; هیچّی **hicci** (*col*)
هیچ کدوم **hic-kodum** neither, none

Exercise 1

Listen to the dialogue between Ali (A) and Parvaneh (P) and put the appropriate letter in the box, true [T] or false [F].

A: معمولاً صبحونه چی میخوری؟
P: هیچ‌وقت صبحونه نمیخورم.
A: من هم همینطور. تو چرا نمیخوری؟ رژیم داری؟
P: نه بابا، رژیم چیه؟
A: پس چرا نمیخوری؟
P: چون تنبلم. تو چرا نمیخوری؟
A: من هم همینطور.

A: **ma`mulan sobhune ci mixori?**
P: **hic-vaqt sobhune nemixoram.**
A: **man (h)am haminto(u)r. to cerā nemixori? reĝim dāri?**
P: **na bābā, reĝim cie?**
A: **pas cerā nemixori?**
P: **con tanbalam. to cerā nemixori?**
A: **man (h)am haminto(u)r.**

1 The relationship between Ali and Parvaneh is formal. [F]
2 Parvaneh never has breakfast because she is on a diet. [ ]
3 Ali never has breakfast because he is lazy. [ ]
4 Their reason for not having breakfast is the same. [ ]

Exercise 2

Write in the blanks the correct form of the verb in brackets.

۱- آخر هفتهٔ گذشته هیچ‌جا ______ (رفتن).

1 **āxar-e hafte-ye gozaŝte hic-jā ______ (raftan).**
Last weekend I didn’t go anywhere.

Example: آخر هفتهٔ گذشته هیچ‌جا نرفتم.
āxar-e hafte-ye gozašte hic-jā naraftam.

۲- آخر هفتهٔ گذشته هیچ‌کار ______ (کردن).
2 **āxar-e hafte-ye gozašte hic-kār ______ (kardan).**
Last weekend I didn't do anything.

۳- دیروز هیچ‌کس به خونهٔ ما ______ (اومدن).
3 **diruz hic-kas be xune-ye mā ______ (umadan).**
Yesterday, no one came to our house.

۴- هیچّی ______ (گفتن).
4 **hicci ______ (goftan).**
He/she didn't say anything.

Exercise 3

Complete these sentences with the help of their English translations.

۱- من هیچ‌چیز دربارهٔ او ______.
1 **man hic-ciz dar bāre-ye u ______.**
I don't know anything about him/her.
Example: من هیچ‌چیز دربارهٔ او نمیدونم.
man hic-ciz dar bāre-ye u nemidunam.

۲- هیچ‌کس ______ من کجا هستم.
2 **hic-kas ______ man kojā hastam.** Nobody knows where I am.

۳- هیچ‌کدوم خوب ______.
3 **hic-kodum xub ______.** Neither is good.

۴- اونها هیچ‌وقت تو خونه ______.
4 **unhā hic-vaqt tu xune ______.** They are never at home.

Exercise 4

Can you say these in Persian?

1 What do you normally have for lunch? Nothing.
2 I never have coffee at night.
3 We rarely go out on Saturdays.
4 Do you ever go to Iranian restaurants? Yes, sometimes.
5 She often comes here with her children.
6 I occasionally go swimming with my friends.

به رستوران بهار خوش آمدید

پیش غذاها

۱ـ ماست و موسیر	۱۵۰۰ ریال
۲ـ ماست و خیار	۱۴۵۰ ریال
۳ـ سالاد فصل	۱۶۰۰ ریال
۴ـ سالاد الیویه	۱۶۵۰ ریال
۵ـ کشک و بادنجان	۱۷۰۰ ریال
۶ـ نان و پنیر و سبزی	۱۴۰۰ ریال
۷ـ ترشی	۱۰۰۰ ریال

غذاهای اصلی

۸ـ چلو کباب مخصوص	۲۰۰۰۰ ریال
۹ـ چلو کباب برگ	۲۰۰۰۰ ریال
۱۰ـ چلو کباب کوبیده	۱۳۵۰۰ ریال
۱۱ـ جوجه کباب	۱۴۵۰۰ریال
۱۲ـ زرشک پلو با مرغ	۱۴۵۰۰ ریال
۱۳ـ چلو خورش قرمه سبزی	۱۰۰۰۰ ریال
۱۴ـ چلو قیمه بادنجان	۱۰۰۰۰ ریال

آشامیدنی‌ها و دسرها

۱۵ـ دوغ	۲۰۰۰ ریال
۱۶ـ کوکاکولا / زمزم	۱۰۰۰ ریال
۱۷ـ آب پرتقال	۲۰۰۰ ریال
۱۸ـ چای	۵۰۰ ریال
۱۹ـ بستنی	۱۲۰۰ ریال
۲۰ـ پالوده شیرازی	۱۰۰۰ ریال

Dialogue 2 Is this seat taken?

The restaurant is full. Two friends have to share a table with two strangers. The waiter (w) then takes their order.

A: ببخشید، اینجا جای کسیه؟
B: بله، رفته دستشویی.
A: ببخشید آقا، میتونیم اینجا بشینیم؟
C: خواهش میکنم. بفرمایید.
W: ببخشید حرفتونو قطع میکنم. غذا سفارش دادهاید؟
A: نه هنوز.
W: حاضرید سفارش بدید؟
A: بله، برای من لطفاً چلوکباب بیارید.
D: برای من لطفاً جوجه کباب بیارید.
W: پیشغذا چی میل دارید؟
A: پنیر و سبزی با نون، لطفاً.
D: برای من سالاد بیارید، لطفاً.
W: نوشیدنی چی بیارم؟
A: دوغ، لطفاً.
D: پپسی، لطفاً.
W: دسر؟
D: بستنی، لطفاً.
A: هنوز تصمیم نگرفتهام. بعداً میگم.

A: **bebaxš̄id, injā jā-ye kasie?**
B: **bale, rafte das(t)šuyi.**
A: **bebaxšid āqā, mitunim injā bešinim?**
C: **xāheš mikonam. befarmāyid.**
W: **bebaxšid harfetun-o qat(`) mikonam. qazā sefāreš dād(e)id?**
A: **na hanuz.**
W: **hāzerid sefāreš bedid?**
A: **bale, barāye man lotfan celo(u)-kabāb biārid.**
D: **barāye man lotfan juje-kabāb biārid.**
W: **piš-qazā ci meil dārid?**
A: **panir o sabzi bā nun, lotfan.**
D: **barāye man sālād biārid, lotfan.**
W: **nušidani ci biāram?**
A: **duq, lotfan.**
D: **pepsi, lotfan.**
W: **deser?**
D: **bastani, lotfan.**
A: **hanuz tasmim nagereft(e)am. ba(`)dan migam.**

A: *Excuse me, is this seat taken? (* lit *Is this place someone (else)'s seat?)*
B: *Yes, he's gone to the toilet.*
A: *Excuse me sir, can we sit here?*
C: *By all means. Please go ahead.*
W: *Sorry to interrupt you. Have you ordered a meal?*
A: *Not yet.*
W: *Are you ready to order?*
A: *Yes, for me, please, the* chelo-kabab. *(* lit *please bring)*
D: *For me, please, the chicken kebab.*
W: *What would you like as a starter?*
A: *Cheese and (fresh) herbs with bread, please.*
D: *Salad for me, please.*
W: *What drink would you like? (* lit *shall I bring?)*
A: *Yoghurt drink, please.*
D: *Pepsi, please.*
W: *Dessert?*
D: *Ice cream, please.*
A: *I haven't decided yet. I'll tell (you) later.*

Vocabulary

جا	**jā**	place, seat
کسی	**kasi**	someone
رفته	**rafte**	has gone
دستشویی	**dastšuyi**	toilet
بشینیم	**bešinim**	(for us) to sit
حرف	**harf**	conversation
قطع کردن (کن)	**qat` kardan (kon)**	to interrupt
سفارش داده‌اید؟	**sefāreš dād(e)id?**	Have you ordered?
سفارش دادن (د)	**sefāreš dādan (d)**	to order
حاضر	**hāzer**	ready
چلوکباب	**celo(u)-kabāb**	rice and grilled kebab
پیش‌غذا	**piš-qazā**	starter
میل دارید	**meil dārid**	would you like
پنیر	**panir**	cheese
سبزی	**sabzi**	fresh herbs
نون	**nun**	*col* for نان **nān** bread
نوشیدنی	**nušidani**	a drink
دوغ	**duq**	yoghurt drink
تصمیم	**tasmim**	decision
نگرفته‌ام	**nagereft(e)am**	I haven't taken
بعداً	**ba`dan**	later
میگم	**migam**	I (will) say

Language points

Present perfect

How to say 'He has gone'

Here is the formula:

Past stem of verb + suffix ه **e** + personal ending

The past stem of the verb رفتن **raftan** 'to go' is رفتـ **raft-**.

من رفته‌ام. **man rafteam.** I have gone.
تو رفته‌ای. **to raftei.** You (*inf*) have gone.
او رفته (است). **u rafte (ast).** S/he has gone.
ما رفته‌ایم. **mā rafteim.** We have gone.
شما رفته‌اید. **šomā rafteid.** You have gone.
اونها رفته‌اند. **un(h)ā rafteand.** They have gone.

Note: For او **u** 'he'/'she', است **ast** is used as a personal ending.

In colloquial Persian, the above forms are reduced and pronounced as follows. Note the stress pattern shown by underlining.

من رفته‌ام. **man raf<u>tam</u>.** I've gone.
تو رفته‌ای. **to raf<u>ti</u>.** You've gone.
او رفته. **u raf<u>te</u>.** He/she's gone.
ما رفته‌ایم. **mā raf<u>tim</u>.** We've gone.
شما رفته‌اید. **šomā raf<u>tid</u>.** You've gone.
اونها رفته‌اند. **un(h)ā raf<u>tand</u>.** They've gone.

It is the stress pattern that distinguishes رفته‌ام **raf<u>tam</u>** 'I've gone' from رفتم **<u>raf</u>tam** 'I went' (see the past simple, pp. 85–6).

As mentioned earlier, with verbs of motion, such as 'to go', 'to come', the preposition به **be** 'to' is often omitted and the verb position precedes the place. Thus, form (B) below is more colloquial:

(A) او به توالت رفته. **u be tuālet rafte.**
He/she's gone to the toilet.

(B) رفته توالت. **rafte tuālet.**
He/she's gone to the toilet.

A similar pattern is used to say, e.g., 'I've been to (a place)', meaning 'I've visited that place':

شما به اسپانیا رفته‌اید؟ **šomā be espāniā raft(e)id?**
Have you been to Spain?

To make the verb negative, we add نـ **na-**, e.g.

من به اسپانیا نرفته‌ام. **man be espāniā naraft(e)am.**
I haven't been to Spain.

من اسپاگتی نخورده‌ام. **man espāgeti naxord(e)am.**
I haven't eaten spaghetti.

Exercise 5

Using the verb خوردن **xordan** 'to eat', give the equivalents of the sentences below. Follow the example.

1 I've eaten Iranian food.
من غذای ایرانی خورده‌ام. **man qazā-ye irāni xord(e)am.**
2 You've eaten Iranian food. __________
3 He/she's eaten Iranian food. __________
4 We've eaten Iranian food. __________
5 They've eaten Iranian food. __________
6 You (*inf*) have eaten Iranian food. __________

Exercise 6

Now make the above sentences negative.

Other items on a typical menu

خورش قرمه‌سبزی **xoreš-e qorme-sabzi**
a stew with herbs and beans

خورش قیمه‌بادنجان **xoreš-e qeime-bādenjan**
a stew with split peas and aubergines

خورش فسنجان **xoreš-e fesenjān**
a stew with crushed walnuts and pomegranate juice

باقلا پلو **bāq(e)lā polou**
steamed rice with broad beans

Complaining in a restaurant

ببخشید، این غذا سرده. **bebaxšid, in qazā sarde.**
Excuse me, this food's cold.

این نوشابه گرمه! **in nušābe garme!** This drink is warm!

این ماهی بو میده. **in māhi bu mide.** This fish smells.

این سالاد/نون تازه نیست. **in sālād/nun tāze nist.**
This salad/bread isn't fresh.

آقا، مردیم از گرسنگی! **āqā, mordim az gorosnegi!**
Sir, we're starving! (*lit* We died of hunger!)

این غذای ما چی شد؟ **in qazā-ye mā ci šod?**
What happened to our meal?

Other useful vocabulary

آقا، صورت‌حساب، لطفاً. **āqā, surat-hesāb, lotfan.**
Sir, (may I have) the bill, please?

کجا باید پول بدم؟ **kojā bāyad pul bedam?**
Where should I pay?

Exercise 7

Can you ask an Iranian friend if:

1 He/she has ever been to America.
2 He/she has seen *Titanic* (film).
3 He/she has ever had (eaten) Chinese food.
4 He/she has had (eaten) lunch/dinner/breakfast.
5 He/she has ever lost something.

Exercise 8

Can you say these in Persian?

1 Where's Mum? She's gone to the supermarket.
2 Where are your parents? They've gone to Iran.
3 Have you seen my new car?
4 Sorry to interrupt you, but you haven't seen my car key, have you? (*lit* haven't you seen?)
5 May I have the bill, please?

Comprehension

You have received a video-taped message from your Iranian friend. For this test, you will only hear the soundtrack.

سلام. میدونید که من همیشه برای شما نامه مینویسم. اما این بار تصمیم گرفتم بجای نامه یک نوار ویدیو بفرستم. باید بگم که هیچ‌وقت جلوی دوربین صحبت نکرده‌ام و به همین دلیل کمی هول شده‌ام. میبخشید. امروز خانم و بچّه‌ها نیستند خونه. همه رفته‌اند مسافرت. اما زیاد هم تنها نیستم چون چند تا از دوست‌هام به دیدنم اومده‌اند. الآن تو اتاق پذیرایی هستند. تو خونهٔ ما اغلب خانمم آشپزی میکنه. من به ندرت غذا درست میکنم. فقط چلوکباب میتونم بپزم. امّا این بار سعی کرده‌ام چند جور غذا درست کنم. آخر نوار میز ناهارخوری‌رو نشون میدم. راستی شما تا حالا غذای ایرانی خورده‌اید؟

salām. midunid ke man hamis̄e barāye s̄omā nāme minevisam. ammā in bār tasmim gereftam bejā-ye nāme yek navār-e vidio bef(e)restam. bāyad begam ke hic-vaqt jelo-ye durbin sohbat nakard(e)am va be hamin dalil kami houl s̄od(e)am. mibaxs̄id. emruz xānom o baccehā nistand xune. hame raft(e)and mosāferat. ammā ziād ham tanhā nistam con cand tā az dust(h)ām be didanam umad(e)and. al(`)ān tu otāq-e pazirāyi hastand. tu xune-ye mā aqlab xānomam ās̄pazi mikone. man be nodrat qazā dorost mikonam. faqat celo(u)-kabāb mitunam bepazam. ammā in bār sa`y kardam cand jur qazā dorost konam. āxar-e navār miz-e nāhārxori-ro nes̄un midam. rāsti s̄omā tā hālā qazā-ye irāni xord(e)id?

1 What does he normally do which he is not doing now?
2 Why is he nervous?
3 In one way, he is alone; but then he is not! Can you solve this puzzle?
4 Who does what often in his home?
5 What brave act has he done today?
6 What promise does he make?
7 What does he want to know at the end?

9 موقعیّت‌های اضطراری
mouqe`iyathā-ye ezterāri

Emergency situations

By the end of this lesson, you should be able to:

- use the Tehran telephone directory
- ask if you can contact your embassy
- ask to talk to your lawyer
- talk about what you were doing yesterday at this time
- describe someone's appearance
- call the police and other emergency services

Dialogue 1 At the police station

A British businessman (B) has just been involved in a car accident. Having obtained his details, the police officer (O) and the businessman have the following exchange.

O: خب، حالا بفرمایید تصادف چطور اتّفاق افتاد.

B: من داشتم با سرعت حدود ۴۰ کیلومتر در ساعت میروندم. این آقا یک دفعه پیچید جلوم.

O: راهنماش روشن بود؟

B: ببخشید، فارسیم زیاد خوب نیست؛ نمیتونم به فارسی توضیح بدم. میتونم به سفارت انگلستان تلفن کنم و خواهش کنم یک مترجم بفرستند؟

O: خواهش میکنم، بفرمایید. تلفن اونجاست.

B: مرسی. در ضمن، ترجیح میدم اوّل با وکیلم صحبت کنم. اشکالی نداره؟

O: خواهش میکنم. به ایشون هم میتونید زنگ بزنید.

O: **xob, hālā befarmāyid tasādof ceto(u)r ettefāq oftād.**

B: **man dāštam bā sor`at-e hodud-e cehel kilumetr dar sā`at mirundam. in āqā yek daf`e picid jelom.**

O: **rāhnamāš roušan bud?**

B: **bebaxšid, fārsim ziād xub nist; nemitunam be fārsi touzih bedam. mitunam be sefārat-e engelestān telefon konam va xāheš konam yek motarjem bef(e)restand?**

O: **xāheš mikonam, befarmāyid, telefon unjāst.**

B: **mersi. dar zemn, tarjih midam avval bā vakilam sohbat konam. eškāli nadāre?**

O: **xāheš mikonam. be išun (h)am mitunid zang bezanid.**

O: *OK, now please tell us how the accident happened.*

B: *I was driving at a speed of about 40 kilometres per hour. This gentleman suddenly turned in front of me.*

O: *Was his indicator on?*

B: *I'm sorry, my Persian isn't that good; I can't explain in Persian. Can I telephone the British Embassy and ask them to send an interpreter?*

O: *By all means, please go ahead. The telephone's there.*

B: *Thank you. Incidentally, I prefer to talk to my lawyer first. Is that OK?*

O: *By all means. You can ring him, too.*

Vocabulary

تصادف	**tasādof**	accident
اتّفاق	**ettefāq**	
افتادن (افتـ)	**oftādan (oft)**	to happen
سرعت	**sor`at**	speed
کیلومتر	**kilumetr**	kilometre
داشتم	**dāštam**	I was
میروندم	**mirundam**	driving
روندن (رونـ)	**rundan (run)**	to drive
یک‌دفعه	**yek-daf`e**	suddenly
جلو	**jelo(u)**	front
راهنما	**rāhnamā**	indicator
روشن	**roušan**	switched on
توضیح	**touzih**	explanation

سفارت	**sefārat**	embassy
انگلستان	**engelestān**	England, Britain
مترجم	**motarjem**	interpreter, translator
فرستادن (فرستـ)	**ferestādan (ferest)**	to send
در ضمن	**dar zemn**	meanwhile
ترجیح دادن (د)	**tarjih dādan (d)**	to prefer
وکیل	**vakil**	lawyer
اشکال	**eškāl**	problem, difficulty
زنگ زدن (زنـ)	**zang zadan (zan)**	to ring/ phone

Language points

Past continuous

How to say 'I was driving'

Verb needed: روندن **rundan** to drive
Here's the formula:

Prefix میـ **mi-** + past stem of verb روند **rund** + personal ending م **am**

میروندم. **mirundam.** I was driving.

Note: The verb داشتن **dāštan** is often used here, as an auxiliary verb, to add an element of continuity or progression:

داشتم میروندم. **dāštam mirundam.** I was driving.

Now consider this sentence, from the dialogue, where an adverbial phrase is sandwiched between the auxiliary verb and the main verb:

من داشتم با سرعت حدود ۴۰ کیلومتر در ساعت میروندم.
man dāštam bā sor`at-e hodud-e cehel kilumetr dar sā`at mirundam.
I was driving at a speed of about 40 kilometres per hour.

Also note how the object can be sandwiched between the two verbs:

داشتم میخوردم. **dāštam mixordam.** I was eating.

داشتم ناهار میخوردم. **dāštam nāhār mixordam.**
I was eating lunch.

دیروز این وقت داشتم ناهار میخوردم.
diruz in vaqt dāštam nāhār mixordam.
Yesterday at this time I was eating lunch.

The auxiliary verb is not used in the negative form:

دیروز این وقت ناهار نمیخوردم.
diruz in vaqt nāhār nemixordam.
Yesterday at this time I was not eating lunch.

Exercise 1

Change these sentences as in the example.

۱- دیشب این وقت داشتم شام میخوردم.

1 **dišab in vaqt dāštam šām mixordam.**
Last night at this time I was eating dinner.
Example: دیشب این وقت داشتم تلویزیون تماشا میکردم.
dišab in vaqt dāštam televizion tamāšā mikardam.
Last night at this time I was watching TV.

۲- دیشب این وقت داشتی شام میخوردی.

2 **dišab in vaqt dāšti šām mixordi.**

۳- دیشب این وقت داشتید شام میخوردید.

3 **dišab in vaqt dāštid šām mixordid.**

۴- دیشب این وقت داشت شام میخورد.

4 **dišab in vaqt dāšt šām mixord.**

۵- دیشب این وقت داشتیم شام میخوردیم.

5 **dišab in vaqt dāštim šām mixordim.**

۶- دیشب این وقت داشتند شام میخوردند.

6 **dišab in vaqt dāštand šām mixordand.**

Exercise 2

Make the new sentences in Exercise 1 negative and then translate them into English.

Example:

۱- دیشب این وقت تلویزیون تماشا نمیکردم.

dišab in vaqt televizion tamāša nemikardam.

Yesterday at this time I was not watching television.

Exercise 3

Your Iranian friend asks you:

دیروز این وقت چکار میکردید؟ **diruz in vaqt cekār mikardid?**

What were you doing yesterday at this time?

With the help of these prompts, answer in Persian.

1 Talking to my wife/husband/friend.
2 Having tea with my guests.
3 Coming here.
4 Listening to the news.
5 Writing a letter.
6 Working with the computer.

Tehran telephone directory: 118

ببخشید، شماره تلفن شرکت ... را میخواستم.

bebaxšid, šomāre telefon-e šerkat-e . . . rā mixāstam.

Excuse me, I wanted the telephone number of a company called . . .

Emergency calls

پدرم حالش به هم خورده.

هرچه زودتر یک آمبولانس بفرستید، لطفا.

pedaram hāleš be ham xorde. harce zudtar yek āmbulāns bef(e)restid, lotfan.

My father has fallen ill. Please send an ambulance as soon as possible.

آتش نشانی؟ **āteš-nešāni?**

(Is that the) Fire Brigade?

خونه‌مون آتش گرفته. کمک کنید، لطفاً.

xunamun āteš (*col* ātiš) gerefte. komak konid, lotfan.

Our house has caught fire. Please help.

خونه‌مونو دزد زده. **xunamun-o dozd zade.**

Our house has been burgled.

قفل درمونو شکسته‌اند. qofl-e daremun-o šekast(e)and.
They have broken the lock to our door.

خونهٔ همسایه‌مون دعواست. xune-ye hamsāyamun da`vāst.
There's a fight in our neighbour's house.

تو خونه‌مون بوی گاز میاد. لطفاً یک نفرو بفرستید.
tu xunamun bu-ye gāz miād. lotfan yek nafar-o bef(e)restid.
There's a smell of gas in our house. Please send someone.

لولهٔ آبمون ترکیده. lule-ye ābemun tarakide.
Our water pipe has burst.

برقمون قطع شده. barqemun qat` šode.
Our electricity has cut out. (We have a power cut.)

گذرنامه‌امو / پاسپورتمو گم کرده‌ام.
gozarnāmam-o/pāsportam-o gom kard(e)am.
I've lost my passport.

Exercise 4

Can you say these in Persian?

1 I saw the accident, but I can't describe it in Persian.
2 My Persian isn't that good. May I phone my embassy?
3 My kitchen is on fire. Please help.
4 My flat has been burgled. Please send someone.
5 My neighbour has collapsed. Please send an ambulance as soon as possible.
6 May I have the telephone number of the police/ambulance/fire brigade, please?

Dialogue 2 Describing appearance

Ahmad (A) has just been pickpocketed. He is now helping the police (P) with their enquiries.

P: شما خودتون جیب‌برو دیدید؟
A: بله.
P: میتونید مشخّصاتشو بگید؟
A: سعی میکنم. قدّش بلندتر از من بود. صورتش گلابی شکل بود. رنگ پوستش سفید بود.
P: موهاش چه رنگ بود؟

A: یادم نیست. فکر میکنم تراشیده بود. اما سبیلش مشکی بود.
P: جثّه‌اش چطور بود؟
A: لاغر بود امّا چارشونه.
P: لباسش یادتون هست؟
A: بله، کت نداشت. یک کاپشن قهوه‌یی داشت با شلوار سرمه‌یی. رنگ پیرهنش یادم نیست.
P: تو دستش چیزی نبود؟
A: چرا، یک ساک آبی داشت.
P: کس دیگه اونجا نبود؟
A: چرا، خیلی‌ها بودند اما اسم و آدرسشونو ندارم.
P: از همکاریتون متشکّرم.
A: خواهش میکنم.

P: **šomā xodetun jib-bor-o didid?**
A: **bale.**
P: **mitunid mošaxxasāteš-o begid?**
A: **sa(`)y mikonam. qaddeš bolandtar az man bud. surateš golābi-šekl bud. rang-e pusteš sefid bud.**
P: **muhāš ce rang bud?**
A: **yādam nist. fekr mikonam tarāšide bud. ammā sebileš meški bud.**
P: **jossaš ceto(u)r bud?**
A: **lāqar bud, ammā cāršune.**
P: **lebāseš yādetun hast?**
A: **bale, kot nadāšt. yek kāpšan-e qahveyi dāšt bā šalvār-e sormeyi. rang-e pirhaneš yādam nist.**
P: **tu dasteš cizi nabud?**
A: **cerā, yek sāk-e ābi dāšt.**
P: **kas-e dige unjā nabud?**
A: **cerā, xeilihā budand ammā esm o ādresešun-o nadāram.**
P: **az hamkāritun mot(a)šakkeram.**
A: **xāheš mikonam.**

P: *Did you see the pickpocket yourself?*
A: *Yes.*
P: *Can you describe him?*
A: *I'll try. He was taller than I (am). His face was pear-shaped. The colour of his skin was white.*
P: *What colour was his hair?*
A: *I can't remember. I think his head was shaved* (lit *he had shaved*). *But his moustache was black.*
P: *What kind of build did he have?*

A: *He was slim but broad-shouldered.*
P: *Do you remember his clothes?*
A: *Yes, he didn't have a jacket. He had a brown bomber jacket with navy-blue trousers. I can't remember the colour of his shirt.*
P: *Wasn't there anything in his hand?*
A: *Yes, he had a blue holdall.*
P: *Wasn't anyone else there?*
A: *Yes there were many people there but I don't have their names and addresses.*
P: *I'm grateful for your cooperation.*
A: *You're welcome.*

Vocabulary

جیب‌بر	**jib-bor**	pickpocket	لاغر	**lāqar**	slim
مشخّصات	**mošaxxasāt**	distinctive features	چارشونه	**cāršune**	broad-shouldered
سعی کردن (کن)	**sa`y kardan (kon)**	to try	لباس	**lebās**	clothes
قدّ	**qadd**	height	کت	**kot**	jacket
بلند	**boland**	tall	یادتون هست؟	**yādetun hast?**	Can you remember?
صورت	**surat**	face	کاپشن	**kāpšan**	bomber jacket
گلابی	**golābi**	pear	قهوه‌یی	**qahveyi**	brown
شکل	**šekl**	shape	شلوار	**šalvār**	trousers
رنگ	**rang**	colour	سرمه‌یی	**sormeyi**	navy blue
پوست	**pust**	skin	پیرهن	**pirhan**	shirt
سفید	**sefid**	white	چرا	**cerā**	yes
یاد	**yād**	memory	ساک	**sāk**	holdall
یادم نیست.	**yādam nist.**	I can't remember.	آبی	**ābi**	blue
تراشیدن (تراش)	**tarāšidan (tarāš)**	to shave	کس	**kas**	person
سبیل	**sebil**	moustache	دیگه	**dige**	else
جثّه	**josse**	build	خیلی‌ها	**xeilihā**	many people
			همکاری	**hamkāri**	cooperation

Language points

Emphatic and reflexive pronouns

How to say 'myself'; 'my own'

Here we use the word خود **xod** 'self'/'own' together with the possessive endings (introduced at pp. 34–5).

خودم **xodam** myself; my own
خودت **xodet** yourself; your own (*inf*)
خودش **xodeš** himself/herself; his/her own; itself/its own
خودمون **xodemun** ourselves; our own
خودتون **xodetun** yourselves; your own
خودشون **xodešun** themselves; their own

من خودم اونهارو دیدم. **man xodam unhā-ro didam.**
I myself saw them, *or*: I saw them myself.

من با چشم‌های خودم اونهارو دیدم.
man bā cešmhā-ye xodam unhā-ro didam.
I saw them with my own eyes.

خودشو تو آینه دید. **xodeš-o tu aine did.**
He saw himself in the mirror.

Exercise 5

Supply the missing word.

1 او ____ نامه‌رو نوشت. **u ____ nāma-ro nevešt.**
He wrote the letter himself.
2 شما ____ احمدو دیدید؟ **šomā ____ ahmad-o didid?**
Did you see Ahmad yourself?
3 ما با ماشین ____ میریم. **mā bā māšin-e ____ mirim.**
We'll go in (*lit* by) our own car.
4 اونها با ماشین ____ میرند. **unhā bā māšin-e ____ mirand.**
They'll go in (*lit* by) their own car.
5 به ____ گفتم: 'صبور باش.' **be ____ goftam: 'sabur bāš.'**
I told myself: 'Be patient.'

Past perfect

How to say 'he had shaved'

Here is the formula:

Past stem of verb +
suffix ه **e** +
بود **bud** +
personal ending (except for third-person singular, which takes no ending.)

Verb needed: تراشیدن **tarāšidan** to shave
Past stem: تراشید **tarāšid**
تراشیده بودم **tarāšide budam** I had shaved
تراشیده بودی **tarāšide budi** you had shaved
تراشیده بود **tarāšide bud** he had shaved

For the negative, we add the prefix نَ **na-** to the main verb:

نتراشیده بود **natarāšide bud** he had not shaved

Exercise 6

Fill in the blanks with the correct form of the verb given.

۱- اوّلین بار ۳ سال پیش غذای ایرانی خوردم.
قبلا غذای ایرانی ______ (خوردن)

1 **avvalin bār se sāl piš qazā-ye irāni xordam.**
qablan qazā-ye irāni ______ (xordan)
I first ate Iranian food three years ago.
I had not eaten Iranian food before.
Example: قبلاً غذای ایرانی نخورده بودم.
qablan qazā-ye irāni naxorde budam.

۲- اوّلین بار ۱۰ سال پیش با شوهرم/ خانمم ملاقات کردم. قبلا او را ______ (دیدن)

2 **avvalin bār dah sāl piš bā šouharam/xānomam molāqāt kardam.**
qablan u rā ______ (didan)
I first met my husband/wife ten years ago.
I had not seen him/her before.

۳- اوّلین بار ۵ سال پیش فارسی صحبت کردم.
قبلا فارسی صحبت ______ (کردن)

3 **avvalin bār panj sāl piš fārsi sohbat kardam.**
qablan fārsi sohbat ______ (kardan)
I first spoke Persian five years ago.
I had not spoken Persian before.

'Yes' to a negative question

'Yes' to a positive question is بله **bale**, to a negative question چرا **cerā**:

Q: شما ایرانی هستید؟ **šomā irāni hastid?** Are you Iranian?
A: بله. **bale.** Yes.
Q: شما ایرانی نیستید؟ **šomā irāni nistid?** Aren't you Iranian?
A: چرا. **cerā.** Yes.

Indefinite pronouns

Note the use of these indefinite pronouns:

کس **kas** person کسی **kasi** someone, a person
کسی با شما کار داره. **kasi bā šomā kār dāre.**
Someone wants to see you. (*lit* Someone has business with you.)
بعضی **ba`zi** some بعضی از **ba`zi az** some of
بعضی از سیب‌ها خرابند. **ba`zi az sibhā xarāband.**
Some of the apples are bad.
بعضی از اونها **ba`zi az unhā** some of them
خیلی **xeili** many خیلی‌ها **xeilihā** many people

Exercise 7

Match these people (a–c) with their descriptions (1–3).

(a)	*(b)*	*(c)*
medium height	tall	short
plump	fat	slim
short black hair	broad-shouldered	long grey hair
pear-shaped face	short blond hair	round-faced

۱- قدّ = بلند؛ جثّه = چاق، چارشونه؛ مو = کوتاه، بور
1 **qadd = boland; josse = cāq, cāršune; mu = kutāh, bur**
۲- قدّ = کوتاه؛ جثّه = لاغر؛ مو = بلند، جوگندمی؛ صورت = گرد
2 **qadd = kutāh; josse = lāqar; mu = boland, jougandomi; surat = gerd**
۳- قدّ = متوسّط؛ جثّه = تپلی؛ مو = کوتاه، مشکی؛ صورت = گلابی‌شکل
3 **qadd = motavasset; josse = topoli; mu = kutāh, meški; surat = golābi-šekl**

Exercise 8

Can you say these in Persian?

1 When did you first go to Iran? 5 years ago.
2 Why did you go to Iran?
3 I had read a few books about your country.
4 I had seen a few Iranian films.
5 I had become interested in Iran.
6 Had you not been to the Middle East before?
7 Yes, I had been to Iraq.

8 Someone wants to see you (*lit* has business with you).
9 Some of the guests want to talk to you.
10 Did you talk to Ahmad yourself?
11 I saw myself in the mirror.

Comprehension

Here's how Ali described what happened to him last night.

من و خانمم داشتیم تو رستوران غذا میخوردیم. حدود ساعت هشت، یک دفعه چراغ‌ها خاموش شد. قبل از اون، دو نفر در میز پهلوی ما غذا میخوردند. بعد از حدود پنج دقیقه چراغ‌ها روشن شد، اما اون دو نفر رفته بودند. کیف من هم ناپدید شده بود. یکی‌شون قدبلند بود و کت و شلوار طوسی داشت. موهاش مشکی بود و کوتاه. سبیل کلفت و عینک آفتابی داشت. دوّمی پشتش به من بود. خوب ندیدمش. اما سرش تاس بود. پیرهنش هم آبی بود.

man o xānomam dās̄tim tu resturān qazā mixordim. hodud-e sā`at-e has̄t, yek daf`e cerāqhā xāmus̄ s̄od. qabl az un, do nafar dar miz-e pahlu-ye mā qazā mixordand. ba`d az hodud-e panj daqiqe cerāqhā rous̄an s̄od, ammā un do nafar rafte budand. kif-e man ham nāpadid s̄ode bud. yekis̄un qad-boland bud va kot o s̄alvār-e tusi dās̄t. muhās̄ mes̄ki bud o kutāh. sebil-e koloft o einak-e āftābi dās̄t. dovvomi pos̄tes̄ be man bud. xub nadidames̄. ammā sares̄ tās bud. pirhanes̄ ham ābi bud.

1 Can you elaborate on the circumstances in which the incident occurred? Where was Ali? Who was he with? What was he doing?
2 What implicit message is he giving the police?
3 Can you describe the appearance of the man the police are now looking for?

10 منزل manzel

Home

By the end of this lesson, you should be able to:

- start, hold and end a telephone conversation
- enquire about rented accommodation
- make longer sentences
- express preference
- apologise for causing inconvenience
- say you are looking for something/someone

Dialogue 1 Answering the phone

The phone rings. Ms Teimuri (T) answers the phone. It's Mr Zandi (Z), a friend of her husband, Ali Keshmiri. (Iranian women often keep their maiden name.)

T: الو؟
Z: ببخشید، منزل آقای کشمیری؟
T: بله، بفرمایید.
Z: سلام، زندی هستم.
T: سلام، حالتون چطوره؟
Z: متشکّرم. علی هست؟
T: نه نیست، متأسّفانه.
Z: از اداره بر نگشته هنوز؟
T: چرا، ساعت ۵ اومد، امّا دوباره رفت بیرون.
Z: میدونید کی میاد خونه؟
T: حدود هشت.
Z: خب، پس بعداً تلفن میکنم.
T: میخواید پیغام بذارید؟
Z: نه، متشکّرم. ببخشید مزاحم شدم.
T: خواهش میکنم.

Z: فعلاً خدا حافظ.
T: خدا حافظ.

T: **alou?**
Z: **bebaxšid, manzel-e āqā-ye kešmiri?**
T: **bale, befarmāyid.**
Z: **salām, zandi hastam.**
T: **salām, hāletun ceto(u)re?**
Z: **mot(a)šakkeram. ali hast?**
T: **na nist, mota(`)assefāne.**
Z: **az edāre bar nagašte hanuz?**
T: **cerā, sā`at-e panj umad, ammā dobāre raft birun.**
Z: **midunid kei miād xune?**
T: **hodud-e hašt.**
Z: **xob, pas ba(`)dan telefon mikonam.**
T: **mixaid peiqām bezārid?**
Z: **na, mot(a)šakkeram. bebaxšid mozāhem šodam.**
T: **xāheš mikonam.**
Z: **fe(`)lan xodā hāfez.**
T: **xodā hāfez.**

T: *Hello?*
Z: *Excuse me, (is that) Mr Keshmiri's home?*
T: *Yes, what can I do for you?*
Z: *Hello, I'm Zandi.*
T: *Hello, how're you?*
Z: *(Fine) thanks. Is Ali in?*
T: *No he's not (in), I'm afraid.*
Z: *Hasn't he come back from the office yet?*
T: *Yes, he came at 5 o'clock, but went out again.*
Z: *Do you know when he'll come home?*
T: *About eight.*
Z: *OK, I'll telephone later, then.*
T: *Do you want to leave a message?*
Z: *No, thanks. Sorry to have bothered you.*
T: *No problem.*
Z: *Goodbye for now.*
T: *Goodbye.*

Vocabulary

منزل **manzel**	home, residence		پیغام **peiqām**	message	
اداره **edāre**	office		گذاشتن **gozāštan**	to leave	
برگشتن **bar gaštan**			(ذار) **(zār)**	(a message)	
(گرد) **(gard)**	to return		مزاحم **mozāhem**	nuisance	
پس **pas**	then, in that case				

Language points

Conjunctions

These are used to join two or more sentences, which are normally of equal weight.

امّا **ammā** but
و **va** (*col* **o**) and
یا X یا Y
هم X (و) هم Y
نه X (و) نه Y

ولی **vali** but
یا **yā** or
yā X yā Y either X or Y
ham X (va) ham Y both X and Y
na X (va) na Y neither X nor Y

Examples:

(a) من ساندویچ خوردم. **man sāndevic xordam.**
I ate a sandwich.
(b) احمد کیک خورد. **ahmad keik xord.**
Ahmad ate some cake.
(a + b) من ساندویچ خوردم امّا احمد کیک خورد.
man sāndevic xordam ammā ahmad keik xord.
I ate a sandwich but Ahmad ate some cake.
(a) علی ساندویچ خورد. **ali sāndevic xord.**
Ali ate a sandwich.
(b) او کیک هم خورد. **u keik ham xord.**
He also ate some cake.
(a + b) علی هم ساندویچ خورد (و) هم کیک.
ali ham sāndevic xord (va) ham keik.
Ali ate both a sandwich and some cake.

More examples:

سوسن نه ساندویچ خورد (و) نه کیک.
susan na sāndevic xord (va) na keik.
Susan ate neither a sandwich nor some (any) cake.

یا ساندویچ میخورم یا کیک. **yā sāndevic mixoram yā keik.**
I'll eat either a sandwich or some cake.

هر دو را نمیخورم. **har do rā nemixoram.**
I won't eat both.

Exercise 1

Join each pair into one sentence using an appropriate conjunction from the list above.

۱- دیشب در یک رستوران بزرگ شام خوردیم.
غذا خوب نبود.

1 **dišab dar yek resturān-e bozorg šām xordim.**
qazā xub nabud.
Last night we ate dinner in a big restaurant.
The food wasn't good.
Example:
دیشب در یک رستوران بزرگ شام خوردیم امّا غذا خوب نبود.
dišab dar yek resturān-e bozorg šām xordim amma qazā xub nabud.
Last night we ate dinner in a big restaurant but the food wasn't good.

۲- برای دسر بستنی خوردم. کیک هم خوردم.

2 **barāye deser bastani xordam. keik ham xordam.**
For dessert I had ice cream. I also had some cake.
How do you say: For dessert I had both ice cream and cake?

۳- مادرم شام نخورد. او دسر هم نخورد.

3 **mādaram šām naxord. u deser ham naxord.**
My mother didn't have dinner. She didn't have a dessert either.
How do you say: My mother had neither dinner nor dessert?

۴- آخر هفتهٔ گذشته کسی به دیدن ما نیومد.
ما هم به دیدن کسی نرفتیم.

4 **āxar-e hafte-ye gozašte kasi be didan-e mā nayumad.**
mā ham be didan-e kasi naraftim.
Last weekend nobody came to see us.
We didn't go to see anyone either.
How do you say: Last weekend, neither did we go to see anyone, nor did anyone come to see us?

More expressions used on the phone

میخواستم با آقای احمدی صحبت کنم.
mixāstam bā āqā-ye ahmadi sohbat konam.
I would like to speak with Mr Ahmadi.

صداتونو خوب نمیشنوم.
sedātun-o xub nemiš(e)navam.
I can't hear your voice well.

لطفاً یک کمی بلندتر صحبت کنید.
lotfan yek kami bolandtar sohbat konid.
Please speak a little louder.

جنابعالی؟ **jenābāli?** (rising tone) Who's speaking?

لطفاً گوشی‌رو نگه دارید. **lotfan guši-ro negah dārid.**
Please hold on. (*lit* Please hold the receiver.)

لطفاً چند لحظه صبر کنید؛ صداشون میکنم.
lotfan cand lahze sabr konid; sedāšun mikonam.
Please wait a few moments; I'll call him.

Exercise 2

Can you say these in Persian?

1 You can have either ice cream or chocolate. You can't have both!
2 Can I have both ice cream and some cake, please?
3 Bear with me a few moments; I'll call her.
4 Can you speak up a little? I can't hear you.
5 Who's speaking? It's Hameed.
6 I'd like to talk to Mr Jamshidi, please.

Dialogue 2 I'm looking for a flat

S, a British lecturer on a two-year teaching assignment at Tehran University, is looking for a flat. A is the estate agent.

S: دنبال یک آپارتمان اجاره‌یی میگردم.
A: چه جور آپارتمانی؟
S: دوخوابه با حموم و توالت جدا و آشپزخونهٔ بزرگ.
A: کجای تهران؟
S: ترجیحاً نزدیک دانشگاه تهران.

A: اونجا، یک آپارتمان دارم که خیلی مناسبه امّا اجاره‌اش یک کمی گرونه.
S: ماهی چنده؟
A: ۱۰۰۰۰۰ تومن.
S: میشه ببینمش؟
A: بله، بفرمایید.

S: **donbāl-e ye(k) āpārtemān-e ejāreyi migardam.**
A: **ce jur āpārtemāni?**
S: **do-xābe bā hamum o tuālet-e jodā va āšpazxune-ye bozorg.**
A: **kojā-ye tehrān?**
S: **tarjihan nazdik-e dānešgāh-e tehrān.**
A: **unjā, ye(k) āpārtemān dāram ke xeili monāsebe ammā ejāraš yek kami gerune.**
S: **māhi cande?**
A: **sad hezār toman.**
S: **miše bebinameš?**
A: **bale, befarmāyid.**

S: *I'm looking for a flat to rent.*
A: *What sort of a flat?*
S: *A two-bedroomed (flat) with separate bathroom and toilet and a large kitchen.*
A: *Whereabouts in Tehran?*
S: *Preferably near Tehran University.*
A: *There, I have a flat which is very suitable but the rent is a bit expensive.*
S: *How much is it per month?*
A: *100,000 tumans.*
S: *Is it possible for me to see it?*
A: *Yes, let's go.*

Vocabulary

... دنبال	**donbāl-e ...**	
گشتن	**gaštan**	to look
(گرد)	**(gard)**	for ...
اجاره‌یی	**ejāreyi**	rented
چه جور	**ce jur**	what kind (of)
دوخوابه	**do-xābe**	two-bedroomed
حموم	**hamum**	(*col* for حمّام **hammām**) bathroom
توالت	**tuālet**	toilet
جدا	**jodā**	separate
آشپزخونه	**āšpazxune**	kitchen
ترجیحا	**tarjihan**	preferably
دانشگاه	**dānešgāh**	university
مناسب	**monāseb**	suitable
ماه	**māh**	month

ماهی	**māhi**	per month	ببینم	**bebinam**	(for me) to see
میشه	**miše**	is it possible	ببینمش	**bebinameš**	(for me) to see it

Language points

Object endings

The possessive endings (introduced at pp. 34–5) can also be used as objects after verbs or prepositions. An example from the dialogue is:

میشه ببینمش؟ **miše bebinameš?** May I see it?

Note how these object endings can be sandwiched between the two elements of a compound verb:

روشن کن **roušan kon** switch on
روشنش کن **roušaneš kon** switch it on
خاموشش کن **xāmušeš kon** switch it off

Note: No را **rā** is used with these object endings.

Examples of object endings with prepositions:

بام **bām** with me	بامون **bāmun** with us
بات **bāt** with you (*inf*)	باتون **bātun** with you
باش **bāš** with him/her/it	باشون **bāšun** with them

Sometimes an 'intrusive' هـ **h** comes between the preposition and the suffix:

بهش گفتم. **beheš goftam.** I told him.

باهش / باهاش بازی میکردم.
bāheš/bāhāš bāzi mikardam. I was playing with him.

How to ask 'What's the matter with . . . ?'

Here's the formula:

چه **ce** what + object ending + ه **e** is

چمه؟	**ceme?**	What's the matter with me?
چته؟	**cete?**	What's the matter with you? (*inf*)
چشه؟	**ceše?**	What's the matter with him/her/it?

چمونه؟ **cemune?**	What's the matter with us?
چتونه؟ **cetune?**	What's the matter with you?
چشونه؟ **cešune?**	What's the matter with them?
هیچّیم نیست. **hiccim nist.**	Nothing's wrong with me.

Exercise 3

Match a number with a letter.

1 میدونم چمه. **midunam ceme.** [ ]
2 میدونم چشه. **midunam cešе.** [ ]
3 میدونم چته. **midunam cete.** [ ]

(a) I know what's wrong with you.
(b) I know what's wrong with me.
(c) I know what's wrong with him/her/it.

Relative clauses

So far we have seen how two sentences of – usually – equal weight are joined by a conjunction (see pp. 128–9). Sometimes we join two sentences one of which contains our main point, while the other is there to provide further information. Consider these:

(a) یک آپارتمان دارم. **yek āpārtemān dāram.**
I have an apartment.
(b) اون خیلی مناسبه. **un xeili monāsebe.**
It is very suitable.

(a + b) یک آپارتمان دارم که خیلی مناسبه.
yek āpārtemān dāram ke xeili monāsebe.
I have an apartment which is very suitable.

You will note that the pronoun اون **un** 'it' was replaced by the relative pronoun که **ke** 'which'/'that'.

Here is another (slightly less colloquial) way of saying (a + b):

آپارتمانی دارم که خیلی مناسبه.
āpārtemāni dāram ke xeili monāsebe.
I have an apartment which is very suitable.

Here is a similar sentence. Focus on the underlined parts:

آپارتمانی دیدم که خیلی مناسبه.
āpārtemāni didam ke xeili monāsebe.
I saw an apartment which is very suitable.

Now let us shift the position of که **ke** 'which' and consider the change in meaning:

آپارتمانی که دیدم خیلی مناسبه.
āpārtemāni ke didam xeili monāsebe.
The apartment which I saw is very suitable.

Conclusion: When immediately followed by the relative pronoun که **ke** 'which', the indefinite article ی **i** 'a/an' can act as a definite article 'the'! (See p. 48 for the indefinite article.)

Here is another example:

ماشینی به من فروختی که راه نمیره.
māšini be man foruxti ke rāh nemire.
You sold me a car which doesn't go.

ماشینی که به من فروختی راه نمیره.
māšini ke be man foruxti rāh nemire.
The car that/which you sold me doesn't go.

Note how these two sentences are joined up:

(a) خانم هنوز نیومده. **xānom hanuz nayumade.**
The lady hasn't come yet.
(b) آدرس شمارو از او گرفتم. **ādres-e šomā-ro az u gereftam.**
I got your address from her.

(a + b) خانمی که آدرس شمارو از او گرفتم، هنوز نیومده.
xānomi ke ādres-e šomā-ro az u gereftam, hanuz nayumade.
The lady from whom I got your address, hasn't come yet.

A more colloquial form for the above sentence would be:

خانمی که آدرستونو ازش گرفتم، هنوز نیومده.
xānomi ke ādresetun-o azaš gereftam, hanuz nayumade.

More examples:

مردی که بهش تلفن کردید اینجاست.
mardi ke beheš telefon kardid injāst.
The man whom you telephoned is here.

روسری(یی) که به من دادید خیلی قشنگه.
rusari(yi) ke be man dādid xeili qašange.
The headscarf which/that you gave me is very pretty.

جمشید، که از همهٔ ما زرنگ‌تر بود، ۱۰ گرفت!
jamšid, ke az hame-ye mā zerangtar bud, dah gereft!
Jamshid, who was cleverer than all of us, got 10 (out of 20)!

پسرم، که در کانادا درس میخونه، دیروز تلفن کرد.
pesaram, ke dar kānādā dars mixune, diruz telefon kard.
My son, who is studying in Canada, telephoned yesterday.
Implication: The speaker has only one son.

اون پسرم که در کانادا درس میخونه دیروز تلفن کرد.
un pesaram ke dar kānādā dars mixune diruz telefon kard.
My son who is studying in Canada telephoned yesterday.
(*lit* That son of mine who . . .)
Implication: The speaker has more than one son.

Note how these sentences are joined up:

(a) دنبال یک ماشین میگردم.
donbāl-e yek māšin migardam. I'm looking for a car.

(b) باید ارزون باشه.
bāyad arzun bāše. It must be cheap.

(a + b) دنبال یک ماشین میگردم که ارزون باشه.
donbāl-e yek māšin migardam ke arzun bāše.
I'm looking for a car that is cheap.

The word باید **bāyad** 'must' has been omitted in (a + b) but its impact remains, i.e. the verb 'to be' remains in the subjunctive. Here's another example:

میخوام خونه‌یی بخرم که دو تا توالت داشته باشه.
mixām xuneyi bexaram ke do tā tuālet dāšte bāše.
I want to buy a house which has two toilets.

Exercise 4

Join each of the following pairs into one sentence using the relative pronoun که **ke** 'that'/'which'/'who'. Follow the example.

۱- در شیراز یک خونه دارم. خیلی قشنگه.

1 **dar širāz yek xune dāram. xeili qašange.**
I have a house in Shiraz. It's very nice.
Example:
در شیراز یک خونه دارم که خیلی قشنگه.
dar širāz yek xune dāram ke xeili qašange.
I have a house in Shiraz which is very nice.

۲- دیروز یک ماشین خریدم. خوب کار نمیکنه.

2 **diruz yek māšin xaridam. xub kār nemikone.**
Yesterday I bought a car. It doesn't work well.
Now say: Yesterday I bought a car which doesn't work well.

۳- بالاخره یک اتوبوس اومد. پر از مسافر بود.

3 **bel`axare yek otobus umad. por az mosāfer bud.**
At last a bus came. It was full of passengers.
Now say: At last there came a bus which was full of passengers.

۴- پدرم دیروز به ایران برگشت. او در لندن کار میکنه.

4 **pedaram diruz be irān bar gas̄t. u dar landan kār mikone.**
My father returned to Iran yesterday. He works in London.
Now say: My father, who works in London, returned to Iran yesterday.

۵- به آژانس تلفن کردم. نزدیک منزلمونه.

5 **be āĝāns telefon kardam. nazdik-e manzelemune.**
I phoned the agency. It's near our home.
Now say: I phoned the agency that is near our home.

Intonation

A shift of stress can create a difference in meaning:

ماهی **māhi** per month *as compared to* ماهی **māhi** fish

Consider examples in English such as:

content *as compared to* content

ویلای فروشی

یک ویلای زیبا و مجهز به کلیه وسایل زندگی

در یکی از بهترین نقاط سرسبز شمال ایران

به فروش میرسد.

تلفن: (حمید آباد) ٦٠٣٨٢٤

Exercise 5

How do you explain to an estate agent that you are looking for a house to rent with the following particulars:

> 3 bedrooms; one bathroom with two toilets; a medium size kitchen; located in central Tehran; preferably near a shopping centre; rent of 120,000 tumans per month or less.

Exercise 6

Can you say these in Persian?

1 What are you looking for?
2 I’m looking for my phone book.
3 Who(m) are you looking for?
4 I’m looking for my son.
5 I’m looking for a new job.
6 The car which you saw wasn’t mine.
7 The man to whom you sold the car is here.
8 I’m looking for a car that is reliable.
9 Next time I’ll buy a house that has ten bedrooms!
10 What’s the matter with you (*inf*)? I have a headache.
11 What’s the matter with your husband?
12 Nothing’s wrong with him. He’s a bit tired.

Comprehension

An Iranian relative left this message on your answering machine.

سلام. علیزاده هستم. از لندن تلفن میکنم. هتلی که گرفته‌ایم خوبه اما خیلی گرونه. لذا دنبال یک آپارتمان میگردیم که سه تا اتاق، خواب، و آشپزخونهٔ بزرگ داشته باشه. میتونی برامون پیدا کنی؟ خیلی ممنون میشم. یک ماه تو لندن میمونیم. اجاره‌اش از ماهی ۵۰۰ پوند بیشتر نشه. ترجیحاً مرکز لندن میخوایم، یا حدّ اقل جایی که به ایستگاه مترو و مرکز خرید و سینما و این جور چیزها نزدیک باشه. میدونی که سرگرمیِ خانمم خریده و سرگرمی بچه‌ها هم سینما. خیلی از لطفت ممنونم. فعلاً خدا حافظ.

salām. alizāde hastam. az landan telefon mikonam. hoteli ke gereft(e)im xube ammā xeili gerune. lezā donbāl-e yek āpārtemān migardim ke se tā otāq-e xāb o āšpazxune-ye bozorg dāšte bāše. mituni barāmun peidā koni? xeili mamnun mišam. yek māh tu

landan mimunim. ejāraš az māhi punsad pond bištar naše. tarjihan markaz-e landan mixaim, yā hadd-e aqal jāyi ke be istgāh-e metro o markaz-e xarid o sinemā o in jur cizhā nazdik bāše. miduni ke sargarmi-e xānomam xaride o sargarmi-e baccehā ham sinemā. xeili az lotfet mamnunam. fe`lan xodā hāfez.

1 What's he looking for and why?
2 What's he asking you to do?
3 What preference does he express and why?

11 گردش
gardes̄
Going out

By the end of this lesson, you should be able to:

- talk about the weather
- talk about likes and dislikes
- talk about your favourite actors/singers
- talk about things you will do if certain conditions are met
- talk about hobbies

Dialogue 1 If the weather gets better . . .

It's Friday morning – weekend in Iran. A man (M) and his wife (W) are talking about what to do.

W: پیش‌بینی هوارو شنیدی؟
M: آره، دو سه درجه سردتر میشه. چطور مگه؟
W: بارون هم میاد؟
M: نه، صبح هوا ابریه، امّا بعد از ظهر ممکنه آفتابی بشه. خب، با این حساب امروز چکار میکنیم؟
W: اگه هوا بهتر بشه، میریم بیرون.
M: اگه نشه چی؟
W: اونوقت تو خونه میمونیم و تلویزیون تماشا میکنیم.

W: **pis̄bini-e havā-ro s̄enidi?**
M: **āre, do se daraje sardtar mis̄e. ceto(u)r mage?**
W: **bārun (h)am miād?**
M: **na, sob(h) havā abrie, ammā ba(`)d az zo(h)r momkene āftābi bes̄e. xob, bā in hesāb emruz cekār mikonim?**
W: **age havā behtar bes̄e, mirim birun.**
M: **age nas̄e ci?**
W: **unvaqt tu xune mimunim o televizion tamās̄ā mikonim.**

W: *Did you hear the weather forecast?*
M: *Yeah, it'll become two (or) three degrees colder. What about it?*
W: *Is it going to rain, too?*
M: *No, it's cloudy in the morning, but it may become sunny in the afternoon. Right, given the situation, what are we doing today?*
W: *If the weather gets better, we'll go out.*
M: *What if it doesn't?*
W: *Then, we'll stay at home and watch TV.*

Vocabulary

پیش‌بینی	**pišbini**	forecast	با این حساب	**bā in hesāb**	given the situation
هوا	**havā**	weather	امروز	**emruz**	today
درجه	**daraje**	degree	اگه	**age**	if
سرد	**sard**	cold	بشه	**beše**	(if) it becomes
بارون	**bārun**	rain	بیرون	**birun**	out
آفتابی	**āftābi**	sunny	نشه	**naše**	(if) it doesn't become
ابر	**abr**	cloud	اونوقت	**unvaqt**	then
ابری	**abri**	cloudy			

Language points

Conditionals: type 1

How to say 'If the weather gets better, we'll go out'

Verbs needed:

Verb 1: شدن (شـ) **šodan (š)** to become/to get
Verb 2: رفتن (ر) **raftan (r)** to go

The verb in the 'if' sentence/clause (verb 1) takes a subjunctive form, i.e. a بـ **be-** prefix (see p. 79). The verb in the result clause (i.e. verb 2) takes a future simple form (see p. 65).

اگه هوا بهتر بشه، میریم بیرون.
age havā behtar beše, mirim birun.
If the weather gets/becomes better, we'll go out.

With some compound verbs, the بـ **be-** prefix is often dropped, e.g.

اگه تلفن کنی، میاد. **age telefon koni, miād.**
If you phone (him), he'll come.

اگه برگردی، خوشحال میشم. **age bar gardi, xoŝhāl miŝam.**
If you return, I'll become happy.

Also note these negative forms:

اگه هوا بهتر نشه، تو خونه میمونیم.
age havā behtar naŝe, tu xune mimunim.
If the weather doesn't get better, we'll stay at home.

اگه هوا بهتر نشه، نمیریم بیرون.
age havā behtar naŝe, nemirim birun.
If the weather doesn't get better, we won't go out.

اگه تلفن نکنی، نمیاد. **age telefon nakoni, nemiād.**
If you don't phone (him), he won't come.

اگه برنگردی، ناراحت میشم. **age bar nagardi, nārāhat miŝam.**
If you don't return, I'll be upset.

Exercise 1

Supply the correct form of the verb given after each sentence. (For help with اومدن **umadan** 'to come', see pp. 55–6 and p. 73.)

۱- اگه ______ خوشحال میشم. خوردن (خور)
1 **age ______ xoŝhāl miŝam. xordan (xor)**
I'll be happy if you eat.
Example: اگه بخورید خوشحال میشم.
age bexorid (*col* **boxorid) xoŝhāl miŝam.**

۲- اگه ______ خوشحال میشم. موندن (مونـ)
2 **age ______ xoŝhāl miŝam. mundan (mun)**
I'll be happy if you stay.

۳- اگه ______ خوشحال میشم. اومدن (ا)
3 **age ______ xoŝhāl miŝam. umadan (ā)**
I'll be happy if you come.

۴- اگه دعوت مارو ______ خوشحال میشیم. قبول کردن (کنـ)
4 **age da`vat-e mā-ro ______ xoŝhāl miŝim. qabul kardan (kon)**
We'll be happy if you accept our invitation.

۵- اگه ______ خوشحال میشیم. برگشتن (گرد)
5 **age ______ xoŝhāl miŝim. bar gaŝtan (gard)**
We'll be happy if he returns.

Exercise 2

Change each sentence in the previous exercise as shown in this example:

۱- اگه نخورید ناراحت میشم.

age naxorid nārāhat mišam. I'll be upset if you don't eat.

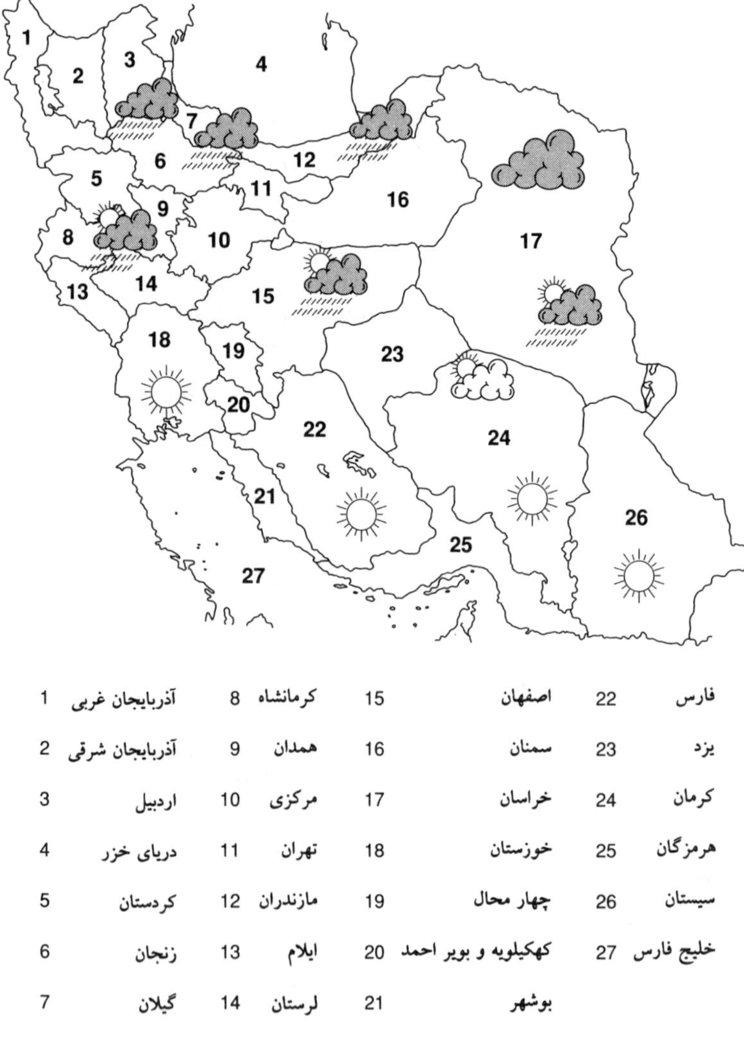

1	آذربایجان غربی	8	کرمانشاه	15	اصفهان	22	فارس
2	آذربایجان شرقی	9	همدان	16	سمنان	23	یزد
3	اردبیل	10	مرکزی	17	خراسان	24	کرمان
4	دریای خزر	11	تهران	18	خوزستان	25	هرمزگان
5	کردستان	12	مازندران	19	چهار محال	26	سیستان
6	زنجان	13	ایلام	20	کهکیلویه و بویر احمد	27	خلیج فارس
7	گیلان	14	لرستان	21	بوشهر		

More 'weather' expressions

بارون / برف میاد. **bārun/barf miād.**
It's raining/snowing.

امروز هوا چند درجه است؟ **emruz havā cand darajast?**
What's the temperature today?

۲۲ درجهٔ سانتیگراد **bist o do daraje-ye sāntigerād**
22 degrees centigrade

۵ درجه زیر صفر **panj daraje zir-e sefr**
5 degrees below zero

هوای تهران خشکه. **havā-ye tehrān xoške.**
Tehran's weather is dry.

هوای لندن مرطوبه. **havā-ye landan martube.**
London's weather is humid.

Exercise 3

Can you say these in Persian?

1 If the weather gets better, we'll go to the park.
2 If you invite them, they'll come.
3 If you don't invite them, they'll be upset.
4 If you get your driving licence, I'll buy you a present.
5 If you tell him (about it), I'll be upset.
6 If you don't take the medicine, you won't get well.
7 What's the weather like today in Tehran?
8 It's snowing. It's 7 degrees below zero.

Dialogue 2 What are your hobbies?

An Iranian (A) is about to visit his British e-mail friend (B) in London. The British friend is ringing to find out what the Iranian's likes and dislikes are so he'll be able to entertain him better. The Iranian, too, asks questions to help him to decide what souvenirs to bring from Iran. Here's part of their conversation.

B: سرگرمی‌هاتون چیه؟

A: خوندن کتاب، تماشای تلویزیون و، اگه هوا خوب باشه، قدم زدن تو پارک. سرگرمی‌های شما چیه؟

B: گوش دادن به موسیقی، رفتن به موزه و، اگه وقت

داشته باشم، آشپزی! غذای ایرانی مورد علاقه‌تون چیه؟

A: چلوکباب. خوراکی‌های ایرانی مورد علاقهٔ شما چیه؟

B: تو غذاها فسنجون؛ تو شیرینی‌ها سوهان و گز.

B: **sargarmihātun cie?**

A: **xundan-e ketāb, tamāšā-ye televizion va, age havā xub bāše, qadam zadan tu pārk. sargarmihā-ye šomā cie?**

B: **guš dādan be musiqi, raftan be muze va, age vaqt dāšte bāšam, āšpazi! qazā-ye irāni-e mo(u)red-e alāqatun cie?**

A: **celo(u)-kabāb. xorākihā-ye irāni-e moured-e alāqe-ye šomā cie?**

B: **tu qazāhā fesenjun, tu šir(i)nihā suhān o gaz.**

B: *What are your hobbies?*

A: *Reading books, watching TV and, if the weather is good, walking in the park. What are your hobbies?*

B: *Listening to music, going to museums and, if I have (the) time, cooking! What's your favourite Iranian dish?*

A: Chelo-kabab. *What are your favourite Iranian foods?*

B: *Among the dishes,* fesenjun, *among the sweets,* suhan *and* gaz.

Vocabulary

خوندن	**xundan**	reading	آشپزی	**āšpazi**	cooking
کتاب	**ketāb**	book	مورد	**mo(u)red-e**	
تماشا	**tamāšā**	watching	علاقه	**alāqe**	favourite
قدم زدن (زن)	**qadam zadan (zan)**	to walk, walking	خوراکی	**xorāki**	food (general)
			فسنجون	**fesenjun**	a meat sauce
گوش دادن (د)	**guš dādan (d)**	to listen, listening	شیرینی‌ها	**šir(i)nihā**	sweets, pastries
			سوهان	**suhān**	a sweet
موزه	**muze**	museum	گز	**gaz**	a sweet

Language points

Contrastive stress

When B asks A a question about A's hobbies, B uses the possessive ending تون **-etun** (**-tun** after a vowel) 'your' in his question:

سرگرمی‌هاتون چیه؟ **sargarmihātun cie?**
What are your hobbies?

When A reciprocates by asking a similar question, he says:

سرگرمی‌های شما چیه؟ **sargarmihā-ye šomā cie?**
What are your hobbies?

Thus stressing شما **šomā** 'you'. This is because the possessive ending تون **-etun** 'your' is not normally stressed and therefore cannot carry the contrastive stress needed for the 'echo' question, while the independent pronoun شما **šomā** 'you' *can* be stressed contrastively. Here are some further examples:

ماشینتون کجاست؟ **māšinetun kojāst?**
Where's your car?

ماشین شما کجاست؟ **māšin-e šomā kojāst?**
Where's your car?

A short cut would be:

مال شما کجاست؟ **māl-e šomā kojāst?**
Where's yours?

(See also pp. 33–5.)

Exercise 4

Answer these questions and reciprocate by asking similar (echo) questions. Follow the example.

1 A: ماشینتون کجاست؟ **māšinetun kojāst?** Where's your car?
B: تو پارکینگ. ماشین شما کجاست؟
tu pārking. māšin-e šomā kojāst?
In the car park. Where's *your* car?

2 A: خونه‌تون کجاست؟ **xunatun kojāst?** Where's your home?
B: ؟ ______ In north London. Where's *your* home?

3 A: ماشینتون چه رنگه؟ **māšinetun ce range?**
What colour is your car?
B: ؟ ______ Blue. What colour is *your* car?

4 A: ماه تولّدتون چیه؟ **māh-e tavallodetun cie?**
What's your month of birth?
B: ؟ ______ September. What's *your* month of birth?

Exercise 5

Rewrite B's replies in the previous exercise using a short cut. Follow the example.

1 B: تو پارکینگ. مال شما کجاست؟
tu pārking. māl-e šomā kojāst?
In the car park. Where's yours?

Conditionals: type 1

With 'to be' and 'to have'

For these two verbs we use their special stems باشـ **bāš** and داشته باشـ **dāšte bāš** respectively (similar to the subjunctive forms introduced at pp. 79–80).

اگه هوا خوب باشه. **age havā xub bāše.**
If the weather is good.

اگه وقت داشته باشم. **age vaqt dāšte bāšam.**
If I have (the) time.

Likes and dislikes

How to say 'I like soup'

من از سوپ خوشم میاد. **man az sup xošam miād.**
I like soup.
تو از سوپ خوشت میاد. **to az sup xošet miād.**
You like soup.
او از سوپ خوشش میاد. **u az sup xošeš miād.**
He/she likes soup.
ما از سوپ خوشمون میاد. **mā az sup xošemun miād.**
We like soup.
شما از سوپ خوشتون میاد. **šomā az sup xošetun miād.**
You like soup.
اونها از سوپ خوششون میاد. **un(h)ā az sup xošešun miād.**
They like soup.

On the above expression, note that:

(a) the word خوش **xoš** 'pleased' is attached to possessive/object endings (see pp. 34–5);
(b) the verb used throughout is میاد **miād** (*lit* 'it comes') from اومدن **umadan** 'to come' (see pp. 55–6).

To say 'I liked . . .', we use the past tense اومد **umad**, e.g.

از سوپ خوشم اومد. **az sup xošam umad.**
I liked the soup.

از سوپ خوشتون اومد؟ **az sup xošetun umad?**
Did you like the soup?

Note the negative forms:

از سوپ خوشم نیومد. **az sup xošam nayumad.**
I didn't like the soup.

از سوپ خوشم نمیاد. **az sup xošam nemiād.**
I don't like soup.

To say 'I dislike soup', replace خوش **xoš** with بد **bad:**

از سوپ بدم میاد. **az sup badam miād.**
I dislike/hate soup.

از سوپ بدم نمیاد. **az sup badam nemiād.**
I don't mind soup.

The verb دوست داشتن (دار) **dust dāštan (dār)** 'to like' is also used to express likes and dislikes of a more permanent nature. Thus, for 'I like soup', we may say either of these:

از سوپ خوشم میاد. = سوپ دوست دارم.
sup dust dāram. = az sup xošam miād.

However, for 'I liked the soup', we say:

از سوپ خوشم اومد. **az sup xošam umad.**

Rather than:

سوپ را دوست داشتم. **sup rā dust dāštam.**

Exercise 6

Complete these sentences, and then make them negative.

۱– من از فیلم‌های پلیسی خوشم میاد.
1 **man az filmhā-ye polisi xošam miād.**
I like detective films.

۲– تو از فیلم‌های پلیسی ______.
2 **to az filmhā-ye polisi ______.**
You like detective films.

۳– او از فیلم‌های پلیسی ______.
3 **u az filmhā-ye polisi ______.**
He/she likes detective films.

4 **mā az filmhā-ye polisi ______.** ۴- ما از فیلم‌های پلیسی ______.
We like detective films.
5 **šoma az filmhā-ye polisi ______.** ۵- شما از فیلم‌های پلیسی ______.
You like detective films.
6 **unhā az filmhā-ye polisi ______.** ۶- اونها از فیلم‌های پلیسی ______.
They like detective films.

Exercise 7

Complete these sentences, and then make them negative.

۱- من از فیلم خوشم اومد.
1 **man az film xošam umad.**
I liked the film.
2 **to az film ______.** ۲- تو از فیلم ______.
You liked the film.
3 **u az film ______.** ۳- او از فیلم ______.
He/she liked the film.
4 **mā az film ______.** ۴- ما از فیلم ______.
We liked the film.
5 **šoma az film ______.** ۵- شما از فیلم ______.
You liked the film.
6 **unhā az film ______.** ۶- اونها از فیلم ______.
They liked the film.

How to say 'what do you like about . . . ?'

از چه چیز ... خوشتون میاد؟ **az ce ciz-e . . . xošetun miād?**
What do you like about . . . ?

از چه چیز ایران خوشتون میاد؟ **az ce ciz-e irān xošetun miād?**
What do you like about Iran?

More colloquial would be:

از چی ایران خوشتون میاد؟ **az ci-e irān xošetun miād?**
What do you like about Iran?

از همه چیز ایران خوشم میاد. **az hame ciz-e irān xošam miād.**
I like everything about Iran.

Exercise 8

Can you say these in Persian?

1 Do you like Iranian food/films? Yes, very much.
2 Did you like the film/meal? Not much.
3 What do you like about Iran?
4 Everything: its food, its scenery, its people.
5 What are your hobbies?
6 Photography, painting, listening to music, sports. What are your hobbies?
7 What's your favourite subject?
8 Fine arts. What's yours?
9 Who's your favourite actor/singer?
10 If you're a good boy, I'll take you to the cinema.
11 If I have money, I'll go to Iran this summer.

Comprehension

Peter has just received this postcard from an Iranian friend who lives in Manchester.

سلام. فقط میخواستم بگم که هفتهٔ آینده اگه هوا خوب باشه برای گردش
به لندن میایم. میدونی که سرگرمی عمدهٔ من تئاتره و از تئاترهای لندن
خیلی خوشم میاد. اگه وقت داشته باشی با ما بیای خوشحال میشیم. با
یک تیر دو نشون میزنیم: هم همدیگه‌رو میبینیم و هم یک نمایشنامهٔ
خوب. به امید دیدار.
علی، ۱۴ مرداد ۱۳۷۸

salām. faqat mixāstam begam ke hafte-ye āyande age havā xub bāše barāye gardeš be landan miaim. miduni ke sargarmi-e omde-ye man te`ātre va az te`ātrhā-ye landan xeili xošam miād. age vaqt dāšte bāši bā mā biai xošhāl mišim. bā yek tir do nešun mizanim: ham hamdiga-ro mibinim va ham yek namāyešnāme-ye xub. be omid-e didār.
Ali, 14 Mordad 1378

1 Where does Peter live? Provide evidence.
2 What's Ali's hobby?
3 What's Ali's plan for next week and what does it depend on?
4 What offer is Ali making and on what condition?
5 What two birds are they going to kill and with what stone?

12 خرید
xarid
Shopping

> **By the end of this lesson, you should be able to:**
>
> - buy things in an Iranian shop
> - go through the rituals of haggling
> - engage in the polite ritual of **ta`ārof**
> - talk about things you would do if . . .
> - talk about things you would have done if . . .

Dialogue 1 Haggling

Haggling is common in small shops in Iran. Shahin (S) is in a clothes shop talking to the assistant (A).

S: آقا، این ژاکت چنده؟
A: اگه چونه نزنید، ۲۰۰۰ تومن. اگه بخواید چونه بزنید، ۳۰۰۰ تومن.
S: کمتر از ۲۰۰۰ تومن نمیشه؟
A: عرض کردم مقطوع ۲۰۰۰ تومن.
S: ژاکتش خوبه؛ ۲۰۰۰ تومن میارزه. اگه پول کافی داشتم میخریدم.
A: چقدر دارید؟
S: ۱۸۰۰ تومن.
A: عیب نداره؛ خدا برکت بده. مبارکه.
S: متشکرم.

S: **āqā, in ĝāket cande?**
A: **age cune nazanid, do hezār toman. age bexaid cune bezanid, se hezār toman.**
S: **kamtar az do hezār toman nemis̄e?**
A: **arz kardam maqtu(`) do hezār toman.**
S: **ĝāketes̄ xube; do hezār toman miarze. age pul-e kāfi dās̄tam mixaridam.**
A: **ceqad(r) dārid?**
S: **hezār o has̄tsad toman.**
A: **eib nadāre; xodā bar(a)kat bede. mobārake.**
S: **mot(a)s̄akkeram.**

S: *Sir, how much is this cardigan?*
A: *If you don't haggle, 2,000 tumans. If you want to haggle, 3,000 tumans.*
S: *Would it not be possible to go below 2,000 tumans?*
A: *As I humbly said (it's) 2,000 tumans fixed.*
S: *The cardigan's good; it is worth 2,000 tumans. If I had enough money (with me) I'd buy (it).*
A: *How much have you got?*
S: *1,800 tumans.*
A: *Doesn't matter; (may) God give (His) blessing. Congratulations!*
S: *Thanks.*

Vocabulary

ژاکت	**ĝāket**	cardigan
چونه زدن	**cune zadan**	
(زنـ)	**(zan)**	to haggle
کمتر	**kamtar**	less
نمیشه	**nemiše**	it's not possible
عرض کردن	**arz kardan**	to say
(کنـ)	**(kon)**	(something) humbly
مقطوع	**maqtu`**	fixed
ژاکتش	**ĝāketeš**	the cardigan (*lit* its cardigan)
میارزه	**miarze**	it's worth
ارزیدن	**arzidan**	
(ارز)	**(arz)**	to be worth
کافی	**kāfi**	enough
برکت	**bar(a)kat**	blessing

Language points

Note how the possessive ending ش **-eš** 'its' is used after ژاکت **ĝāket** 'cardigan' to produce ژاکتش **ĝāketeš** meaning 'the cardigan'.

Conditionals: type 2

How to say 'If I knew Persian well, I would understand what he says'

Let us simplify the sentence and split it into two parts:

(a) If I knew
(b) I would understand

The verbs we need are:

Verb 1: دونستن **dunestan** to know
Past stem: دونستـ **dunest**
Verb 2: فهمیدن **fahmidan** to understand
Past stem: فهمید **fahmid**

For both verbs, we use the past stem prefixed with میـ **mi-** with the appropriate personal ending(s) added on:

(a) اگه میدونستم **age midunestam** If I knew
(b) میفهمیدم **mifahmidam** I would understand

(a + b) اگه میدونستم، میفهمیدم
age midunestam, mifahmidam
If I knew, I would understand

Now the full sentence:

اگه فارسی خوب میدونستم، میفهمیدم چی میگه.
age fārsi xub midunestam, mifahmidam ci mige.
If I knew Persian well, I would understand what he says.

Note: In such conditional sentences, the verbs بودن **budan** 'to be' and داشتن **dāstan** 'to have' do not normally take a میـ **mi-** prefix.

اگه فارسیم خوب بود، میفهمیدم چی میگه.
age fārsim xub bud, mifahmidam ci mige.
If my Persian was good, I would understand what he says.

اگه بچّه داشتی، میفهمیدی چی میگم.
age bacce dāsti, mifahmidi ci migam.
If you had children, you would understand what I'm saying.

اگه من جای شما بودم، میرفتم.
age man jā-ye somā budam, miraftam.
(*lit*) If I were in your place, I would go.

اگه بچّه‌ام اینجا بود، نگرانی نداشتم.
age baccam injā bud, negarāni nadāstam.
If my child was/were here, I would have no worries.

اگه دخترم اینجا بود، بهتر بود.
age doxtaram injā bud, behtar bud.
If my daughter was/were here, it would be better.

اگه یک برادر داشتم، دیگه غمی نداشتم.
age yek barādar dāstam, dige qami nadāstam.
If I had a brother, I wouldn't have any other anxiety.

اگه پول داشتم، ماشین میخریدم.
age pul dāstam, māsin mixaridam.
If I had money, I would buy a car.

Now a sentence from the above dialogue:

اگه پول کافی داشتم، میخریدم.
age pul-e kāfi dāstam, mixaridam.
If I had enough money, I would buy (it).

Note: In a conditional sentence, when the verb in the result clause is a request, the verb in the 'if' clause is normally in the simple past:

اگه چیزی لازم داشتید، صدا کنید.
age cizi lāzem dāstid, sedā konid.
Call (me) if you need something. (*lit* . . . if you needed . . .)

Compare these two forms:

(a) اگه دیدمش، بهش میگم. **age didameš, beheš migam.**
If I should see him, I'd tell him (about it).

(b) اگه ببینمش، بهش میگم. **age bebinameš, beheš migam.**
If I see him, I'll tell him (about it).

Use of past tense in the 'if' clause makes (a) less likely than (b).

Exercise 1

Translate these sentences into English.

۱- اگه پدرم اینجا بود، بهتر بود.

1 **age pedaram injā bud, behtar bud.**

۲- اگه من جای تو بودم، اون کارو نمیکردم.

2 **age man jā-ye to budam, un kār-o nemikardam.**

۳- اگه آدرسشو داشتم، بهت میدادم.

3 **age ādreseš-o dāštam, behet midādam.**

۴- اگه با من کار داشتی، این تکمه‌رو فشار بده.

4 **age bā man kār dāšti, in tokma-ro fešār bede(h).**

۵- اگه فارسی خوب میدونستم، با مادر شوهرم به فارسی صحبت میکردم.

5 **age fārsi xub midunestam, bā mādar šouharam be fārsi sohbat mikardam.**

۶- اگه تلفن کرد، پیغامتو بهش میدم.

6 **age telefon kard, peiqāmet-o beheš midam.**

۷- اگه تلفن کنه، پیغامتو بهش میدم.

7 **age telefon kone, peiqāmet-o beheš midam.**

Exercise 2

Complete these sentences with the correct form of the verb in brackets.

۱- اگه ______ ، لطفاً این کتابو بهش بده. (اومدن)

1 **age ______ , lotfan in ketāb-o beheš bede. (umadan)**
If he comes, please give him this book.
Example: اگه اومد، لطفاً این کتابو بهش بده.
age umad, lotfan in ketāb-o beheš bede.

۲- اگه تلفن ______ ، بگو همونجا بمونه تا من بیام. (کردن)

2 **age telefon ______ , begu hamunjā bemune tā man biām. (kardan)**
If he phones, tell him to stay right there until I come.

۳- اگه علی‌رو ______ ، شماره تلفنمو بهش بده. (دیدن)
3 **age ali-ro ______ , šomāre telefonam-o beheš bede. (didan)**
If you see Ali, give him my phone number.

۴- اگه شما جای من بودید، چکار ______ ؟ (کردن)
4 **age šomā jā-ye man budid, cekār ______ ? (kardan)**
What would you do if you were in my place?

Conditionals: type 3

How to say 'If you had come earlier, we would have gone together'

Verbs needed:

1: اومدن **umadan** to come   Past stem: اومد **umad**
2: رفتن **raftan** to go   Past stem: رفت **raft**

Additional vocabulary: با هم **bā ham** together

The same form is often used for conditionals types 2 and 3. Thus, for both verbs, we use the past stem prefixed with میـ **mi-**, with the appropriate personal ending(s) added on:

اگه زودتر میومدی، با هم میرفتیم.
age zudtar miumadi, bā ham miraftim.
If you had come earlier, we would have gone together.

Alternatively, the verb in the 'if' clause can be rendered in the past perfect (see pp. 122–3):

اگه زودتر اومده بودی، با هم میرفتیم.
age zudtar umade budi, bā ham miraftim.
If you had come earlier, we would have gone together.

Exercise 3

Match a number with a letter and then translate into English.

1 اگه اون ساندویچ فاسدو میخوردی   [d]
age un sāndevic-e fāsed-o mixordi.
If you'd eaten that rotten sandwich, you'd have become ill.

2 اگه موضوع‌رو به پدرم میگفتی   [ ]
age mouzu(ʽ)-ro be pedaram migofti.

3 اگه دیرتر از خونه حرکت میکردیم   [ ]
age dirtar az xune harkat mikardim.

4 اگه پنج دقیقه زودتر میومدی   [ ]
age panj daqiqe zudtar miumadi.

5 اگه با من ازدواج نمیکردی [ ]
age bā man ezdevāj nemikardi.

(a) خودکشی میکردم. **xodkos̄i mikardam.**
(b) برادرمو میدیدی. **barādaram-o mididi.**
(c) ناراحت میشدم. **nārāhat mis̄odam.**
(d) مریض میشدی. **mariz mis̄odi.**
(e) به موقع نمیرسیدیم. **be mouqe` nemiresidim.**

Exercise 4

Can you say these in Persian?

1 What would you do if you were in my place?
2 If my father were here, he would become angry.
3 If I had a lot of money, I'd travel around the world.
4 If you'd shaved your beard, I wouldn't have recognised you.
5 If I hadn't taken the antibiotic, I wouldn't have got better.
6 Excuse me sir, how much is this rug/carpet/can of caviar?
7 Isn't this car worth 2,000,000 tumans?
8 It is worth (the price), but it's expensive for me.
9 What would you do if you were a millionaire?
10 I'd build a hospital for sick children.

Dialogue 2 In a corner shop

Participants: customer (C) and assistant (A)

C: آقا ببخشید، این خیارها کیلویی چنده؟
A: قلمی‌ها کیلویی هشتاد تومن، تپلی‌ها کیلویی پنجاه تومن.
C: تخم مرغ‌هارو دونه‌یی میفروشید یا کیلویی؟
A: دونه‌یی ۲۰ تومن.
C: یک کیلو خیار قلمی و ده تا تخم مرغ لطف کنید.
A: بفرمایید.
C: مرسی. چند شد؟
A: بفرمایید، قابلی نداره.
C: خواهش میکنم، چقدر شد؟
A: دویست و هشتاد تومن.
C: ببخشید پول خرد ندارم. فقط یک هزار تومنی دارم.
A: عیب نداره. بفرمایید، این هم بقیّهٔ پولتون، هفتصد و بیست تومن.

C: **āqā bebaxs̄id, in xiār(h)ā kiluyi cande?**
A: **qalami(h)ā kiluyi has̄tād toman, topoli(h)ā kiluyi panjā(h) toman.**
C: **toxm-e morq(h)ā-ro duneyi mif(o)rus̄id yā kiluyi?**

A: **duneyi bist toman.**
C: **yek kilu xiār-e qalami o dah tā toxm-e morq lotf konid.**
A: **befarmāyid.**
C: **mersi. cand šod?**
A: **befarmāyid, qābeli nadāre.**
C: **xāheš mikonam, ceqadr šod?**
A: **devist o haštād toman.**
C: **bebaxšid pul-e xord nadāram. faqat ye(k) hezār tomani dāram.**
A: **eib nadāre. befarmāyid, in (h)am baqiye(-ye) puletun, haftsad o bist toman.**

C: *Excuse me sir, how much are these cucumbers per kilo?*
A: *The slim ones (are) 80 tumans per kilo, the plump ones 50 tumans per kilo.*
C: *Do you sell the eggs by number or by weight (* lit *by kilo)?*
A: *20 tumans each.*
C: *Please give (me) one kilo of slim cucumbers and ten eggs.*
A: *Here you are.*
C: *Thanks. How much did it come to?*
A: *Be my guest, it's not worth a mention.*
C: *I insist, how much did it come to?*
A: *280 tumans.*
C: *I'm sorry I haven't got anything smaller (* lit *small money). I only have a 1,000-tuman (note).*
A: *Doesn't matter. There we are, here's your change, 720 tumans.*

Vocabulary

خیار	**xiār**	cucumber	کیلویی	**kiluyi**	by kilo/weight
کیلو	**kilu**	kilo	دونه‌یی	**duneyi**	each
کیلویی	**kiluyi**	per kilo	لطف کنید	**lotf konid**	kindly give
قلمی	**qalami**	slim	لطف کردن	**lotf kardan**	to give
تپلی	**topoli**	plump	(کن)	**(kon)**	kindly
تپلی‌ها	**topolihā**	plump ones	قابلی	**qābeli**	it is not worthy
تخم	**toxm-e**		نداره	**nadāre**	(of you)
مرغ	**morq**	hen's egg	هزار	**hezār**	
دونه	**dune**	number	تومن	**toman**	1,000 tumans
دونه‌یی	**duneyi**	by number	هزار	**hezār**	1,000-tuman
میفروشید	**mif(o)rušid**	you sell	تومنی	**tomani**	(note)
فروختن	**foruxtan**		این هم	**in ham**	here's
(فروش)	**(foruš)**	to sell			(*lit* this also)
			بقیّه	**baqiye**	the rest; change

Language points

Intonation

Note the difference in the stress pattern of کیلویی **kiluyi** 'per kilo' and کیلویی **kiluyi** 'by kilo'/'weight'. (The underlined syllable is stressed.) The ending ـی **i** (or یی **yi** after vowels) is unstressed when it means 'per'/'each' and stressed when it means 'by'.

کیلویی چنده؟ **kiluyi cande?** How much is it per kilo?
کیلویی میفروشید؟ **kiluyi mif(o)rusid?** Do you sell it by kilo?
دونه‌یی چند؟ **duneyi cand?** How much (for) each?
دونه‌یی میفروشید؟ **duneyi mif(o)rusid?**
Do you sell (them) by number?

Note the stressed ending ـی **i** in a different function:

هزار تومن **hezār toman** 1,000 tumans
هزار تومنی **hezār tomani** a 1,000-tuman (note)
اسکناس هزار تومنی **eskenās-e hezār tomani** a 1,000-tuman note
پنج ریال **panj riāl** 5 rials
پنج ریالی **panj riāli** a 5-rial (coin)
سکّهٔ پنج ریالی **sekke-ye panj riāli** a 5-rial coin
ده پوندی **dah pondi** a £10 (note)

Exercise 5

Can you translate the following shopping list into Persian?

15 eggs; 1 kilo of tomatoes; 2 kilos of cucumbers; half a kilo of cheese; 2 watermelons; 3 loaves/pieces of bread

Exercise 6

Using the shopping list in the previous exercise, ask the shopkeeper:

1 for the price of each item
2 to give you the required amount/number.

Ta`ārof (colloquially pronounced **tārof**) is a politeness ritual or formula observed by a host and a guest, and more generally by: (a) the person offering something; and (b) the person being offered something. If you compliment an Iranian on one of his belongings, he may say to you: پیشکش **piškeš** 'gift' (meaning: 'you can have it as a gift'.) This is often a **tārof** never to be taken seriously by the person being offered the thing in question. A 'no-thank-you' reply would be sufficient. If the offer is serious, and not just a politeness ritual, the offerer insists several times. So when a host says to his guest: **تعارف نميکنم tārof nemikonam** (*lit* I'm not using **tārof**) he is really saying: I'm not just being polite; my offer is genuine; I mean what I say. When a guest says the same sentence to his host, he is really saying: I'm not just being polite; my declining is genuine; I'm not resisting in the expectation of further insistence on your part; I'm not standing on ceremony. In Dialogue 2, A is making a **tārof** when he says:

> **بفرمایید، قابلی نداره. befarmāyid, qābeli nadāre.**
> Be my guest, it's not worth a mention.

To which C correctly replies:

> **خواهش میکنم، چقدر شد؟ xāhes̄ mikonam, ceqadr s̄od?**
> I insist, how much did it come to?

Exercise 7

You have just complimented an Iranian friend on his 'Nice briefcase!' and have received this reply: **پیشکش! pis̄kes̄!**

1 What is he saying? 2 How should you respond?

Exercise 8

Translate these sentences into English.

۱– آقا، این پرتقال‌ها کیلویی چنده؟
1 **āqā, in porteqāl(h)ā kiluyi cande?**
۲– آقا، این مرغ‌هارو کیلویی میفروشید یا دونه‌یی؟
2 **āqā, in morq(h)ā-ro kiluyi mif(o)rus̄id yā duneyi?**
۳– پنج کیلو برنج لطف کنید و دو تا مرغ.
3 **panj kilu berenj lotf konid va do tā morq.**
۴– جمعاً چقدر شد؟
4 **jam`an ceqadr s̄od?**
۵– بفرمایید، قابلی نداره.
5 **befarmāyid, qābeli nadāre.**

Exercise 9

Can you say these in Persian?

1 OK, how much do I owe you?
2 Be my guest. It's not worth a mention.
3 I insist, how much did it come to?
4 5,000 tumans.

5 Here you are.
6 A 200-tuman note.
7 A 10-rial coin.
8 Will you kindly pass/give the sugar?

Comprehension

Here is an account of what happened to Masoud in his own words.

دیروز با دوستم رفتم خرید. احمد اصلاً خجالتی نیست، اما من خیلی کمرو هستم. خوب شد که احمد همراهم بود. یک پالتو خریدم برای پدرم و یک کلاه زمستونی هم برای خودم. پدرم وقتی پالتورو دید خیلی خوشحال شد، اما حسّ کردم که از رنگش زیاد خوشش نیومد. آخه پدرم همیشه میگه رنگ‌های روشن مال جوون‌هاست. پالتورو که پس بردیم، صاحب فروشگاه پرسید: پالتو چشه؟ گفتم: هیچیش نیست، فقط رنگش برای پدرم خیلی روشنه. فروشنده گفت: عیب نداره، پدرتونو جوونتر نشون میده. من دیگه نمیدونستم چی بگم. اما احمد بلافاصله گفت: پدر دوستم از این رنگ خوشش نمیاد. شما اگه جای او بودید، این پالتورو به پدرتون تحمیل میکردید؟ فروشنده جوابی نداشت و فورا پالتورو پس گرفت.

diruz bā dustam raftam xarid. ahmad aslan xejālati nist, ammā man xeili kamru hastam. xub šod ke ahmad hamrā(ha)m bud. yek pālto xaridam barāye pedaram va yek kolāh-e zemestuni ham barāye xodam. pedaram vaqti pālto-ro did xeili xošhāl šod, ammā hes kardam ke az rangeš ziād xošeš nayumad. āxe pedaram hamiše mige ranghā-ye roušan māl-e javunhāst. pālto-ro ke pas bordim, sāheb-e forušgāh porsid: pālto ceše? goftam: hicciš nist, faqat rangeš barāye pedaram xeili roušane. forušande goft: eib nadāre, pedaretun-o javuntar nešun mide. man dige nemidunestam ci begam. ammā ahmad belāfāsele goft: pedar-e dustam az in rang xošeš nemiād. šomā age jā-ye u budid, in pālto-ro be pedaretun tahmil mikardid? forušande javābi nadāšt va fouran pālto-ro pas gereft.

1 What difference in character is there between Masoud and Ahmad?
2 Why was Masoud happy to have Ahmad with him on that day?
3 What would have happened if Ahmad had not been there?
4 Can you spot examples of evasion, reasoning and conviction in the story?

13 خدمات
xadamāt
Services

> **By the end of this lesson, you should be able to:**
>
> - buy stamps and send an item by registered mail
> - ask if it's possible to do something
> - use a passive construction
> - enquire about exchange rates; change dollars into rials
> - say something must/should have happened
> - talk about things you had/didn't have to do

Dialogue 1 At the post office

Participants: customer (c) and assistant (A).

C: ببخشید، پول نقدو میشه با پست فرستاد؟
A: نه، متأسّفانه. میتونید با حوالهٔ پستی بفرستید.
C: این نامه‌رو میخواستم سفارشی کنم.
A: برای کجاست؟
C: کانادا.
A: بذارید رو(ی) ترازو لطفاً.
C: بفرمایید.
A: پول تمبرش میشه صد و پنجاه تومن.
C: بفرمایید. در ضمن، یک سؤال داشتم. دو هفته پیش، یک بسته با پست سفارشی به انگلستان فرستادم. فکر میکنید تا حالا رسیده؟
A: باید رسیده باشه. معمولاً ظرف یک هفته میرسه.
C: خیلی ممنون. خدا حافظ

C: **bebaxšid, pul-e naqd-o miše bā post ferestād?**
A: **na, mota`assefāne. mitunid bā havāle-ye posti bef(e)restid.**
C: **in nāma-ro mixāstam sefāreši konam.**
A: **barāye kojāst?**
C: **kānādā.**
A: **bezārid ru(ye) tarāzu lotfan.**
C: **befarmāyid.**
A: **pul-e tam(b)reš miše sad o panjāh toman.**
C: **befarmāyid. dar zemn, yek so`āl dāštam. do hafte piš, yek baste bā post-e sefāreši be engelestān ferestādam. fekr mikonid tā hālā reside?**
A: **bāyad reside bāše. ma`mulan zarf-e yek hafte mirese.**
C: **xeili mamnun. xodā hāfez.**

C: *Excuse me, is it possible to send cash by post?*
A: *I'm afraid not. You can send (it) by postal order.*
C: *I would like to send this letter by registered mail.*
A: *Where to?*
C: *Canada.*
A: *Put it on the scale, please.*
C: *Here you are.*
A: *The postage comes to 150 tumans.*
C: *Here you are. Incidentally, I have (*lit *had) a question. Two weeks ago, I sent a parcel by registered mail to England. Do you think it's got there by now?*

A: *It must/should have arrived. It normally gets there within a week.*
C: *Much obliged. Goodbye.*

Vocabulary

نقد	**naqd**	cash
میشه	**miše**	is it possible
شدن (شـ)	**šodan (š)**	to be possible; to become
پست	**post**	post, mail
فرستادن (فرستـ)	**ferestādan (ferest)**	to send
حواله	**havāle**	order
پستی	**posti**	postal
نامه	**nāme**	letter
سفارشی	**sefāreši**	registered
سفارشی کردن (کنـ)	**sefāreši kardan (kon)**	to register
ترازو	**tarāzu**	scale
تمبر	**tam(b)r**	stamp
در ضمن	**dar zemn**	incidentally
بسته	**baste**	parcel
فکر کردن (کنـ)	**fekr kardan (kon)**	to think
رسیدن (رسـ)	**residan (res)**	to reach/arrive
ظرف	**zarf-e**	within

Language points

Impersonal construction

How to say 'Is it possible to send . . . ?'

The verb شدن (شـ) **šodan (š)** which normally means 'to become' is used here with a particular meaning: 'to be possible'. The actual form used is میشه **miše** 'it is possible':

میشه فرستاد؟ **miše ferestād?**
Is it possible to send? (Can one send?)

Note that the verb following میشه **miše** comes in its past stem form without any suffix. More examples:

اینجا میشه نشست؟ **injā miše nešast?** Can one sit here?
نوشیدنی میشه برد تو سینما؟ **nušidani miše bord tu sinemā?**
Can one take a drink inside the cinema? (i.e. do the regulations permit?)

Exercise 1

How do you ask whether you can do the following in Persian?

1 Smoke in the hall?
2 Send medicine by post?
3 Park the car there/here?

How to say 'It must have arrived (by now)'

Here is the formula:

باید **bāyad** must +
past stem of verb +
suffix ه **e** +
باشـ **bāš** +
personal ending

The verb we need is رسیدن **residan** to arrive. Its past stem is رسید **resid**.

باید رسیده باشه. **bāyad reside bāše.**
It must/should have arrived.

تا حالا باید رسیده باشه. **tā hālā bāyad reside bāše.**
It must/should have arrived by now. (The speaker is guessing.)

Compare with the following.

How to say 'They should have arrived (by now)'

This is when the speaker is concerned as to why 'they have not arrived yet'. Here we use a different formula:

باید **bāyad** should +
prefix میـ **mi-** +
past stem of the verb +
personal ending (except for third-person singular)

This gives us:

تا حالا باید میرسیدند. **tā hālā bāyad miresidand.**
They should have arrived by now. (The speaker knows/thinks that they have not arrived yet.)

Also note these forms:

باید برم. **bāyad beram.** I must/should go.
نباید برم. **nabayad beram.** I mustn't/shouldn't go.
باید میرفتم. **bāyad miraftam.** I had to go, *or* I should have gone. (But I didn't.)
نباید میرفتم. **nabāyad miraftam.**
I shouldn't have gone. (But I did.)
مجبور نبودم برم. **majbur nabudam beram.**
I didn't have to go. (*lit* I wasn't obliged to go.)

Exercise 2

Match a letter with a number:

1 **bāyad da`vateš mikardi.** ۱- باید دعوتش میکردی.
2 **bāyad unhā-ro dide bāši.** ۲- باید اونهارو دیده باشی.
3 **un harf-o nabāyad mizadi.** ۳- اون حرفو نباید میزدی.
4 **davā-ro bāyad mixordi.** ۴- دوارو باید میخوردی.
5 **šir-o nabāyad mixordi.** ۵- شیرو نباید میخوردی.

(a) You must have seen them.
(b) You should have taken (*lit* eaten) the medicine.
(c) You should have invited him.
(d) You shouldn't have had the milk.
(e) You shouldn't have said it (*lit* that word).

Other relevant expressions

پست عادی **post-e ādi** ordinary mail
تلگرام **telegrām** telegram
ایمیل **imeil** e-mail
فاکس / فکس **fāks/faks** fax

فتوکپی **fotokopi** photocopy
از ... فتوکپی گرفتن (گیر) **az . . . fotokopi gereftan (gir)**
to take a photocopy of . . .
برای این کارت‌پستال چقدر تمبر لازمه؟
barāye in kārt-postāl ceqadr tambr lāzeme?
How much stamps/postage is needed for this postcard?

Exercise 3

Can you say these in Persian?

1 I should have gone with them. (But I didn't.)
2 He shouldn't have eaten that sandwich. (It was off.)
3 You must have had *chelo-kabab*.
4 How much stamps/postage is needed for this letter?
5 Is it possible to take a sandwich/drink into the theatre?
6 Can one smoke in/on the aeroplane?
7 Is it possible to send this parcel by registered mail?
8 Where can I take some photocopies?
9 Where can I send a fax/an e-mail?

Dialogue 2 Exchanging currencies

Participants: customer (C) and assistant (A).

C: ببخشید، نرخ دلار چیه امروز؟
A: فروش ۸۵۰ تومن، خرید ۸۳۰ تومن.
C: میخواستم ۵۰۰ دلار به ریال تبدیل کنم.
A: این فرمو لطفاً پر کنید.
C: بفرمایید، این فرم، این هم ۵۰۰ دلار.
A: این فرم، مثل اینکه، امضا نشده. این رسید(و) هم لطفاً امضا کنید.
C: معذرت میخوام. ... بفرمایید.
A: متشکّرم، بفرمایید. این پول قبلاً با ماشین شمرده شده، ولی خودتون هم لطفاً بشمرید.
C: چشم ... درسته، خیلی ممنون.

C: **bebaxšid, nerx-e dolār cie emruz?**
A: **foruš haštsad o panjāh toman, xarid haštsad o si toman.**
C: **mixāstam punsad dolār be riāl tabdil konam.**
A: **in form-o lotfan por konid.**
C: **befarmāyid, in form, in (h)am punsad dolār.**
A: **in form, mesl-e inke, emzā našode. in resid(-o) ham lotfan emzā konid.**
C: **ma`zerat mixām. . . . befarmāyid.**
A: **mot(a)šakkeram, befarmāyid. in pul qablan bā māšin šomorde šode, vali xodetun ham lotfan beš(o)morid.**
C: **cašm . . . doroste, xeili mamnun.**

C: *Excuse me, what's the (exchange) rate for the (US) dollar today?*
A: *Selling 850 tumans, buying 830 tumans.*
C: *I wanted to change $500 into rials.*
A: *Please fill in this form.*
C: *Here you are; here's the form, (and) here's the $500.*
A: *This form, it seems, has not been signed. Would you please also sign this receipt?*
C: *I beg your pardon . . . Here you are.*
A: *Thanks, here you are. This money has already been counted by the machine, but please also count (it) yourself.*
C: *By all means . . . It's correct, much obliged.*

Vocabulary

نرخ	**nerx**	rate	امضا کردن	**emzā kardan**	
دلار	**dolār**	dollar	(کن)	**(kon)**	to sign
فروش	**foruš**	selling	مثل اینکه	**mesl-e inke**	it seems
خرید	**xarid**	buying	امضا	**emzā**	
تبدیل	**tabdil**		شدن (ش)	**šodan (š)**	to be signed
کردن	**kardan**		بشمرید	**beš(o)morid**	count
(کن)	**(kon)**	to change	شمردن	**šomordan**	
فرم	**form**	form	(شمر)	**(šomor)**	to count
پر کردن	**por kardan**		شمرده	**šomorde**	
(کن)	**(kon)**	to fill	شدن (ش)	**šodan (š)**	to be counted
امضا(ء)	**emzā(`)**	signature	چشم	**cašm**	by all means

Exercise 4

These are what C in the preceding dialogue did in the bank earlier today, but they are mixed up. Can you put them in order by putting a letter (a–f) in each box?

1 پولو (پول را) به من داد. **pul-o (pul rā) be man dād.** [ ]
2 فرم و ۵۰۰ دلارو دادم. **form o punsad dolar-o dādam.** [ ]
3 نرخ دلارو پرسیدم. **nerx-e dolār-o porsidam.** [ ]
4 پولو شمردم. **pul-o šomordam.** [ ]
5 رسیدو امضا کردم. **resid-o emzā kardam.** [ ]
6 یک فرم پر کردم. **yek form por kardam.** [ ]

Language points

The passive

How to say 'to be counted'

The Persian equivalent for 'to count' is شمردن **šomordan**. Here is the formula to produce the equivalent of 'to be counted':

Past stem of the verb شمرد **šomord** +
suffix ه **-e** +
verb 'to become' شدن **šodan**

The result:

شمرده شدن (ش) **šomorde šodan (š)**
to be counted (*lit* to become counted)

An example from the above dialogue:

این پول قبلاً با ماشین شمرده شده.
in pul qablan bā māšin šomorde šode.
This money has already been counted by the machine.

More examples:

پختن	**poxtan**	to cook
پخته شدن	**poxte šodan**	to be cooked

این کباب خوب پخته نشده.
in kabāb xub poxte našode.
This kebab has not been cooked well.

کشتن	**koštan**	to kill
کشته شدن	**košte šodan**	to be killed

کندی در سال ۱۹۶۳ کشته شد.
kenedi dar sāl-e hezār o nohsad o šast o se košte šod.
Kennedy was killed in the year 1963.

Also note these pairs:

امضا کردن **emzā kardan** to sign
امضا شدن **emzā šodan** to be signed

باز کردن **bāz kardan** to open
باز شدن **bāz šodan** to be opened

Exercise 5

Using the above formula, fill in the blanks.

1	خوردن **xordan**	to eat
	______	to be eaten
2	بستن **bastan**	to close
	______	to be closed
3	دیدن **didan**	to see
	______	to be seen
4	شنیدن **šenidan**	to hear
	______	to be heard
5	گفتن **goftan**	to say; to tell
	______	to be said; to be told

Exercise 6

Can you translate these sentences into English?

1 . ببخشید صداتون شنیده نمیشه **bebaxšid sedātun šenide nemiše.**
2 . سرتون تو عکس دیده نمیشه **saretun tu aks dide nemiše.**
3 . مرغ خوب پخته نشده **morq xub poxte našode.**

Other major currencies

پوند **pond** pound sterling
مارک آلمان **mārk-e ālmān** German mark
فرانک فرانسه **ferānk-e farānse** French franc
ین ژاپن **yen-e ĝāpon** Japanese yen

Exercise 7

Can you say these in Persian?

1 Martin Luther King was killed in 1968.
2 The meat has not been cooked well.
3 Suddenly the door was closed.
4 Where's my sandwich? Sorry, it was eaten!
5 Excuse me, this cheque has not been signed.

Comprehension

Ali (A) is making an enquiry at his local bank. This is the conversation he has with the clerk (C).

A: ببخشید، نرخ ارز برای امروز اعلام شده؟
C: باید شده باشه. یک لحظه صبر کنید ... ببخشید، ساعت ۱۱ اعلام میشه. چی دارید؟
A: ۱۰۰۰ پوند میخوام تبدیل کنم.
C: نرخ خرید دیروز ۱۲۰۰ تومن بود. برای نرخ امروز میتونید به شمارهٔ ۳۸۷۰۳۱۱ تلفن کنید.
A: متأسفانه عجله دارم. با همون نرخ دیروز میشه فروخت؟
C: بله، این فرمو پر کنید (و) ببرید باجه ۳.

A: **bebaxšid, nerx-e arz barāye emruz e`lām šode?**
C: **bāyad šode bāše. yek lahze sabr konid . . . bebaxšid, sā`at-e yāzdah e`lām miše. ci dārid?**

A: **hezār pond mixām tabdil konam.**

C: **nerx-e xarid-e diruz hezār o devist toman bud. barāye nerx-e emruz mitunid be šomāre-ye si o hašt, haftād, sisad o yāzdah telefon konid.**

A: **mota`assefāne ajale dāram. bā hamun nerx-e diruz miše foruxt?**

C: **bale. in form-o por konid (va) bebarid bāje-ye se.**

1 What does Ali want to do?
2 What compromise does he have to make, and why?

14 سلامت و بهداشت salāmat o behdāšt

Health and hygiene

By the end of this lesson, you should be able to:

- use polite titles
- talk about ailments
- ask a chemist for medicine for a minor illness
- make a major apology
- report what someone has said

Dialogue 1 Hello doctor

Parviz (P) is talking to his doctor (D).

P: سلام آقای دکتر. خیلی معذرت میخوام که دیر اومدم.
D: سلام. بفرمایید بشینید.
P: متشکّرم. حالم خیلی بده آقای دکتر.
D: مشکل چیه؟
P: سرم دائم درد میکنه. گلوم همیشه خشکه. قبل از غذا دلم درد میگیره. بینیم اغلب گرفته است. شب‌ها به سختی نفسِ میکشم. نمیذاره بخوابم.
D: دهانتونو باز کنید لطفاً. بگید آ ... مرسی. سه تا دارو براتون مینویسم. هفتهٔ آینده بیاید ببینیم نتیجه چی شده.

P: **salām āqā-ye doktor. xeili ma`zerat mixām ke dir umadam.**
D: **salām. befarmāyid bešinid.**
P: **mot(a)šakkeram. hālam xeili bade āqā-ye doktor.**
D: **moškel cie?**
P: **saram dā`em dard mikone. galum hamiše xoške. qabl az qazā delam dard migire. binim aqlab gereftast. šabhā be saxti nafas mikešam. nemizāre bexābam.**
D: **dahānetun-o bāz konid lotfan. begid ā . . . mersi. se tā dāru barātun minevisam. hafte-ye āyande biaid bebinim natije ci šode.**

P: *Hello (*lit *Mr) Doctor. I'm very sorry I am (*lit *came) late.*
D: *Hello. Do sit down.*
P: *Thank you. I'm very unwell doctor.*
D: *What's the problem?*
P: *My head constantly aches. My throat is always dry. Before a meal, my stomach begins to ache. My nose is often blocked. At night I breathe with difficulty. It's stopping me from sleeping. (*lit *It does not let me sleep.)*
D: *Open your mouth please. Say 'Ah . . .' Thank you. I'm writing out three medicines for you. Come (back) next week and we'll see what the outcome is.*

Vocabulary

معذرت	**ma`zerat**		مشکل	**moškel**	problem
میخوام	**mixām**	I apologise	سر	**sar**	head
دیر	**dir**	late	دائم	**dā`em**	constantly

درد کردن (کن)	**dard kardan (kon)**	to ache	نفس کشیدن (کش)	**nafas kešidan (keš)**	to breathe
گلو	**galu**	throat	نمیذاره	**nemizāre**	it doesn't let
خشک	**xošk**	dry	گذاشتن (ذار)	**gozāštan (zār)**	to let, to allow
دل	**del**	stomach, heart	بخوابم	**bexābam**	(for me) to sleep
درد گرفتن (گیر)	**dard gereftan (gir)**	to begin to ache	دهان	**dahān**	mouth
بینی	**bini**	nose	دارو	**dāru**	medicine
گرفته	**gerefte**	blocked	آینده	**āyande**	next
به سختی	**be saxti**	with difficulty	نتیجه	**natije**	result

Language points

Titles

آقای **āqā-ye** Mr and خانم **xānom-e** Ms

We use the above words before most titles, which is not only a sign of politeness but also an indication of gender:

آقای / خانم دکتر احمدی **āqā-ye/xānom-e doktor ahmadi**
(*lit*) Mr/Ms Doctor Ahmadi

آقای / خانم مهندس هوشنگی
āqā-ye/xānom-e mohandes hušangi
(*lit*) Mr/Ms Engineer Hooshangi (This is a common title for someone with an engineering degree.)

آقای / خانم مدیر **āqā-ye/xānom(-e) modir**
Mr/Ms Director/Head Teacher/Principal

Noun derivation

To turn an adjective into a noun we add the stressed suffix ـی **i**

سخت **saxt** difficult, hard
سختی **saxti** difficulty, hardship, hardness

The pattern به سختی **be saxti** used in the dialogue means 'with difficulty'. If the noun ends with the vowel **e**, the ending گی **-gi** is used instead:

تشنه **tešne** thirsty — تشنگی **tešnegi** thirst
گرسنه **gorosne** hungry — گرسنگی **gorosnegi** hunger

If the noun ends with the vowel ـی **i**, various forms may be used depending on the origin of the word. Words borrowed from Arabic normally have their own noun forms:

غنی **qani** rich — غنا **qanā** richness
سخی **saxi** generous — سخاوت **saxāvat** generosity
ملّی **melli** national — ملّیّت **melliyat** nationality

For words of Persian origin we sometimes add بودن **budan** 'being':

ابری **abri** cloudy
ابری بودن **abri budan** cloudiness (i.e. the fact that it is cloudy)

After other vowels, the suffix یی **-yi** is normally used:

زیبا **zibā** beautiful — زیبایی **zibāyi** beauty
خوشرو **xošru** cheerful — خوشرویی **xošruyi** cheerfulness

Exercise 1

Can you convert these adjectives into nouns?

1 خوشحال **xošhāl** happy → خوشحالی **xošhāli** happiness
2 شاد **šad** joyful → ______ joy
3 حسود **hasud** jealous → ______ jealousy
4 پررو **por-ru** cheeky → ______ cheekiness
5 خسته **xaste** tired → ______ tiredness
6 آواره **āvāre** homeless → ______ homelessness
7 بارونی **bāruni** rainy → ______ raininess (i.e. the fact that it is rainy)

More symptoms or conditions . . .

کمر درد **kamar dard** backache
گلو درد **galu dard** sore throat
کم اشتها **kam eštehā** having little appetite
حسّاسیّت **hassāsiyat** allergy
اسهال **eshāl** diarrhoea
سرما خوردن (خور) **sarmā xordan (xor)** to catch a cold
عطسه کردن **atse kardan** to sneeze
گوش درد **guš dard** earache
بیخوابی **bixābi** sleeplessness, insomnia
آسم **āsm** asthma
استفراغ **estefrāq** vomiting
یبوست **yobusat** constipation
سرفه کردن **sorfe kardan** to cough
تب داشتن (دار) **tab dāštan (dār)** to have a temperature

از بینیم آب میاد. **az binim āb miād.** My nose is streaming. (*lit* Water is coming from my nose.)

سینه‌ام چرک کرده. **sinam cerk karde.** I have a chest infection.

Exercise 2

Match a letter with a number.

۱- خیلی کم اشتها شده‌ام.
1 **xeili kam ēstehā šod(e)am.**

۲- شب‌ها از گوش درد نمیتونم بخوابم.
2 **šabhā az guš dard nemitunam bexābam.**

۳- به گرد و خاک خونه حسّاسیّت دارم.
3 **be gard o xāk-e xune hassāsiyat dāram.**

۴- گلوم هنوز درد میکنه.
4 **galum hanuz dard mikone.**

۵- استفراغ و اسهال با هم خطرناکه.
5 **estefrāq o eshāl-e bā ham xatarnāke.**

۶- هر وقت سیب میخورم یبوست میگیرم.
6 **har vaqt sib mixoram yobusat migiram.**

(a) My throat is still painful/sore.
(b) I've lost much of my appetite.
(c) Vomiting and diarrhoea together are dangerous.
(d) At night I can't sleep because of earache.
(e) Whenever I eat apples I get constipation.
(f) I am allergic to house dust.

Exercise 3

Can you say these in Persian?

1 When I go into a park, I sneeze a lot.
2 When I do some hoovering, I cough a lot.
3 At night, my nose gets blocked. I can't breathe. It doesn't let me sleep.
4 During the night, I need to go to the toilet several times.

Dialogue 2 At the pharmacy

Ali (A) is talking to his local chemist (C).

A: ببخشید، برای گلودرد چی دارید؟
C: سه نوع شربت داریم و دو نوع قرص مکیدنی.
A: از شربت‌ها کدوم بهتره؟

C: والله، مشتری‌ها بیشتر اینو میخرند.
A: خیلی خوب، همونو لطف کنید. در ضمن، برای سرماخوردگی چی دارید؟
C: برای خودتون میخواید؟
A: نه، برای پسرم. ده سالشه. امروز صبح گفت حالم خوب نیست؛ نمیرم مدرسه. فکر میکنم سرما خورده.
C: بفرمایید. هر چهار ساعت یکی از این قرص‌ها بهش بدید و یک قاشق هم از این شربت.
A: خیلی ممنون. چند شد؟
C: دویست تومن.
A: بفرمایید.

A: **bebaxšid, barāye galu-dard ci dārid?**
C: **se nou(`) šarbat dārim va do nou(`) qors-e makidani.**
A: **az šarbat(h)ā kodum behtare?**
C: **vāllā, moštari(h)ā bištar in-o mixarand.**
A: **xeili xub, hamun-o lotf konid. dar zemn, barāye sarmāxordegi ci dārid?**
C: **barāye xodetun mixaid?**
A: **na, barāye pesaram. dah sālešе. emruz sobh goft hālam xub nist; nemiram madrese. fekr mikonam sarmā xorde.**
C: **befarmāyid. har c(ah)ār sā`at yeki az in qorshā beheš bedid va yek qāšoq ham az in šarbat.**
A: **xeili mamnun. cand šod?**
C: **devist toman.**
A: **befarmāyid.**

A: *Excuse me, what have you got for a sore throat?*
C: *We have three types of syrup and two kinds of sucking tablets.*
A: *Of/among the syrups, which one is better?*
C: *Well, customers buy this one more often.*
A: *Very well, give me that one, please. Meanwhile, what have you got for a cold?*
C: *Is it for yourself?*
A: *No, for my son. He's 10 years old. This morning he said he wasn't feeling well; (and therefore) he wouldn't go to school. I think he's got a cold.*
C: *Here you are. Every four hours, give him one of these tablets and also one spoonful of this syrup.*
A: *Much obliged. How much did it come to?*
C: *Two hundred tumans.*
A: *Here you are.*

Vocabulary

نوع	**nou`**	kind, type, sort	همون	**hamun**	that same one
شربت	**šarbat**	syrup	سرماخوردگی	**sarmāxordegi**	(the state of having caught) a cold
قرص	**qors**	tablet, pill			
مکیدن (مک)	**makidan** (**mak**)	to suck			
مکیدنی	**makidani**	suckable	ده سالشه	**dah sālešе**	he's 10 years old
والله	**vāllā**	well, to be honest, (*lit* by God)	قاشق	**qāšoq**	spoon(ful)
مشتری	**moštari**	customer			

Language points

Reported speech

How to say 'He said he was ill'

Consider these sentences:

(a) Peter said: 'I'm ill'.
(b) Peter said (that) he was ill.

A Persian equivalent for (b) would be similar to (a), only without the quotation marks:

(a) پیتر گفت: 'مریضم.' **piter goft: 'marizam.'**
Peter said: 'I'm ill'.
(b) پیتر گفت (که) مریضم. **piter goft (ke) marizam.**
Peter said (that) he was ill. (*lit* Peter said (that) I'm ill.)

In Persian reported speech, person and particularly tense do not normally change. Thus, sentence (b) may also take this form:

پیتر گفت (که) مریضه. **piter goft (ke) marize.**
Peter said (that) he was ill. (*lit* Peter said (that) he's ill.)

Here is a sentence from the dialogue:

گفت حالم خوب نیست؛ نمیرم مدرسه.
goft hālam xub nist; nemiram madrese.
He said he wasn't feeling well (and therefore) he wouldn't go to school. (*lit* He said I'm not feeling well . . . I won't go . . .)

Exercise 4

Change these sentences into reported forms.

۱- احمد گفت: 'خسته‌ام.'

1 **ahmad goft: 'xasteam'.** Ahmad said: 'I'm tired'.
Example: احمد گفت (که) خسته‌ام.
ahmad goft (ke) xasteam. Ahmad said (that) he was tired.

۲- برادرم گفت: 'ماشینمو فروختم.'

2 **barādaram goft: 'māšinam-o foruxtam'.**
My brother said: 'I sold my car'.
My brother said (that) he had sold his car . . .

۳- حسن گفت: 'نمیدونم تلویزیون چشه.'

3 **hasan goft: 'nemidunam televizion češe'.**
Hassan said: 'I don't know what's wrong with the TV'.
Hassan said (that) he didn't know what was wrong with the TV . . .

۴- مهمون‌ها گفتند: 'ما گرسنه‌ایم.'

4 **mehmunhā goftand: 'mā gorosneim'.**
The guests said: 'We are hungry'.
The guests said (that) they were hungry.

۵- او پرسید: 'ساعت چنده؟'

5 **u porsid: 'sā`at čande?'**
He asked: 'What's the time?'
He asked what the time was . . .

More medicines

For medicines taken orally, we use the verb خوردن (خور) **xordan (xor)** (*lit* to eat).

شربت سرفه **šarbat-e sorfe** cough syrup
مسکّن **mosakken** pain-killer
آنتی بیوتیک **ānti biutik** antibiotic

For کرم **kerem** 'cream', we use مالیدن (مال) **mālidan (māl)** 'to rub'.
For آمپول **āmpul** 'injection', we use زدن (زن) **zadan (zan)** 'to hit/jab'.

Exercise 5

Match these medicines with the conditions they treat.

1 **xeili sorfe mikonam.** ۱- خیلی سرفه میکنم.
2 **sin(e)am čerk karde.** ۲- سینه‌ام چرک کرده.

3 **sar-dard-e s̄adid dāram.**   **۳– سردرد شدید دارم.**
4 **azolāt-e pos̄tam dard mikone.**   **۴– عضلات پشتم درد میکنه.**

(a) **آنتی بیوتیک ānti biutik** [ ]
(b) **قرص مسکّن qors-e mosakken** [ ]
(c) **کرم kerem** [ ]
(d) **شربت سرفه s̄arbat-e sorfe** [ ]

Exercise 6

Can you say these in Persian?

1 Excuse me, what have you got for toothache/backache?
2 Which of these toothpastes is better?
3 What's the matter with you?
4 It seems I've got a cold.
5 She said she had missed the 9 o'clock train.
6 He asked if I was married.
7 What did you say?
8 I told him I was engaged.

Comprehension

Listen to this dialogue and answer the questions in English.

A: میدونی که حدود یک ساعت تأخیر داری؟
B: جداً عذر میخوام. قرار بود با احمد بیام. دو ساعت پیش تلفن کرد گفت ماشینو فروخته‌ام؛ بدون ماشین نمیتونم بیام؛ خیلی خسته‌ام. من هم چون تأخیر داشتم قطارو از دست دادم.
A: تو گفتی اگه دیر شد تلفن میکنم.
B: واقعاً معذرت میخوام. تو حالت بهتره؟
A: نه، تب دارم. تموم بدنم درد میکنه. از شدّت درد نمیتونم بخوابم.
B: چیزی خورده‌ای؟
A: نه، اشتها ندارم.
B: دکتر دوا نداد؟
A: چرا، یک قرص مکیدنی داد، یک شربت سرفه و یک آمپول پنی‌سیلین.
B: به پنی‌سیلین حسّاسیّت نداری؟
A: نه خوشبختانه.
B: خوش به حالت!

A: **miduni ke hodud-e yek sā`at ta`xir dāri?**

B: **jeddan ozr mixām. qarār bud bā ahmad biām. do sā`at piš telefon kard goft māšin-o foruxt(e)am; bedun-e māšin nemitunam biām; xeili xast(e)am. man ham con ta`xir dāštam qatār-o az dast dādam.**

A: **to gofti age dir šod telefon mikonam.**

B: **vāqe`an ma`zerat mixām. to hālet behtare?**

A: **na, tab dāram. tamum-e badanam dard mikone. az šeddat-e dard nemitunam bexābam.**

B: **cizi xord(e)i?**

A: **na, eštehā nadāram.**

B: **doktor davā nadād?**

A: **cerā, yek qors-e makidani dād, yek šarbat-e sorfe va yek āmpul-e penisilin.**

B: **be penisilin hassāsiyat nadāri?**

A: **na, xošbaxtāne.**

B: **xoš be hālet!**

1 Can you identify two instances of apology?
2 Who promised to do what?
3 What explanation does he give for his failure to fulfil his promise?
4 What is the matter with A?
5 How do we know that B envies A?

15 روابط با دیگران ravābet bā digarān

Relations with other people

By the end of this lesson, you should be able to:

- use polite words for giving and receiving gifts
- offer congratulations and best wishes on happy occasions
- make a social phone call
- send your regards to someone
- express pleasant surprise
- suggest a joint activity
- arrange to meet a friend

Dialogue 1 Giving and receiving gifts

Siam (S) is celebrating his birthday. Hameed (H), one of his friends, has just arrived.

H: صیام جان، این قابل تو نیست. تولّدت مبارک.
S: خیلی ممنون حمید جان. صاحبش قابله. خیلی زحمت کشیدی.
H: خواهش میکنم.
S: خب، داداش چطوره؟
H: خوبه، مرسی. سلام میرسونه. خب، پس بقیّه کجاند؟
S: هنوز نیومده‌اند. تو اوّلین 'مشتری' هستی.

H: **siām jān in qābel-e to nist. tavallodet mobārak.**
S: **xeili mamnun hamid jān. sāhebeš qābele. xeili zahmat kešidi.**
H: **xāheš mikonam.**

S: **xob, dādāš ceto(u)re?**
H: **xube, mersi. salām miresune. xob, pas baqiye kojānd?**
S: **hanuz nayumad(e)and. to avvalin 'moštari' hasti.**

H: *Dear Siam, this is just a little something for you* (lit *this is not worthy of you*). *Happy birthday.*
S: *(I'm) most grateful dear Hameed. Its owner (i.e. giver of the gift) is worthy. You've gone to a lot of trouble.*
H: *Not at all.*
S: *Right, how's (your) brother?*
H: *He's fine, thanks. He sends his regards. Well, where are the others, then?*
S: *They haven't come yet. You are the first 'customer' (metaphorically).*

Vocabulary

قابل	**qābel**	worthy	زحمت	**zahmat**	trouble
تولّد	**tavallod**	birth(day)	زحمت کشیدن (کش)	**zahmat kešidan (keš)**	to take trouble
مبارک	**mobārak**	(may it be) blessed	داداش	**dādāš**	brother (*col*)
تولّدت مبارک	**tavallodet mobārak**	Happy birthday to you	اوّلین	**avvalin**	first
صاحب	**sāheb**	owner; (offerer)			

Language points

How to say 'first customer'

There are two ways of saying this:

(a) مشتری اوّل **moštari-e avval**
(b) اوّلین مشتری **avvalin moštari**

There is not much difference between the two, but note the different position of the noun, as well as the presence of **ezāfe** in (a). Also, note that the ordinal number takes an ین **-in** suffix when it precedes the noun, as in (b). The (b) way seems to feature in more formal contexts:

پنجمین سالگرد ازدواج **panjomin sālgard-e ezdevāj**
fifth wedding anniversary
سوّمین سمینار زبانشناسی **sevvomin seminār-e zabānšenāsi**
third seminar on linguistics

The opposite of اوّل **avval** 'first' is آخر **āxar** 'last'.

روز آخر **ruz-e āxar** last day
آخرین روز **āxarin ruz** last day

Also note these special time phrases:

اوایل اکتبر **avāyel-e oktobr** early October (first few days)
اواسط اکتبر **avāset-e oktobr** mid-October (middle few days)
اواخر اکتبر **avāxer-e oktobr** late October (last few days)

Exercise 1

Put the ordinal number before the noun and make any necessary changes.

1 روز اوّل سال **ruz-e avval-e sāl** first day of the year
  Example: اوّلین روز سال **avvalin ruz-e sāl**
2 روز آخرِ سال **ruz-e āxar-e sāl** last day of the year
3 هفتهٔ دومِ سال **hafte-ye dovvom-e sāl** second week of the year
4 ماه سوّمِ سال **māh-e sevvom-e sāl** third month of the year
5 فصل چهارم سال **fasl-e c(ah)ārom-e sāl** fourth season of the year

How to say 'Happy New Year'/'Birthday', etc.

Here is the formula:

Occasion + مبارک **mobārak** may it be blessed

Here are some examples:

سال نو مبارک **sāl-e nou mobārak** Happy New Year
تولّدت مبارک **tavallodet mobārak** Happy Birthday to you (*inf*)
تولّدتون مبارک **tavallodetun mobārak** Happy Birthday (*f*)
سالگرد ازدواجتون مبارک **sālgard-e ezdevājetun mobārak**
Happy Wedding Anniversary

Note: The above pattern is used to offer good wishes on a much longer list of occasions than is customary in English. These include when a friend has, e.g., a new pair of shoes, a new haircut, etc. So when an Iranian friend says to you:

کفش نو مبارک. **kafš-e nou mobārak.**
(*lit* Congratulations on (your) new shoes.)

He is not being sarcastic!

Exercise 2

Today, you received this card through the post.

دوست عزیز
کریسمس و سال نو مبارک!
سهراب هاشمی

dust-e aziz
kerismas va sāl-e nou mobārak!
sohrāb-e hāšemi

1 Who is it from?
2 What relation is he to you?
3 What does it say?

Exercise 3

Produce a reply to the above card sending a similar message.

A related expression

A Persian equivalent for 'to congratulate someone on something' is:

[گو] (گـ) تبریک گفتن 'someone' را به 'something'
'something' **rā be** 'someone' **tabrik goftan (g) [gu]**

سالگرد ازدواجتان را به شما تبریک میگویم.
sālgard-e ezdevājetān rā be šomā tabrik miguyam.
I congratulate you on your wedding anniversary.

A colloquial form of this would be:

سالگرد ازدواجتونو بهتون تبریک میگم.
sālgard-e ezdevājetun-o behetun tabrik migam.

He sends his regards!

Consider the expression سلام میرسونه **salām miresune** 'He sends his regards', as used in the preceding dialogue. When someone asks after the health of a close friend or relative, the normal response is to say they are fine followed by the above expression, which literally means: 'He/she sends his/her regards'. This is purely a politeness formula. Here are some more related expressions:

به خانواده سلام برسونید. **be xānevāde salām beresunid.**
Give (my) regards to (your) family.

A reply would be چشم **cašm** (By all means).

احمد سلام رسوند. **ahmad salām resund.**
Ahmad sent (his) regards.

Wish you had been there!

When we talk about a pleasant experience, we normally use an expression which literally translates: 'Your place was vacant', *or*: 'You were missed'. The message is: 'I wish you had been there so you would share the experience'. Below is the expression in its various forms.

جات خالی (بود). **jāt xāli (bud).** (*col/inf*)
جاتون خالی (بود). **jātun xāli (bud).** (*col/f*)
جایت خالی بود. **jāyat xāli bud.** (*l/inf*)
جایتان خالی بود. **jāyetān xāli bud.** (*l/f*)

Examples:

جاتون خالی، غذا خیلی خوشمزه بود.
jātun xāli, qazā xeili xošmaze bud.
Wish you were there, the food was very tasty.

تعطیلات خوش گذشت؟ **ta`tilāt xoš gozašt?**
Did you enjoy the holiday?

بله، جاتون خالی بود. **bale, jātun xāli bud.**
Yes, wish you had been there.

Exercise 4

Can you do these in Persian?

1 Use the first line in Dialogue 1 (p. 181) to congratulate your spouse on your wedding anniversary and present him/her with a gift.
2 Respond to the above.
3 Say happy birthday to an older relative.
4 Say happy new house/home to a friend.
5 Write a brief message to family friends congratulating them on their tenth wedding anniversary.
6 Respond to questions like: 'How's your family?'
7 Ask your friend to give your regards to his parents.
8 Tell a friend that you had a pleasant time at a party.

Dialogue 2 Arranging to meet

Ali (A) rings his friend Behrooz (B) to arrange an outing.

A: سلام بهروز جان.
B: سلام. به به! چه عجب از این طرف‌ها! خانم (و) بچّه‌ها خوبند؟
A: همه خوبند. سلام میرسونند. شما چطورید؟
B: بچّه‌ها خوبند، اما خانمم یک کمی سرش درد میکنه. رو کاناپه دراز کشیده.
A: عصر خانمم میاد دیدنش.
B: خیلی ممنون. خب، چطور شد که یاد ما کردی؟
A: گفتم زنگ بزنم حالتو بپرسم؛ در ضمن پیشنهاد کنم که اگه حالشو داشته باشی امشب بریم سینما.
B: فکر بدی نیست. من هم امشب برنامه‌یی ندارم. کجا همدیگه‌رو ببینیم؟
A: ساعت ۸ جلوی سینما آسیا، خوبه؟

B: عالیه.
A: به خانمت سلام برسون.
B: چشم، تو هم همینطور.
A: حتماً. فعلاً خدا حافظ.
B: قربانت.

A: **salām behruz jān.**
B: **salām. bah bah! ce ajab az in taraf(h)ā! xānom (o) baccehā xuband?**
A: **hame xuband. salām miresunand. šomā ceto(u)rid?**
B: **baccehā xuband, ammā xānomam yek kami sareš dard mikone. ru kānāpe derāz kešide.**
A: **asr xānomam miād didaneš.**
B: **xeili mamnun. xob, ceto(u)r šod ke yād-e mā kardi?**
A: **goftam zang bezanam hālet-o beporsam; dar zemn pišnahād konam ke age hāleš-o dāšte bāši emšab berim sinemā.**
B: **fekr-e badi nist. man ham emšab barnāmeyi nadāram. kojā hamdiga-ro bebinim?**
A: **sā`at-e hašt jelo-ye sinemā āsiā, xube?**
B: **ālie.**
A: **be xānomet salām beresun.**
B: **cašm, to ham haminto(u)r.**
A: **hatman. fe`lan xodā hāfez.**
B: **qorbānet.**

A: *Hello dear Behruz.*
B: *Hello. Wow! What a surprise to hear from you in this part of the world! Are (your) wife and children well?*
A: *Everyone's fine. They send their regards. How are you?*
B: *The children are fine, but my wife has a slight headache. She's lying on the sofa.*
A: *My wife will come to see her this evening.*
B: *Thank you very much. What made you think of us?* (lit *How come you remembered us?*)
A: *I thought* (lit *I told (myself)*) *I'd give you a ring to ask how you are; meanwhile to suggest that we go to the cinema if you're in the mood.*
B: *It's not a bad idea. I don't have a plan for tonight either. Where shall we meet each other?*
A: *8 o'clock outside the Asia Cinema, is that OK?*
B: *That's excellent.*
A: *Give my regards to your wife.*
B: *By all means, you too.*
A: *Certainly. Goodbye for now.*
B: *Cheerio.*

Vocabulary

به به !	**bah bah!**	Wow! How lovely!	زنگ زدن (زن)	**zang zadan (zan)**	to ring
عجب	**ajab**	surprise	پرسیدن (پرس)	**porsidan (pors)**	to ask/enquire
طرفها	**tarafhā**	sides; quarters; area	پیشنهاد کردن (کن)	**pišnahād kardan (kon)**	to suggest
کاناپه	**kānāpe**	sofa, settee	حال	**hāl**	mood
دراز کشیدن (کش)	**derāz kešidan (keš)**	to lie down	برنامه	**barnāme**	plan
چطور شد	**ceto(u)r šod**	how come	همدیگه	**hamdige**	each other
یاد ... کردن	**yād-e . . . kardan**	to remember . . .	عالی	**āli**	excellent
گفتم	**goftam**	I told (myself); I thought	قربانت	**qorbānet**	cheerio

Language points

Long time no see/hear from!

The expression چه عجب از این طرفها ! **ce ajab az in taraf(h)ā!** literally means 'What a surprise (to see you pass) through these quarters!' We say this to friends or relatives who visit or phone us after a long gap in communication.

'I'm sitting' v. 'I'm eating'

Here is an exciting piece of grammar! Verbs needed:

نشستن (شین) **nešastan (šin)** to sit down
خوردن (خور) **xordan (xor)** to eat

In English, both verbs 'to sit' and 'to eat' are usually put in the present continuous form to describe a current situation, as in:

(a) I'm sitting on the settee.
(b) I'm eating a sandwich.

A purely grammatical equivalent for (a) and (b) in Persian would be:

(A) من دارم روی کاناپه میشینم.
man dāram ru-ye kānāpe mišinam.

(B) من دارم ساندویچ میخورم.
man dāram sāndevic mixoram.

(See p. 67 for the present continuous tense.)

In terms of meaning, however, while (B) is an acceptable equivalent, (A) is not. This is because (A) means 'I'm in the process of sitting down', i.e. the act of 'sitting' has not been completed yet. One explanation is that the verb نشستن **nešastan** means 'to sit down', i.e. 'to get into a seated position'. Thus, when it is put into a continuous form, it means the person is still in the process of doing the action. To produce the equivalent of 'I'm sitting' in Persian, we actually say 'I have sat down', to show that the act of 'sitting' has been completed. (See pp. 110–11 for present perfect tense.) Compare:

(a) من نشسته‌ام. **man nešasteam.** (*col* **nešas<u>tam</u>**)
I'm sitting. (*lit* I've sat down.)

(b) من دارم میشینم. **man dāram mišinam.**
I'm sitting down. (i.e. I'm in the process of sitting down.)

There are quite a few other verbs which fall into this category. Among them are:

ایستادن (ایستـ)	**istādan (ist)**	to stand up
خوابیدن (خوابـ)	**xābidan (xāb)**	(to go) to sleep
پوشیدن (پوشـ)	**pušidan (puš)**	to wear, to put on
دراز کشیدن (کشـ)	**derāz kešidan (keš)**	to lie down

Examples:

رضا خوابیده (است). **rezā xābide (ast).**
Reza is sleeping. (*lit* Reza has gone to sleep.)

Negative:

رضا نخوابیده (است). **rezā naxābide (ast).**
Reza isn't sleeping. (*lit* Reza has not gone to sleep.)

Alternatively, we can use the word خواب **xāb** meaning 'asleep':

رضا خوابه. **rezā xābe.** Reza's asleep.
رضا خواب نیست. **rezā xāb nist.** Reza isn't asleep.

Here is a sentence from the preceding dialogue:

روکاناپه دراز کشیده. **ru kānāpe derāz keside.** She's lying on the sofa.

Exercise 5

Complete each sentence with the correct form of the verb in brackets.

۱- اونها کنار پنجره ______ (ایستادن).

1 **unhā kenār-e panjare ______ (istādan).**
They are standing by the window.

۲- بچّه‌ها ______ (خوابیدن).

2 **baccehā ______ (xābidan).**
The children are sleeping.

۳- بهترین لباسشو ______ (پوشیدن).

3 **behtarin lebāseš-o ______ (pušidan).**
He's wearing his best clothes.

۴- رو(ی) تخت ______ (دراز کشیدن).

4 **ru(-ye) taxt ______ (derāz kešidan).**
I'm lying on the bed.

How to say 'I was sitting on the settee'

For this, we say the equivalent of 'I had sat on the settee' (see pp. 122–3). Thus:

رو(ی) کاناپه نشسته بودم. **ru(-ye) kānāpe nešaste budam.**

The negative form is:

رو(ی) کاناپه ننشسته بودم.
ru(-ye) kānāpe nan(e)šaste budam.
I was not sitting on the settee. (*lit* I had not sat on the settee.)

Exercise 6

Change the sentences in the previous exercise into the past tense. Example:

۱- اونها کنار پنجره ایستاده بودند.

1 **unhā kenār-e panjare istāde budand.**
They were standing by the window.

Are you in the mood for . . . ?

Here is the expression we need:

حال ... (را) داشتن (دار) **hāl-e . . . (rā) dāštan (dār)**
to be in the mood for . . . ; to feel like doing . . . (*lit* to have the mood for . . .)

This expression is used mostly in questions or negatives:

امروز حال فوتبال (را) ندارم.
emruz hāl-e futbāl (rā) nadāram.
I'm not in the mood for football today.

امشب حال رفتن به سینما را ندارم.
emšab hāl-e raftan be sinemā rā nadāram.
Tonight I'm not in the mood for going to the cinema.

Note how we can say the same sentence with the verb in the subjunctive form:

امشب حالش را ندارم به سینما بروم.
emšab hālaš rā nadāram be sinemā beravam.
Tonight I'm not in the mood to go to the cinema.

The colloquial form is:

امشب حالشو ندارم برم سینما.
emšab hāleš-o nadāram beram sinemā.

In the preceding dialogue, A says:

اگه حالشو داشته باشی ... **age hāleš-o dāšte bāši . . .**
If you're in the (right) mood for it . . . (or: If you feel like it . . .)

Exercise 7

Can you translate these sentences into English?

۱- حالشو داری امشب بریم کنسرت؟

1 **hāleš-o dāri emšab berim konsert?**

۲- نه امشب حالشو ندارم. باشه فردا شب.

2 **na emšab hāleš-o nadāram. bāše fardā šab.**

۳- حالشو دارید امروز بعد از ظهر بریم شنا؟

3 **hāleš-o dārid emruz ba`d az zohr berim šenā?**

How to say 'to go/come to see someone'

Here are the patterns:

به دیدن 'someone' رفتن (ر)
be didan-e 'someone' **raftan (r)** 'to go to see someone'
به دیدن 'someone' اومدن (ا)
be didan-e 'someone' **umadan (ā)** 'to come to see someone'

Examples:

دیروز به دیدن علی رفتم. **diruz be didan-e ali raftam.**
Yesterday I went to see Ali.

دیروز به دیدن او رفتم. **diruz be didan-e u raftam.**
Yesterday I went to see him.

دیروز به دیدنش رفتم. ***diruz be didanes̄ raftam.**
Yesterday I went to see him.

دیروز رفتم دیدنش. ****diruz raftam didanes̄.**
Yesterday I went to see him.

دیروز علی به دیدن من اومد. **diruz ali be didan-e man umad.**
Yesterday Ali came to see me.

دیروز علی به دیدنم اومد. ***diruz ali be didanam umad.**
Yesterday Ali came to see me.

دیروز علی اومد دیدنم. ****diruz ali umad didanam.**
Yesterday Ali came to see me.

*More colloquial register
**Most colloquial register

The form used in the dialogue:

عصر خانمم میاد دیدنش. **asr xānomam miād didanes̄.**
My wife will come to see her this evening.

is a shortened form for:

عصر خانمم به دیدن او میاد.
asr xānomam be didan-e u miād.

Exercise 8

Rewrite these sentences in colloquial form, as in the example. (For object endings, see p. 132.)

۱- دیروز به دیدن او رفتم. ← دیروز رفتم دیدنش.

1 **diruz be didan-e u raftam. → diruz raftam didanes̄.**
I went to see him yesterday.

۲- دیشب به دیدن من اومد. ← ______

2 **dis̄ab be didan-e man umad.** He came to see me last night.

۳- امشب به دیدن اونها میرم. ← ______

3 **ems̄ab be didan-e unhā miram.** Tonight I'll go to see them.

Exercise 9

Can you say these in Persian?

1 He's lying on the bed and watching TV.
2 I'm wearing my Sunday best. What are you wearing?
3 Please be quiet; the children are sleeping.
4 They are standing by the fire and drinking hot chocolate.
5 My brother is watching the news and my mother is sitting beside him.
6 Last weekend my Iranian friend came to see me.
7 Yesterday I went to see my uncle.
8 Do you feel like going to the theatre tonight?
9 Do you have any plans for this evening?
10 When and where shall we meet?

Comprehension

Marjan has just received this letter from Zahra.

مرجان عزیز
سلام. امیدوارم حال تو و خانواده خوب باشد. خیلی ممنون از هدیهٔ قشنگی که برایم فرستادی. حیف که در جشن تولّدم نبودی. جایت خالی بود.
من هم سالگرد ازدواجت را به تو و شوهرت تبریک میگویم. الآن که دارم این نامه را برایت مینویسم، پرویز روی تخت دراز کشیده و (به) موسیقی گوش میکند و سودابه هم کنار میز ایستاده و مرا (من را) تماشا میکند. میدانم که با داشتن بچهٔ کوچک همیشه کمبود وقت داری، ولی اگر حال نامه نوشتن را داشتی، خوشحال میشویم دستخطّ زیبایت را ببینیم. پرویز و سودابه سلام میرسانند. سلام من را هم به شوهرت برسان و دختر قشنگت را هم ببوس. به امید دیدار. زهرا ۲۳ شهریور ۱۳۷۸

marjān-e aziz
salām. omidvāram hāl-e to va xānevāde xub bās̄ad. xeili mamnun az hedye-ye qas̄angi ke barāyam ferestādi. heif ke dar

jašn-e tavallodam nabudi. jāyat xāli bud. man ham sālgard-e ezdevājat rā be to va šouharat tabrik miguyam. al`ān ke dāram in nāme rā barāyat minevisam, parviz ruy-e taxt derāz kešide va (be) musiqi guš mikonad va sudābe ham kenār-e miz istāde va marā (man rā) tamāšā mikonad. midānam ke bā dāštan-e bacce-ye kucek hamiše kambud-e vaqt dāri, vali agar hāl-e nāme neveštan rā dāšti, xoshāl mišavim dastxatt-e zibāyat rā bebinim. parviz va sudābe salām miresānand. salām-e man rā ham be šouharat beresān va doxtar-e qašangat rā ham bebus.
be omid-e didār.
zahrā 23 šahrivar 1378

1 Is their relationship formal/informal? Provide evidence.
2 Why is Zahra thanking Marjan?
3 What regret is she expressing?
4 How do we know Zahra has had a pleasant experience?
5 What do we know about Marjan's family?
6 What is Zahra congratulating Marjan on?
7 Who was with Zahra when she was writing this letter?
8 What were they doing at the time?
9 What compliment is Zahra paying Marjan?

16 کار و زبان‌های خارجی

kār va zabānhā-ye xāreji

Business and foreign languages

By the end of this lesson, you should be able to:

- arrange a business meeting (date and time)
- end a telephone conversation or personal call politely
- express disagreement
- use the Iranian calendar (week, months, seasons)
- talk about the skills or things you can or cannot do
- say how long you have been doing something

Dialogue 1 A business appointment

Mr Amiri's secretary (A) rings Mr Karimi's secretary (K) to arrange a meeting between the two business counterparts.

A: ببخشید، دفتر آقای کریمی؟
K: بله، من منشی‌شون هستم. بفرمایید.
A: سلام، من از دفتر آقای امیری تلفن میکنم.
K: سلام خانم، چه فرمایشی دارید؟
A: آقای امیری مایل بودند با آقای کریمی ملاقات کنند.
K: اجازه بدید تقویمشونو نگاه کنم. برای کی میخواند؟
A: هرچه زودتر بهتر. ترجیحاً این هفته.
K: این هفته که غیر ممکنه، متأسّفانه. هفتهٔ آینده چطوره؟
A: چه روزی؟

سه شنبه ۲۱ فروردین. :K
خوبه، چه ساعتی؟ :A
سه تا چهار بعد از ظهر خوبه؟ :K
بله، خوبه. خیلی ممنون. :A
خواهش میکنم. :K

A: **bebaxšid, daftar-e āqā-ye karimi?**
K: **bale, man monšišun hastam. befarmāyid.**
A: **salām, man az daftar-e āqā-ye amiri telefon mikonam.**
K: **salām xānom, ce farmāyeši dārid?**
A: **āqā-ye amiri māyel budand bā āqā-ye karimi molāqāt konand.**
K: **ejāze bedid taqvimešun-o negāh konam. barāye kei mixānd?**
A: **harce zudtar behtar. tarjihan in hafte.**
K: **in hafte ke qeir-e momkene, mota(`)assefāne. hafte-ye āyande ceto(u)re?**
A: **ce ruzi?**
K: **se šanbe bist o yek-e farvardin.**
A: **xube, ce sā`ati?**
K: **se tā c(ah)ār-e ba`d az zohr xube?**
A: **bale, xube. xeili mamnun.**
K: **xāheš mikonam.**

A: *Excuse me, (is that) Mr Karimi's office?*
K: *Yes, I'm his secretary. Please go ahead.*
A: *Hello, I'm calling from Mr Amiri's office.*
K: *Hello madam, what can I do for you?*
A: *Mr Amiri would like to have a meeting with Mr Karimi.*
K: *Let me have a look in his diary. When does he want it for?*
A: *The sooner the better. Preferably this week.*
K: *As far as this week is concerned, it is impossible, I'm afraid. How about next week?*
A: *What day?*
K: *Tuesday 21 Farvardin.*
A: *That's fine, what time?*
K: *Will 3 to 4 in the afternoon be OK?*
A: *Yes, it's fine. Much obliged.*
K: *You're welcome.*

Vocabulary

دفتر	**daftar**	office	مایل	**māyel**	inclined, interested
منشی	**monši**	secretary			
فرمایش	**farmāyeš**	business (*lit* command)	ملاقات	**molāqāt**	meeting

... با	**bā ...**	to meet	هرچه زودتر	**harce zudtar**	the sooner
ملاقات	**molāqāt**	with ...	بهتر	**behtar**	the better
کردن (کن)	**kardan (kon)**		غیر	**qeir-e**	
تقویم	**taqvim**	diary, calendar	ممکن	**momken**	impossible
نگاه کردن (کن)	**negāh kardan (kon)**	to look	فروردین	**farvardin**	Farvardin (1st month in Iranian calendar)

Language points

What can I do for you?

For the above expression we normally say:

> **چه فرمایشی دارید؟ ce farmāyeši dārid?**
> (*lit* What command do you have?)

Also note the following exchange which is used when leaving someone or ending a telephone conversation:

(a) **خب، فرمایشی ندارید؟ xob, farmāyeši nadārid?**
OK, do you not have any (other) business with me?

(b) **عرضی ندارم، متشکّرم. arzi nadāram, mot(a)šakkeram.**
No (*lit* I have no submission to make), thank you.

Note: (a) is used by the visitor or caller. Also, make sure that you do not switch subjects! We always use (a) in reference to others and (b) in reference to ourselves.

Exercise 1

1 You have been talking to a business counterpart on the phone. How do you end the conversation politely?
2 You have been visiting an Iranian partner. How do you take leave politely?
3 How would you respond in either of the above situations?

Special use of که **ke**

The generic meaning of **که ke** is 'that', 'which', 'who'. However, in the following examples (the first taken from the previous dialogue) the word که **ke** means 'as far as' [the stated thing] 'is concerned'.

این هفته که غیر ممکنه.
in hafte ke qeir-e momkene.
As far as this week is concerned, it's impossible.

من که با این موضوع مخالفم.
man ke bā in mouzu` moxālefam.
As far as I am concerned, I'm opposed to this matter, *or*:
As for me, I disagree with this matter.

Exercise 2

Translate these sentences into English.

1 **mā ke jāmun xube.** ۱- ما که جامون خوبه.
2 **pul ke mas`aleyi nist.** ۲- پول که مسئله‌یی نیست.
۳- من که از مکانیک اتومبیل هیچّی نمیدونم.
3 **man ke az mekānik-e otomobil hicci nemidunam.**

The Iranian calendar

The Iranian year has 365 days and normally begins on 21 March. It has 12 months: 1–6 have 31 days each; 7–11 have 30 days each; month 12 has 29 days except in leap years when it has 30 days. Here is the full list:

بهار **bahār** spring:	1	فروردین	**farvardin** Farvardin
	2	اردیبهشت	**ordibehešt** Ordibehesht
	3	خرداد	**xordād** Khordad
تابستان **tābestān** summer:	4	تیر	**tir** Tir
	5	مرداد	**mordād** Mordad
	6	شهریور	**šahrivar** Shahrivar
پاییز **pāyiz** autumn:	7	مهر	**mehr** Mehr
	8	آبان	**ābān** Aban
	9	آذر	**āzar** Azar
زمستان **zemestān** winter:	10	دی	**dey** Dey
	11	بهمن	**bahman** Bahman
	12	اسفند	**esfand** Esfand

March 2001		ذیحجه ۱۴۲۱		**اسفند ۱۳۷۹**
Saturday	17	۲۱	**۲۷**	شنبه
Sunday	18	۲۲	**۲۸**	یکشنبه
Monday	19	۲۳	**۲۹**	دوشنبه
		روز ملی شدن صنعت نفت - تعطیل		
Tuesday	20	۲۴	**۳۰**	سه شنبه
Wednesday	21	۲۵	**۱**	چهارشنبه
		عید نوروز - تعطیل		**فروردین ۱۳۸۰**
Thursday	22	۲۶	**۲**	پنجشنبه
		عید نوروز - تعطیل		
Friday	23	۲۷	**۳**	جمعه

Exercise 3

1 You want to visit Iran next spring. Can you identify the months?
2 Your Iranian friend is visiting you during the summer. Name the months.
3 You want to go on a skiing holiday in Iran. Name the months.
4 Schools open in the first month of autumn. Name the month.

Exercise 4

Can you say these in Persian?

1 Excuse me, is this the Koorosh Company? Yes, what can I do for you?
2 Where are you phoning from? I'm phoning from Iran.
3 As for me, I know nothing about computers.
4 I'll see you next week/summer/spring.
5 Next winter I'm going to Iran to ski.

6 Last autumn, my Iranian friend came to London.
7 I'd like to meet you. When?
The sooner the better. How about this afternoon?
That's excellent. What time? Is 3 p.m. any good?
That's fine. I'll see you at 3 then.

Dialogue 2 A job interview

Peter Jackson (J) is attending a job interview for a vacancy with an Iranian company. (I is the interviewer.)

I: چندتا زبان بلدید؟
J: انگلیسی، که زبان مادریمه، و فرانسه. یک کمی هم فارسی بلدم.
I: شکسته‌نفسی میکنید. فارسیتون خیلی خوبه.
J: لطف دارید.
I: چند وقته (که) فارسی میخونید؟
J: روی هم پنج ساله که فارسی میخونم: سه سال در لندن و دو سال هم تو آمریکا.
I: تا حالا ترجمه کرده‌اید؟
J: کتاب ترجمه نکرده‌ام، امّا مکاتبات بازرگانی ترجمه کرده‌ام.
I: کدوم براتون راحت‌تره: ترجمه از فارسی به انگلیسی یا بالعکس؟
J: انگلیسی به فارسی برام آسونتره، مخصوصاً اگه فرهنگ لغت در دسترس نباشه.
I: چرا میخواید برای این شرکت کار کنید؟
J: به دو دلیل: اوّل اینکه به کار ترجمه علاقه دارم. دوّم اینکه دوست دارم چند سال در ایران زندگی کنم.
I: خب، شما اگه سؤالی دارید بفرمایید.
J: بله، یک جمله تو این فرم هست که نمیفهمم. ممکنه لطفاً برام ترجمه‌اش کنید؟
I: سعی میکنم.

I: **cand tā zabān baladid?**
J: **engelisi, ke zabān-e mādarime, va farānse. yek kami ham fārsi baladam.**
I: **šekaste-nafsi mikonid. fārsitun xeili xube.**
J: **lotf dārid.**
I: **cand vaqte (ke) fārsi mixunid?**
J: **ru-ye ham panj sāle ke fārsi mixunam: se sāl dar landan va do sāl ham tu āmrikā.**
I: **tā hālā tarjome kard(e)id?**
J: **ketāb tarjome nakard(e)am, ammā mokātebāt-e bāzargāni tarjome kard(e)am.**

I: **kodum barātun rāhattare: tarjome az fārsi be engelisi yā bel`aks?**

J: **engelisi be fārsi barām āsuntare, maxsusan age farhang-e loqat dar dastras nabāše.**

I: **cerā mixaid barāye in šerkat kār konid?**

J: **be do dalil: avval inke be kār-e tarjome alāqe dāram. dovvom inke dust dāram cand sāl dar irān zendegi konam.**

I: **xob, šomā age so`āli dārid befarmāyid.**

J: **bale, yek jomle tu in form hast ke nemifahmam. momkene lotfan barām tarjomaš konid?**

I: **sa`y mikonam.**

I: *How many languages do you speak?*

J: *English, which is my mother tongue, and French. I also know a bit of Persian.*

I: *You're being modest. Your Persian is very good.*

J: *That's (very) kind of you.*

I: *How long have you been learning Persian?*

J: *I've been learning Persian for five years in total: three years in London and two years in America.*

I: *Have you done (any) translation so far?*

J: *I haven't translated any books, but I have translated business correspondence.*

I: *Which is easier for you: translating from Persian into English or vice versa?*

J: *English into Persian is easier for me, particularly if a dictionary is not available.*

I: *Why do you want to work for this company?*

J: *For two reasons: first, I'm interested in translation work. Second, I'd like to live in Iran for a few years.*

I: *Right, if you have any questions, please go ahead.*

J: *Yes, there is one sentence in this form which I don't understand. Would you translate it for me, please?*

I: *I'll try.*

Vocabulary

زبان	**zabān**	language	شکسته‌نفسی کردن (کن)	**šekaste-nafsi kardan (kon)**	to be modest (self-deprecate)
زبان مادری	**zabān-e mādari**	mother tongue			

چند وقته	**cand vaqte**	how long is it?	براتون	**barātun**	for you
میخونید	**mixunid**	you are studying	راحت	**rāhat**	easy, comfortable
خوندن (خونـ)	**xundan (xun)**	to study; to read	بالعکس	**bel`aks**	vice versa
روی هم	**ru-ye ham**	in total	برام	**barām**	for me
پنج ساله که	**panj sāle ke**	it's five years that	آسون	**āsun**	easy
ترجمه	**tarjome**	translation	مخصوصاً	**maxsusan**	particularly
ترجمه کردن (کنـ)	**tarjome kardan (kon)**	to translate	فرهنگ لغت	**farhang-e loqat**	dictionary
مکاتبات	**mokātebāt**	correspondence	در دسترس	**dar dastras**	available
بازرگانی	**bāzargāni**	commercial, business	دلیل	**dalil**	reason
			علاقه	**alāqe**	interest
			جمله	**jomle**	sentence

Language points

How to say 'Can you do X?'

The key word used is بلد **balad**, which means 'able to do' (the stated thing). It is used with the verb 'to be'.

من ... بلد هستم. **man . . . balad hastam.** I can do . . .
من تنیس بلد هستم. **man tenis balad hastam.**
I can play tennis. (*lit* I am able to do/play tennis.)

من تنیس بلدم. **man tenis baladam.** (Reduced) I can play tennis.

Negative form:

من تنیس بلد نیستم. **man tenis balad nistam.**
I can't play tennis.

Since this is a highly productive pattern, here it is in full:

من X بلدم. **man X baladam.** I can do X.
تو X بلدی. **to X baladi.** You (*inf*) can do X.
او X بلده. **u X balade.** He/she can do X.
ما X بلدیم. **mā X baladim.** We can do X.
شما X بلدید. **šomā X baladid.** You can do X.
اونها X بلدند. **un(h)ā X baladand.** They can do X.

Examples:

شنا بلدید؟ **šenā baladid?** Can you swim?
رانندگی بلدید؟ **rānandegi baladid?** Can you drive?
دوچرخه سواری بلدید؟ **docarxe savāri baladid?**
Can you ride a bicycle?

انگلیسی بلدید؟ **engelisi baladid?** Can you speak English?
فارسی بلدید؟ **fārsi baladid?** Can you speak Persian?

Exercise 5

At a store in Tehran, you have been asked to fill in a form. Ask an Iranian:

1 If he/she speaks English.
2 If he/she can translate a sentence that you don't understand.

Exercise 6

Can you translate these sentences into English?

1 **man tenis xub baladam.**	۱– من تنیس خوب بلدم.
2 **šomā violon baladid?**	۲– شما ویولن بلدید؟
3 **barādaram šenā balade.**	۳– برادرم شنا بلده.
4 **mā fārsi xub baladim.**	۴– ما فارسی خوب بلدیم.
5 **šomā rānandegi baladid?**	۵– شما رانندگی بلدید؟
6 **man asb savāri balad nistam.**	۶– من اسب سواری بلد نیستم.
7 **u mekāniki balad nist.**	۷– او مکانیکی بلد نیست.

'I've been learning Persian for 5 years'

Literally, we say the equivalent of: 'It is five years that I am learning Persian'. (See present continuous tense, p. 67.)

Thus:

پنج ساله که فارسی میخونم. **panj sāle (ke) fārsi mixunam.**
I've been learning Persian for five years.

The word که **ke** 'that' is often dropped in colloquial Persian. To emphasise the length of time something has been going on, we use the verb داشتن **dāštan** 'to have' as an auxiliary verb:

سه ساله (که) داره عکّاسی میخونه.
se sāle (ke) dāre akkāsi mixune.
He's been learning photography for three (long?) years. (Perhaps

suggesting that 'He still can't take a good picture!)

The verb خوندن **xundan** also means 'to sing', as in:

چهار ساعته که داره میخونه! **c(ah)ār sā`ate (ke) dāre mixune!**
He's been singing for four hours (non-stop)! (Suggesting admiration or boredom!)

Also note these forms:

یک ساعته که اینجا نشسته‌ام. **yek sā`ate ke injā nešast(e)am.**
I've been sitting here for an hour.

دو ساعته که اینجا ایستاده‌ام. **do sā`ate ke injā istād(e)am.**
I've been standing here for two hours.

سه ساعته که منتظره. **se sā`ate ke montazere.**
He's been waiting for three hours.

ده ساعته که خوابه. **dah sā`ate ke xābe.**
He's been sleeping/asleep for ten hours.

چند وقته که اینجایید؟ **cand vaqte ke injāyid?**
How long have you been here?

Exercise 7

Match a letter with a number.

1 سه ساله که اینجاییم. **se sāle ke injāyim.** [d]
2 پنج ساعته که خوابه. **panj sā`ate ke xābe.** [ ]
3 دو ساعته که منتظریم. **do sā`ate ke montazerim.** [ ]
4 چهار ساله که داری آلمانی میخونی.
c(ah)ār sāle ke dāri ālmāni mixuni. [ ]
5 ده ساله که تو لندن زندگی میکنیم.
dah sāle ke tu landan zendegi mikonim. [ ]
6 سه ساعته که اینجا نشسته‌ام.
se sā`ate ke injā nešast(e)am. [ ]
7 دو ساعته که اینجا ایستاده‌ام.
do sā`ate ke injā istād(e)am. [ ]

(a) I've been standing here for two hours.
(b) We've been living in London for ten years.
(c) He's been sleeping for five hours.
(d) We've been here for three years.
(e) We've been waiting for two hours.
(f) I've been sitting here for three hours.
(g) You've been learning German for four years.

Exercise 8

Read Dialogue 2 above (see pp. 200–01) and answer these questions. (Try not to look at the English translations!)

1 Can you spot an instance of modesty or understatement?
2 Who is complimenting whom and on what?
3 Can you identify an example of irony?
4 What does J say, which goes against the accepted norms in translation?
5 How does he qualify this?

Exercise 9

Can you say these in Persian?

1 Can you speak Spanish? No, I can speak French.
2 Can he play the piano? Yes, he's a good pianist.
3 Can you ride a motorbike? No, but I can ride a bicycle.
4 Can you translate this sentence into English/Persian for me, please?
5 How long have you been standing here?
6 How long have you been sitting here?
7 How long have you been waiting?
8 How long have you been learning English?
9 How long have you been living in England?

Comprehension

Following the interview in Dialogue 2 above (see pp. 200–01), Peter Jackson received this letter from the Iranian company.

انتشارات حافظ
تهران، خیابان حافظ، پلاک ۷۹۰
تلفن ۳۸۰۱۵۶
فکس ۳۸۰۱۵۷

تاریخ: ۱۶ آبان ۱۳۷۹

جناب آقای جکسون

با سلام و تشکر از اینکه در مصاحبهٔ روز یک‌شنبه ۱۵ آبان ۱۳۷۹ شرکت کردید، از شما دعوت میشود در روز شنبه ۲۸ آبان ۱۳۷۹، ساعت هشت و نیم صبح به این شرکت مراجعه فرمایید. مدیر شرکت مایل است با شما در بارهٔ جزئیّات کار، میزان حقوق و سایر شرایط استخدام مذاکره کند.

اگر وقت پیشنهادی برای شما مناسب نیست، لطفاً هرچه زودتر با شمارهٔ تلفن فوق تماس بگیرید و موضوع را به منشی شرکت اطّلاع دهید. در ضمن، فرم پیوست را پر کنید و حد اکثر تا تاریخ ۲۵ آبان ۱۳۷۹ به آدرس این شرکت ارسال فرمایید.

ارادتمند

احسان جعفری

entešārāt-e hāfez
tehrān, xiābān-e hāfez, pelāk-e 790
telefon 380156
fax 380157

tārix: 16 ābān 1379

jenāb-e āqā-ye jakson

bā salām va tašakkor az inke dar mosāhebe-ye ruz-e yekšanbe pānzdah-e ābān-e hezār o sisad o haftād o noh šerkat kardid, az šomā da`vat mišavad dar ruz-e šanbe bist o hašt-e ābān-e hezār o sisad o haftād o noh, sā`at-e hašt o nim-e sobh be in šerkat morāje`e farmāyid. modir-e šerkat māyel ast bā šomā dar bāre-ye joz`iyāt-e kār, mizān-e hoquq va sāyer-e šarāyet-e estexdām mozākere konad.

agar vaqt-e pišnahādi barāye šomā monāseb nist, lotfan harce zudtar bā šomāre-ye telefon-e fouq tamās begirid va mouzu` rā be monši-e šerkat ettelā` dahid. dar zemn, form-e peivast rā por konid va hadd-e aksar tā tārix-e bist o panj-e ābān-e hezār o sisad o haftād o noh be ādres-e in šerkat ersāl farmāyid.

erādatmand

ehsān-e ja`fari

1 When was J interviewed?
2 How long after the interview was the letter written?
3 What is the writer asking J to do and why?
4 What option is the writer giving J?
5 If J decides to choose a different option, how can he inform the writer?
6 What deadline is given and what is it about?

Key to the exercises

Lesson 1

Exercise 1

1b; 2c; 3a; 4f; 5d; 6e

Exercise 2

1 روز بخیر **ruz bexeir** 2 عصر بخیر **asr bexeir** 3 سفر بخیر **safar bexeir** 4 ظهر بخیر **zohr bexeir**

Exercise 3

من خوشحال هستم. **man xošhāl hastam.** I am happy.
تو خوشحال هستی. **to xošhāl hasti.** You (*inf*) are happy.
او خوشحال است. **u xošhāl ast.** He/she is happy.
آن خوشحال است. **ān xošhāl ast.** It is happy.
ما خوشحال هستیم. **mā xošhāl hastim.** We are happy.
شما خوشحال هستید. **šomā xošhāl hastid.** You are happy.
آنها خوشحال هستند. **ānhā xošhāl hastand.** They are happy.

Exercise 4

1 سلام، آقا. من پیتر براون هستم. **salām, āqā. man piter berāwn hastam.** آها بله، این پیغام برای شماست. **āhā bale, in peiqām barāye šomāst.** 2 این بسته برای خانم احمدی است. **in baste barāye xānom-e ahmadi ast.** 3 این هدیه برای شماست. **in hedye barāye šomāst.** 4 این هدیه برای آقای احمدی است. **in hedye barāye āqā-ye ahmadi ast.** 5 ایشون خانم احمدی هستند. **išun xānom-e ahmadi hastand.**

Comprehension

1 Late afternoon. 2 Ahmadi. 3 A ticket and a message. 4 A good journey for A.

Lesson 2

Exercise 1

(من) خوشحالم.	**(man) xošhālam.**	I'm happy.
(تو) خوشحالی.	**(to) xošhāli.**	You (*inf*)'re happy.
(او) خوشحاله.	**(u) xošhāle.**	He/she's happy.
(اون) خوشحاله.	**(un) xošhāle.**	It's happy.
(ما) خوشحالیم.	**(mā) xošhālim.**	We're happy.
(شما) خوشحالید.	**(šomā) xošhālid.**	You're happy.
(اونها) خوشحالند.	**(unhā) xošhāland.**	They're happy.

Exercise 2

1 نیستم **nistam** 2 نیستیم **nistim** 3 نیستی **nisti** 4 نیستند **nistand** 5 نیستید **nistid** 6 نیست **nist**

Exercise 3

1 حال احمد چطوره؟ **hāl-e ahmad ceto(u)re?** خوبه، مرسی. **xube, mersi.** 2 حال مامان / بابا چطوره؟ **hāl-e māmān/bābā ceto(u)re?** خوبند، مرسی. **xuband, mersi.** 3 چطوری؟ **ceto(u)ri?** بد نیستم، مرسی. **bad nistam, mersi.**

Exercise 4

1 ماشین او **māšin-e u** 2 ماشین ما **māšin-e mā** 3 تلفن او **telefon-e u** 4 آپارتمان شما **āpārtemān-e šomā** 5 منزل اونها **manzel-e unhā** 6 ماشین شما **māšin-e šomā**

Exercise 5

1 بوی خوب **bu-ye xub** 2 موی بلند **mu-ye boland** 3 موی خوب **mu-ye xub** 4 فیلم بد **film-e bad** 5 موی بور **mu-ye bur** 6 موی مشکی **mu-ye meški** 7 بابای خوب **bābā-ye xub**

Exercise 6

1 ماشینش **māšineš** 2 ماشینمون **māšinemun** 3 تلفنش **telefoneš** 4 آپارتمانتون **āpārtemānetun** 5 منزلشون **manzelešun** 6 ماشینتون **māšinetun**

Exercise 7

1 من هم همینطور. **man ham haminto(u)r.** 2 ما هم همینطور. **mā ham haminto(u)r.** 3 پیتر هم همینطور. **piter ham haminto(u)r.** 4 من هم همینطور. **man ham haminto(u)r.** 5 او(ن) هم همینطور. **u(n) ham haminto(u)r.** 6 من هم همینطور. **man ham haminto(u)r.**

Exercise 8

1 اسمتون **esmetun** 2 آدرستون **ādresetun** 3 ملّیّتتون **melliyatetun** 4 شماره تلفنتون **šomāre telefonetun** 5 تاریخ تولّدتون **tārix-e tavallodetun**

Exercise 9

1 حال مادرتون چطوره؟ **hāl-e mādaretun ceto(u)re?** خوبند، مرسی. **xuband, mersi.** 2 ماشینتون کجاست؟ **māšinetun kojāst?** اینجاست. **injāst.** 3 کارتون چیه؟ **kāretun cie?** من دکترم. **man doktoram.** 4 این کیه؟ **in kie?** اون برادرمه. **un barādarame.** 5 اون چیه؟ **un cie?** ناهارمه. **nāhārame.** 6 این ماشین کیه؟ **in māšin-e kie?** مال منه. **māl-e mane.** 7 آپارتمانتون قشنگه. **āpārtemānetun qašange.** مرسی **mersi.**

Comprehension

1 London 2 Parents, brother and sister 3 Tehran Hotel 4 Fairly happy, small but nice

Lesson 3

Exercise 1

1 تهرانی **tehrāni** 2 لندنی **landani** 3 ایتالیایی **itāliāyi** 4 پاریسی **pārisi** 5 مشهدی **mašhadi** 6 اصفهانی **esfahāni**

Exercise 2

1 شما ایرانی هستید؟ **šomā irāni hastid?** 2 شما متأهّل هستید؟ **šomā mota`ahhel hastid?** 3 محلّ تولّدتون کجاست؟ **mahall-e tavallodetun kojāst?** 4 محلّ کارتون کجاست؟ **mahall-e kāretun kojāst?** 5 خانمتون / شوهرتون کجایی هستند؟ **xānometun/šouharetun kojāyi hastand?** 6 سرگرمی‌هاتون چیه؟ **sargarmihātun cie?**

Exercise 3

1 آپارتمان‌ها **āpārtemānhā** flats 2 ماشین‌ها **māšinhā** cars 3 روزنامه‌ها **ruznāmehā** newspapers 4 ایرانی‌ها / ایرانیان **irānihā/ irāniān** Iranians 5 دوست‌ها / دوستان **dusthā/dustān** friends

Exercise 4

1 شما کجایی هستید؟ **šomā kojāyi hastid?** 2 من فرانسوی / ایتالیایی / آلمانی / اسپانیایی هستم. **man farānsavi/itāliāyi/ālmāni/ espāniāyi hastam.** 3 من لندنی / منچستری هستم. **man landani/ mancesteri hastam.** 4 محلّ تولّدم لندن / پاریس / نیویورک است. **mahall-e tavallodam landan/pāris/nioyork ast.**

Exercise 5

1c; 2a; 3f; 4b; 5d; 6e

Exercise 6

1 من پول ندارم. **man pul nadāram.** 2 تو بلیت نداری. **to belit nadāri.** 3 او ۲۵ سال نداره. **u bist o panj sāl nadāre.** 4 ما اتاق خالی نداریم. **mā otāq-e xāli nadārim.** 5 شما وقت ندارید. **šomā vaqt nadārid.** 6 اونها تلفن ندارند. **unhā telefon nadārand.**

Exercise 7

1 ماشین قشنگی دارید. **māšin-e qašangi dārid.** حیاط قشنگی دارید. **hayāt-e qašangi dārid.** خونهٔ قشنگی دارید. **xune-ye qašangi dārid.** 2 ببخشید، وقت ندارم. **bebaxšid, vaqt nadāram.** 3 چند سال داره؟ **cand sāl dāre?** سی سال داره **si sāl dāre.** 4 ایشون دوستم پیتر هست. **išun dustam piter hast.** انگلیسیه. **engelisie.** ایشون مادرم هستند. **išun mādaram hastand.** 5 خوشوقتم. **xošvaqtam.** من هم همینطور. **man ham haminto(u)r.** 6 چند تا دوست ایرانی دارید؟ **cand tā**

dust-e irāni dārid? 7 .پنج تا دوست ایرانی دارم **panj tā dust-e irāni dāram.**

Comprehension

1 Parviz Alizadeh. 2 He's a (civil) servant. 3 She's an English teacher. 4 Iranian. 5 America. 6 A flat in Tehran. 7 He says the flat is قشنگ **qašang** nice/pretty. 8 He goes to the cinema; she paints. 9 Islam.

Lesson 4

Exercise 1

1 روبروی **ruberu-ye**; 2 پهلوی **pahlu-ye**; 3 روی **ru-ye**; 4 زیر **zir-e**; 5 جلوی **jelo-ye**; 6 پشت **pošt-e**; 7 بالای **bālā-ye**

Exercise 2

(a) اوّل **avval**; (b) دوّم **dovvom**; (c) سوّم **sevvom**; (d) نهم **nohom**; (e) بیست و یکم **bist o yekom**; (f) هفتادم **haftādom**

Exercise 3

انگلستان، لندن، کد پستی SW1، خیابان داونینگ، پلاک ۱۰
engelestān, landan, kod-e posti-e SW1, xiābān-e dāwning, pelāk-e dah

Exercise 4

۱ – احمد روزهای شنبه، دوشنبه و چهارشنبه به دانشگاه میره.
1 **ahmad ruzhā-ye šanbe, došanbe va c(ah)āršanbe be dānešgāh mire.** ۲ – روزهای یک‌شنبه پیانو میزنه. 2 **ruzhā-ye yekšanbe piāno mizane.** ۳ – روزهای سه شنبه تو کتابخونه کتاب میخونه. 3 **ruzhā-ye sešanbe tu ketābxune ketāb mixune.** ۴ – پنج‌شنبه شب با دوستهاش شام میخوره. بعد به سینما میرند. 4 **panjšanbe šab bā dust(h)āš šām mixore. ba`d be sinemā mirand.** ۵ – صبح جمعه به استخر شنا میره. 5 **sobh-e jom`e be estaxr-e šenā mire.**

Exercise 5

1b; 2e; 3d; 4a; 5c

Exercise 6

(a) هفتاد و یک، صفر، بیست و شش، هشتاد و سه haftād o yek, sefr, bist o šeš, haštād o se (b) سی و چهار، سیزده، پونصد و نه si o c(ah)ār, sizdah, punsad o noh (c) چهل و چهار، پنجاه و پنج، دو صفر cel o c(ah)ār, panjāh o panj, do sefr (d) هفتصد و هشتاد و پنج، سی و چهار، دوازده haftsad o haštād o panj, si o c(ah)ār, davāzdah (e) هفتصد و هشتاد و نه، صفر، ششصد و سی و پنج haftsad o haštād o noh, sefr, šešsad o si o panj (f) پنجاه، سی و شش، هفتصد و نود و هفت panjāh, si o šeš, haftsad o navad o haft

Exercise 7

1 آدرس احمد چیه؟ ādres-e ahmad cie? تهران، کد پستی ۱۶۳۷۲، خیابان حافظ، پلاک ۲۴ tehrān, kod-e posti-e šānzdah sisad o haftād o do, xiābān-e hāfez, pelāk-e bist o c(ah)ār 2 فندک دارید؟ fandak dārid? بله، امّا خرابه، متأسّفانه. bale, ammā xarābe, mota`assefāne. 3 آپارتمانتون کدوم طبقه‌است؟ āpārtemānetun kodum tabaqast? طبقهٔ چهارم. tabaqe-ye c(ah)ārom. 4 ساندویچم کجاست؟ sāndevicam kojāst? رو(ی) میز، تو(ی) آشپزخونه‌است. ru(-ye) miz, tu(-ye) āšpazxunast. 5 پستخونه روبرو(ی) پمپ بنزین، پهلو(ی) سینماست. postxune ruberu(-ye) pomp-e benzin, pahlu(-ye) sinemāst. 6 قلمت زیر صندلیه. qalamet zir-e sandalie. 7 شما هر روز به اینجا میاید؟ šomā har ruz be injā miaid? 8 نمیدونه (ما) کجاییم. nemidune (mā) kojāyim. 9 میدونند (ما) اینجاییم؟ midunand (mā) injāyim? 10 میدونید کیه؟ midunid kie? 11 میدونید این چیه؟ midunid in cie?

Exercise 8

1 از az 2 کوچکتر kucektar 3 بزرگتر bozorgtar

Exercise 9

1 بدترین فیلم badtarin film 2 گرونترین اتومبیل geruntarin otomobil 3 ارزونترین آپارتمان arzuntarin āpārtemān 4 بزرگترین شهر bozorgtarin šahr 5 جوونترین زن javuntarin zan 6 مسنّترین مرد mosenntarin mard

Exercise 10

1 شما خواهر کوچکتر دارید؟ šomā xāhar-e kucektar dārid? 2 من

من سه سال از خواهرم بزرگترم. **man se sāl az xāharam bozorgtaram.** 3 شما بزرگترین عضو خانواده هستید؟ **šomā bozorgtarin ozv-e xānevāde hastid?** 4 پدرم دو سال از عمه‌ام کوچکتره. **pedaram do sāl az amm(e)am kucektare.** 5 به نظر من بهترین غذای ایرانی چلوکبابه. **be nazar-e man behtarin qazā-ye irāni celo(u)-kabābe.** 6 نزدیکترین سوپرمارکت کجاست؟ **nazdiktarin supermārket kojāst?** 7 بهترین رستوران کجاست؟ **behtarin resturān kojāst?** 8 من تلویزیون تماشا نمیکنم. **man televizion tamāšā nemikonam.** 9 (به) رادیو گوش میکنم. **(be) rādio guš mikonam.**

Comprehension

1 Hoseini's residence, no. 15 Narges Lane, Sa`di Street, Shiraz 18248. 2 There's a petrol station opposite the lane, a pizza shop on the right, and a bakery on the left. There's a post box in front of her house. 3 Her room is the largest in the house. Her sister's room is smaller but nicer than hers. 4 She thinks Shajarian is the best singer in Iran.

Lesson 5

Exercise 1

1 میام **miām** 2 میای **miai/** میاید **miaid** 3 میاد **miād** 4 میایم **miaim** 5 میاند **miānd**

Exercise 2

1 فردا میام خونه‌تون. **fardā miām xunatun.** 2 سال دیگه/آینده میرم ایران. **sāl-e dige/āyande miram irān.** 3 آخر هفتهٔ آینده به مهمونیم میای؟ **āxar-e hafte-ye āyande be mehmunim miai?** **(OR:** ... میای مهمونیم؟ **... miai mehmunim?)**

Exercise 3

1 جمعه‌ها میریم سینما. **jom`ehā mirim sinemā.** 2 ماهی دو بار میاد منزل ما. **māhi do bār miād manzel-e mā.** 3 سالی یک بار میرم ایران. **sāli yek bār miram irān.** 4 هر روز دیر میاد اداره. **har ruz dir miād edāre.**

Exercise 4

1d; 2a; 3b; 4c

Exercise 5

1 من دارم سوپ میخورم. man dāram sup mixoram. 2 ما داریم تنیس بازی میکنیم. mā dārim tenis bāzi mikonim. 3 تو داری تلویزیون تماشا میکنی. to dāri televizion tamāšā mikoni. 4 او داره نامه مینویسه. u dāre nāme minevise. 5 شما دارید به رادیو گوش میکنید. šomā dārid be rādio guš mikonid.

Exercise 6

1 چه مدّت اینجا میمونید؟ ce moddat injā mimunid? یک ماه اینجا میمونم. yek māh injā mimunam. 2 کجا میمونید / اقامت میکنید؟ kojā mimunid/eqāmat mikonid? یک آپارتمان اجاره میکنم. yek āpārtemān ejāre mikonam. 3 الآن داری چکار میکنی؟ alān dāri cekār mikoni? دارم (به) اخبار گوش میکنم. dāram (be) axbār guš mikonam. دارم روزنامه میخونم. dāram ruznāme mixunam. 4 آخر هفته چکار میکنی؟ āxar-e hafte cekār mikoni? هیچّی. تو خونه میمونم. hicci. tu xune mimunam.

Exercise 7

1 (not needed) 2 را rā 3 (not needed) 4 را rā (needed for both blanks) 5 را rā

Exercise 8

1 Correct 2 لطفاً بچّه‌هاتونو بیارید. lotfan baccehātun-o biārid. 3 Correct 4 لطفاً به اتاق ده برید. lotfan be otāq-e dah berid.

Exercise 9

1 Let's go to a restaurant tonight. 2 Now let's have dinner. 3 Now let's go to sleep. 4 Now let's sit down and see what grandad has to say. 5 OK, now let's watch television for a little while.

Exercise 10

1 لطفاً پنجره‌رو ببند. lotfan panjara-ro beband. 2 لطفاً درو باز کن. lotfan dar-o bāz kon. 3 لطفاً یک کمی آب بیار. lotfan yek kami āb biār. 4 لطفاً چای درست کن. lotfan cai dorost kon. 5 لطفاً اون نمکدونو بده. lotfan un namakdun-o bede. 6 میوه بخور. mive boxor. 7 اونجا نشین. unjā našin. 8 پهلو(ی) من بشین. pahlu(-ye)

man besin. 9 .پنجره‌رو نبند panjara-ro naband. 10 .درو باز نکن dar-o bāz nakon. 11 .چراغو خاموش نکن cerāq-o xāmus nakon. 12 .چراغو روشن کن cerāq-o rousan kon. 13 تلویزیونو خاموش کن. television-o xāmus kon. 14 .زود برگرد خونه zud bar gard xune.

Exercise 11

1 شام چی بخوریم؟ sām ci boxorim? 2 .من ساندویچ میخورم man sāndevic mixoram. 3 .من ساندویچو میخورم man sāndevic-o mixoram. 4 .من هیچی نمیخورم man hicci nemixoram. 5 .به احمد نگو be ahmad nagu. 6 .به مهمونیش نرو be mehmunis narou. 7 .به حرفش گوش نکن be harfes gus nakon. 8 .چشمهاتو ببند / باز کن cesm(h)āt-o beband/bāz kon. 9 .مهمونی خوش بگذره mehmuni xos begzare. 10 آخر هفته خوش بگذره. āxar-e hafte xos begzare. 11 من و پدرم تابستون آینده میریم ایران. man o pedaram tābestun-e āyande mirim irān. 12 بعد از ظهر بریم سوپرمارکت؟ ba`d az zohr berim supermārket? 13 چند نفرید؟ cand nafarid? چهار نفریم: من و خانمم و دو تا بچّه. c(ah)ār nafarim: man o xānomam va do tā bacce. 14 .لطفا بیاید خونه‌مون و بچّه‌هاتونو هم بیارید lotfan biaid xunamun va baccehātun-o ham biārid.

Comprehension

1 He wants to know where he should put the suitcase. He's asked to put it in the boot. 2 Because he knows the place. 3 Two weeks. 4 Australia. 5 200 tumans. 6 He thanks him and wishes him a nice time.

Lesson 6

Exercise 1

1 ببندم bebandam 2 بدونم bedunam 3 ببینی bebini 4 باز کنید bāz konid 5 تلفن کنم telefon konam 6 باشید bāsid 7 داشته باشم dāste bāsam

Exercise 2

1 .شاید پول خرد داشته باشم sāyad pul-e xord dāste bāsam.

2 . ممکنه ماشین نداشته باشند momkene māšin nadāšte bāšand. 3 . باید تلفن داشته باشه bāyad telefon dāšte bāše. 4 ممکنه در منزل نباشند . momkene dar manzel nabāšand.

Exercise 3

1 بیام **biām** 2 بیاید **biaid** 3 بیاد **biād** 4 بیایم **biaim** 5 بیاند **biānd**

Exercise 4

1 میتونم اخبارو ببینم؟ **mitunam axbār-o bebinam?** خواهش میکنم. **xāheš mikonam.** 2 این فیلمو باید همین حالا ببینی؟ **in film-o bāyad hamin hālā bebini?** نه، میتونم فردا ببینم. **na, mitunam fardā bebinam.** 3 بهتر نیست اینجا بشینیم؟ **behtar nist injā bešinim?** 4 شاید شماره تلفنشو/آدرسشو داشته باشم. **šāyad šomāre telefoneš-o/ādreseš-o dāšte bāšam.** 5 باید صبر داشته باشی. **bāyad sabr dāšte bāši.** 6 باید خیلی خوشحال باشید. **bāyad xeili xošhāl bāšid.**

Exercise 5

1 شنبه رفتم منزل دوستم. **šanbe raftam manzel-e dustam.** 2 تلویزیون تماشا کردیم. **televizion tamāšā kardim.** 3 بعد رفتیم سینما. **ba`d raftim sinemā.** 4 یک شنبه پدر و مادرم به خونهٔ من اومدند. **yek šanbe pedar o mādaram be xune-ye man umadand.** 5 با هم ناهار خوردیم. **bā ham nāhār xordim.**

Exercise 6

1 به **be** 2 از **az** 3 از **az** 4 با **bā**; به **be**

Exercise 7

1 دستت درد نکنه. **dastet dard nakone.** 2 سرت درد نکنه **saret dard nakone.**

Exercise 8

1 I want two double rooms with a shower, please. 2 I want (a) second-class hotel. 3 Preferably, it should be in the town centre. 4 How much is this room per night? 5 Does this price include breakfast as well?

Exercise 9

1 . یک اتاق یک نفره با دوش میخوام، برای دو هفته **yek otāq-e yek nafare bā duš mixām, barāye do hafte.** 2 این قیمت شامل شام هم میشه؟ **in qeimat šāmel-e šām ham miše?** . نه، اون جداست **na, un jodāst.** 3 . میخواستم دو تا جا برای مشهد رزرو کنم **mixāstam do tā jā barāye mašhad rezerv konam.** 4 میتونم یک سؤال از شما بپرسم؟ بفرمایید. **mitunam yek so`āl az šomā beporsam? befarmāyid.** 5 میتونم با مدیر هتل صحبت کنم؟ **mitunam bā modir-e hotel sohbat konam?** 6 . چراغهای حمّام خرابه **cerāqhā-ye hammām xarābe.** 7 . دوش آب نداره **duš āb nadāre.** 8 منتظر چی / کی هستی؟ **montazer-e ci/ki hasti?** 9 . منتظر اخبارم **montazer-e axbāram.** 10 . منتظر دوستم هستم **montazer-e dustam hastam.** 11 از من عصبانی هستی؟ **az man asabāni hasti?** 12 از درآمدت راضی هستی؟ **az darāmadet rāzi hasti?** 13 بله، امّا از رئیسم راضی نیستم! **bale, ammā az ra`isam rāzi nistam.** 14 . فردا به شما تلفن میکنم **fardā be šomā telefon mikonam.**

Comprehension

1 He booked a large double room but was given a single room with an additional bed. He wanted a room with a bathroom and a tub, but got a room with a shower. The phone's not working either. 2 He says he's really sorry and ashamed. 3 He offers to give the guest a large double room, which will be available in the evening. 4 Initially, he intended to stay for three weeks, but, given the situation, he might stay less than a week. 5 Noisy neighbours. 6 To show the new room to the guest. 7 Because he's waiting for a phone call from England.

Lesson 7

Exercise 1

R: ببخشید، این فکسو میتونید برام بخونید، لطفاً؟
bebaxšid, in faks-o mitunid barām bexunid, lotfan?

YOU: خواهش میکنم. از کیه؟ **xāheš mikonam. az kie?**

R: . از دوست استرالیاییم **az dust-e osterāliāyim. . . .**

R: . خیلی ممنون **xeili mamnun.**

YOU: . خواهش میکنم **xāheš mikonam.**

Exercise 2

A .خیابون دوّم دست چپ. داخل خیابون، پستخونه دست چپه **xiābun-e dovvom dast-e cap. dāxel-e xiābun, postxune dast-e cape.** B .مستقیم برید. بعد از چهارراه، مرکز تلفن دست راسته **mostaqim berid. ba`d az c(ah)ār-rāh, markaz(-e) telefon dast-e rāste.** C بپیچید تو خیابون اوّل دست راست. بعد مستقیم برید تا خیابون اول دست چپ. سوپرمارکت سر نبشه. **bepicid tu xiābun-e avval dast-e rāst. ba`d mostaqim berid tā xiābun-e avval dast-e cap. supermārket sar-e nabše.**

Exercise 3

1 ساعت چنده، لطفاً؟ **sā`at cande, lotfan?** 2 .شش و نیم **šeš o nim.** 3 .یک ربع به سه **yek rob` be se.** 4 .یک و ربع **yek o rob`.** 5 .پنج دقیقه به دوازده **panj daqiqe be davāzdah.** 6 یازده و پنج دقیقه. **yāzdah o panj daqiqe.** 7 .ببخشید، ساعت ندارم **bebaxšid, sā`at nadāram.** 8 ببخشید، پستخونه کجاست؟ **bebaxšid, postxune kojāst?** 9 از اینجا تا ایستگاه چقدر راه است؟ **az injā tā istgāh ceqadr rāh ast/rāst?** 10 .پیاده نیم ساعت **piāde nim sā`at.** 11 .با ماشین پنج دقیقه **bā māšin panj daqiqe.**

Exercise 4

1 Are there (any) Iranians in your town? 2 Is there an Iranian restaurant in your area? 3 Is there a television in your classroom? 4 Is there (any) ice cream in the freezer? 5 There was but I ate (it).

Exercise 5

1 .بعد از اینکه کلاس تموم شد، میرم خونه **ba`d az inke kelās tamum šod, miram xune.** 2 .بعد از اینکه کلاس تموم شد، رفتم خونه **ba`d az inke kelās tamum šod, raftam xune.** 3 قبل از اینکه کلاس شروع بشه، ناهار میخورم. **qabl az inke kelās šoru` beše, nāhār mixoram.** 4 .قبل از اینکه کلاس شروع بشه، ناهار خوردم **qabl az inke kelās šoru` beše, nāhār xordam.** 5 دیشب قبل از اینکه بخوابم به ایران تلفن کردم. **dišab qabl az inke bexābam be irān telefon kardam.**

Exercise 6

1 ببخشید، این اطراف پستخونه / کلانتری / کتابخونه / سوپرمارکت هست؟ **bebaxšid, in atrāf postxune/kalāntari/ketābxune/supermārket**

hast? 2 **تو یخچال شیر هست؟ tu yaxcāl šir hast?** 3 **تو محلّهٔ شما ایرانی هست؟ tu mahalle-ye šomā irāni hast?** 4 **پارسال پنج تا ایرانی تو کلاسم بود. pārsāl panj tā irāni tu kelāsam bud.** 5 **قبل از اینکه بری بیرون، چراغهارو خاموش کن. qabl az inke beri birun, cerāqhā-ro xāmuš kon.** 6 **قبل از اینکه ادارهرو ترک کنم، به احمد تلفن کردم. qabl az inke edāra-ro tark konam, be ahmad telefon kardam.** 7 **بعد از اینکه همهٔ مهمونها اومدند، شام میخوریم. ba`d az inke hame-ye mehmunhā umadand, šām mixorim.**

Comprehension

1 Jalal. 2 Atlas Hotel. 3 He's happy with it, except for the traffic noise. 4 He's going to the cinema with his wife. 5 7 p.m. 6 To have dinner. 7 Touring the city. 8 6 p.m., an hour before the film starts, so that there will be time for a chat. 9 In the restaurant opposite the Hafez cinema.

Lesson 8

Exercise 1

1F; 2F; 3T; 4T

Exercise 2

1 **نرفتم naraftam** 2 **نکردم nakardam** 3 **نیومد nayumad** 4 **نگفت nagoft**

Exercise 3

1 **نمیدونم nemidunam** 2 **نمیدونه nemidune** 3 **نیست nist** 4 **نیستند nistand**

Exercise 4

1 **معمولاً ناهار چی میخوری؟ ma`mulan nāhār ci mixori? هیچّی. hicci.** 2 **هیچوقت شب قهوه نمیخورم. hic-vaqt šab qahve nemixoram.** 3 **شنبهها به ندرت میریم بیرون. šanbehā be nodrat mirim birun.** 4 **شما هیچوقت به رستوران ایرانی میرید؟ šomā hic-vaqt be resturān-e irāni mirid? بله، بعضی وقتها. bale, ba`zi vaqthā.** 5 **او اغلب با بچّههاش میاد اینجا. u aqlab bā baccehāš miād**

injā. 6 گاهی با دوستهام میرم شنا. gāhi bā dusthām miram šenā.

Exercise 5

1 من غذای ایرانی خوردهام. man qazā-ye irāni xord(e)am. 2 شما غذای ایرانی خوردهاید. šomā qazā-ye irāni xord(e)id. 3 او غذای ایرانی خورده (است). u qazā-ye irāni xorde (ast). 4 ما غذای ایرانی خوردهایم. mā qazā-ye irāni xord(e)im. 5 اونها غذای ایرانی خوردهاند. unhā qazā-ye irāni xord(e)and. 6 تو غذای ایرانی خوردهای. to qazā-ye irāni xord(e)i.

Exercise 6

1 من غذای ایرانی نخوردهام. man qazā-ye irāni naxord(e)am. 2 شما غذای ایرانی نخوردهاید. šomā qazā-ye irāni naxord(e)id. 3 او غذای ایرانی نخورده (است). u qazā-ye irāni naxorde (ast). 4 ما غذای ایرانی نخوردهایم. mā qazā-ye irāni naxord(e)im. 5 اونها غذای ایرانی نخوردهاند. unhā qazā-ye irāni naxord(e)and. 6 تو غذای ایرانی نخوردهای. to qazā-ye irāni naxord(e)i.

Exercise 7

1 شما هیچوقت (به) آمریکا رفتهاید؟ šomā hic-vaqt (be) āmrikā raft(e)id? 2 فیلم تایتنیکو دیدهاید؟ film-e taitanik-o did(e)id? 3 هیچوقت غذای چینی خوردهاید؟ hic-vaqt qazā-ye cini xord(e)id? 4 ناهار / شام / صبحانه خوردهاید؟ nāhār/šām/sobhāne xord(e)id? 5 هیچوقت چیزی گم کردهاید؟ hic-vaqt cizi gom kard(e)id?

Exercise 8

1 مامان کجاست؟ māmān kojāst? رفته سوپرمارکت. rafte supermārket. 2 پدر (و) مادرتون کجاند؟ pedar (o) mādaretun kojānd? رفتهاند ایران. raft(e)and irān. 3 ماشین جدیدمو دیدهاید؟ māšin-e jadidam-o did(e)id? 4 ببخشید حرفتونو قطع میکنم، سوئیچ ماشینمو ندیدهاید؟ bẹbaxšid harfetun-o qat` mikonam, su`ic-e māšinam-o nadid(e)id? 5 صورتحساب، لطفا. surat-hesāb, lotfan.

Comprehension

1 He normally writes a letter (but now he's sending a video tape). 2 Because he's never spoken in front of a camera. 3 His wife and children are away; but some friends are with him. 4 His wife does the

cooking. He cooks chelo-kebab. 5 He has prepared several dishes. 6 To show the dining table at the end of the tape. 7 If I have ever had Iranian food.

Lesson 9

Exercise 1

1 .دیشب این وقت داشتم تلویزیون تماشا میکردم **dis̆ab in vaqt dās̆tam televizion tamās̆ā mikardam.** 2 دیشب این وقت داشتی تلویزیون تماشا میکردی. **dis̆ab in vaqt dās̆ti televizion tamās̆ā mikardi.** 3 .دیشب این وقت داشتید تلویزیون تماشا میکردید **dis̆ab in vaqt dās̆tid televizion tamās̆ā mikardid.** 4 دیشب این وقت داشت تلویزیون تماشا میکرد. **dis̆ab in vaqt dās̆t televizion tamās̆ā mikard.** 5 .دیشب این وقت داشتیم تلویزیون تماشا میکردیم **dis̆ab in vaqt dās̆tim televizion tamās̆ā mikardim.** 6 دیشب این وقت داشتند تلویزیون تماشا میکردند. **dis̆ab in vaqt dās̆tand televizion tamās̆ā mikardand.**

Exercise 2

1 .دیشب این وقت تلویزیون تماشا نمیکردم **dis̆ab in vaqt televizion tamās̆ā nemikardam.** Last night at this time I was not watching TV. 2 .دیشب این وقت تلویزیون تماشا نمیکردی **dis̆ab in vaqt televizion tamās̆ā nemikardi.** Last night at this time you (*inf*) were not watching TV. 3 .دیشب این وقت تلویزیون تماشا نمیکردید **dis̆ab in vaqt televizion tamās̆ā nemikardid.** Last night at this time you (*f*) were not watching TV. 4 .دیشب این وقت تلویزیون تماشا نمیکرد **dis̆ab in vaqt televizion tamās̆ā nemikard.** Last night at this time he/she was not watching TV. 5 .دیشب این وقت تلویزیون تماشا نمیکردیم **dis̆ab in vaqt televizion tamās̆ā nemikardim.** Last night at this time we were not watching TV. 6 .دیشب این وقت تلویزیون تماشا نمیکردند **dis̆ab in vaqt televizion tamās̆ā nemikardand.** Last night at this time they were not watching TV.

Exercise 3

1 .داشتم با خانمم / شوهرم / دوستم صحبت میکردم **dās̆tam bā xānomam/s̆ouharam/dustam sohbat mikardam.** 2 داشتم با مهمونهام چای میخوردم. **dās̆tam bā mehmunhām cai mixordam.** 3 .داشتم میومدم اینجا **dās̆tam miumadam injā.** 4 داشتم (به)

اخبار گوش میدادم/میکردم. dāštam (be) axbār guš midādam/ mikardam. 5 داشتم نامه مینوشتم. dāštam nāme minevestam. 6 داشتم با کامپیوتر کار میکردم. dāštam bā kāmpiuter kār mikardam.

Exercise 4

1 تصادفو دیدم امّا نمیتونم به فارسی توضیح بدم. tasādof-o didam ammā nemitunam be fārsi touzih bedam. 2 فارسیم زیاد خوب نیست. میتونم به سفارتم تلفن کنم؟ fārsim ziād xub nist. mitunam be sefāratam telefon konam? 3 آشپزخونه‌ام آتش گرفته. لطفاً کمک کنید. āšpazxun(e)am āteš gerefte. lotfan komak konid. 4 آپارتمانمو دزد زده. لطفاً یک نفرو بفرستید. āpārtemānam-o dozd zade. lotfan yek nafar-o bef(e)restid. 5 همسایه‌ام غش کرده. لطفاً هرچه زودتر یک آمبولانس بفرستید. hamsāy(e)am qaš karde. lotfan harce zudtar yek āmbulāns bef(e)restid. 6 شماره تلفن پلیس/آمبولانس/آتش‌نشانی‌رو میخواستم، لطفاً. šomāre telefon-e polis/ āmbulāns/āteš-nešāni-ro mixāstam, lotfan.

Exercise 5

1 خودش xodeš 2 خودتون xodetun 3 خودمون xodemun 4 خودشون xodešun 5 خودم xodam

Exercise 6

1 نخورده بودم naxorde budam 2 ندیده بودم nadide budam 3 نکرده بودم nakarde budam

Exercise 7

(a) 3 (b) 1 (c) 2

Exercise 8

1 اوّلین بار کی به ایران رفتید؟ avvalin bār kei be irān raftid? پنج سال پیش panj sāl piš. 2 چرا به ایران رفتید؟ cerā be irān raftid? 3 چند تا کتاب دربارهٔ کشورتون خونده بودم. cand tā ketāb darbāre-ye kešvaretun xunde budam. 4 چند تا فیلم ایرانی دیده بودم. cand tā film-e irāni dide budam. 5 به ایران علاقه‌مند شده بودم. be irān alāqemand šode budam. 6 قبلاً به خاور میانه نرفته بودید؟ qablan be xāvar-e miāne narafte budid? 7 چرا، به عراق

رفته بودم. cerā, be erāq rafte budam. 8 کسی با شما کار داره. kasi bā šomā kār dāre. 9 بعضی از مهمونها میخواند با شما صحبت کنند. ba`zi az mehmunhā mixānd bā šomā sohbat konand. 10 شما خودتون با احمد صحبت کردید. šomā xodetun bā ahmad sohbat kardid? 11 خودمو تو(ی) آینه دیدم. xodam-o tu(-ye) aine didam.

Comprehension

1 Ali and his wife were having a meal in a restaurant. 2 He's implying that his briefcase was probably stolen by the two people at the next table. 3 He was tall, wearing a grey suit. He had short black hair, a thick moustache and was wearing sunglasses.

Lesson 10

Exercise 1

1 دیشب در یک رستوران بزرگ شام خوردیم امّا غذا خوب نبود. dišab dar yek resturān-e bozorg šām xordim ammā qazā xub nabud. 2 برای دسر هم بستنی خوردم و هم کیک. barāye deser ham bastani xordam va ham keik. 3 مادرم نه شام خورد و نه دسر. mādaram na šām xord va na deser. 4 آخر هفتهٔ گذشته نه کسی به دیدن ما اومد و نه ما به دیدن کسی رفتیم. āxar-e hafte-ye gozašte na kasi be didan-e mā umad va na mā be didan-e kasi raftim.

Exercise 2

1 یا بستنی میتونی بخوری یا شکلات. هر دورو نمیتونی بخوری. yā bastani mituni boxori yā šokolāt. har do-ro nemituni boxori. 2 میتونم هم بستنی بخورم و هم یک کمی کیک، لطفاً؟ mitunam ham bastani boxoram va ham yek kami keik, lotfan? 3 چند لحظه صبر کنید، صداشون میکنم. cand lahze sabr konid, sedāšun mikonam. 4 ممکنه یک کمی بلندتر صحبت کنید؟ صداتونو نمیشنوم. momkene yek kami bolandtar sohbat konid? sedātun-o nemiš(e)navam. 5 جنابعالی؟ jenābāli? حمید هستم. hamid hastam. 6 میخواستم با آقای جمشیدی صحبت کنم، لطفاً. mixāstam bā āqā-ye jamšidi sohbat konam, lotfan.

Exercise 3

1b; 2c; 3a

Exercise 4

1 . در شیراز یک خونه دارم که خیلی قشنگه **dar širāz yek xune dāram ke xeili qašange.** 2 . دیروز یک ماشین خریدم که خوب کار نمیکنه **diruz yek māšin xaridam ke xub kār nemikone.** 3 . بالاخره یک اتوبوس اومد که پر از مسافر بود **bel`axare yek otobus umad ke por az mosāfer bud.** 4 . پدرم، که در لندن کار میکنه، دیروز به ایران برگشت **pedaram, ke dar landan kār mikone, diruz be irān bar gašt.** 5 . به آژانسی که نزدیک منزلمونه تلفن کردم **be âgânsi ke nazdik-e manzelemune telefon kardam.**

Exercise 5

دنبال یک خونهٔ اجاره‌یی میگردم که این مشخّصاتو داشته باشه: سه تا اتاق خواب؛ یک حمّام با دو تا توالت؛ یک آشپزخونهٔ متوسّط؛ در مرکز تهران؛ ترجیحاً نزدیک مرکز خرید؛ اجاره ماهی صد و بیست هزار تومن یا کمتر.

donbāl-e yek xune-ye ejāre-yi migardam ke in mošaxxasāt-o dāšte bāše: se tā otāq-e xāb; yek hammām bā do tā tuālet; yek āšpazxune-ye motavasset; dar markaz-e tehrān; tarjihan nazdik-e markaz-e xarid; ejāre māhi sad o bist hezār toman yā kamtar.

Exercise 6

1 دنبالِ چی میگردی؟ **donbāl-e ci migardi?** 2 دنبال دفتر تلفنم میگردم. **donbāl-e daftar-e telefonam migardam.** 3 دنبال کی میگردی؟ **donbāl-e ki migardi?** 4 دنبال پسرم میگردم. **donbāl-e pesaram migardam.** 5 دنبال یک کار تازه میگردم. **donbāl-e yek kār-e tāze migardam.** 6 ماشینی که دیدید مال من نبود. **māšini ke didid māl-e man nabud.** 7 مردی که ماشینو بهش فروختید اینجاست. **mardi ke māšin-o beheš foruxtid injāst.** 8 دنبال ماشینی میگردم که قابل اطمینان باشه. **donbāl-e māšini migardam ke qābel-e etminān bāše.** 9 دفعهٔ دیگه خونه‌یی میخرم که ده تا اتاق خواب داشته باشه. **daf`e-ye dige xuneyi mixaram ke dah tā otāq-e xāb dāšte bāše.** 10 چته؟ **cete?** سرم درد میکنه. **saram dard mikone.** 11 شوهرتون چشه؟ **šouharetun ceše?** 12 هیچّیش نیست. یک کمی خسته‌است. **hiccis nist. yek kami xastast.**

Comprehension

1 He's looking for a flat because the hotel where he's staying is too expensive. 2 To find a flat with three bedrooms and a large kitchen. Rent under £500 per month. 3 He prefers to have a flat in central London or near the tube and shopping centre, cinemas, etc., because his wife's hobby is shopping and his children's hobby is (going to the) cinema.

Lesson 11

Exercise 1

1 بخورید **boxorid** 2 بمونید **bemunid** 3 بیاید **biaid** 4 قبول کنید **qabul konid** 5 برگرده **bar garde**

Exercise 2

1 اگه نخورید ناراحت میشم. **age naxorid nārāhat mišam.** 2 اگه نمونید ناراحت میشم. **age namunid nārāhat mišam.** 3 اگه نیاید ناراحت میشم. **age nayaid nārāhat mišam.** 4 اگه دعوت مارو قبول نکنید ناراحت میشیم. **age da`vat-e mā-ro qabul nakonid nārāhat mišim.** 5 اگه بر نگرده ناراحت میشیم. **age bar nagarde nārāhat mišim.**

Exercise 3

1 اگه هوا بهتر بشه، میریم پارک. **age havā behtar beše, mirim pārk.** 2 اگه دعوتشون کنی، میاند. **age da`vatešun koni, miānd.** 3 اگه دعوتشون نکنی، ناراحت میشند. **age da`vatešun nakoni, nārāhat mišand.** 4 اگه گواهینامتو (گواهینامه‌ات را) بگیری، یک هدیه برات میخرم. **age gavāhinamat-o (gavāhināmeat rā) begiri, yek hedye barāt mixaram.** 5 اگه بهش بگی ناراحت میشم. **age beheš begi, nārāhat mišam.** 6 اگه دوارو نخوری، خوب نمیشی. **age davā-ro naxori, xub nemiši.** 7 امروز هوای تهران چطوره؟ **emruz havā-ye tehrān ceto(u)re?** 8 برف میاد. هفت درجه زیر صفره. **barf miād. haft daraje zir-e sefre.**

Exercise 4

1 تو پارکینگ. ماشین شما کجاست؟ **tu pārking. māšin-e šomā**

kojāst? 2 خونهٔ شما کجاست؟ (در) شمالِ لندن. **(dar) šomāl-e landan. xune-ye šomā kojāst?** 3 آبی. ماشین شما چه رنگه؟ **ābi. māšin-e šomā ce range?** 4 سپتامبر. ماه تولد شما چیه؟ **septāmbr. māh-e tavallod-e šomā cie?**

Exercise 5

1 تو پارکینگ. مال شما کجاست؟ **tu pārking. māl-e šomā kojāst?** 2 (در) شمال لندن. مال شما کجاست؟ **(dar) šomāl-e landan. māl-e šomā kojāst?** 3 آبی. مال شما چه رنگه؟ **ābi. māl-e šomā ce range?** 4 سپتامبر. مال شما چیه؟ **septāmbr. māl-e šomā cie?**

Exercise 6

1 خوشم میاد **xošam miād** 2 خوشت میاد **xošet miād** 3 خوشش میاد **xošeš miād** 4 خوشمون میاد **xošemun miād** 5 خوشتون میاد **xošetun miād** 6 خوششون میاد **xošešun miād**
For the negative, replace میاد **miād** with نمیاد **nemiād**.

Exercise 7

1 خوشم اومد **xošam umad** 2 خوشت اومد **xošet umad** 3 خوشش اومد **xošeš umad** 4 خوشمون اومد **xošemun umad** 5 خوشتون اومد **xošetun umad** 6 خوششون اومد **xošešun umad**
For the negative, replace اومد **umad** with نیومد **nayumad**.

Exercise 8

1 شما از غذای / فیلم‌های ایرانی خوشتون میاد؟ **šomā az qazā-ye/ filmhā-ye irāni xošetun miād?** بله، خیلی. **bale, xeili.** 2 از فیلم / غذا خوشتون اومد؟ **az film/qazā xošetun umad?** نه زیاد. **na ziād.** 3 از چه چیز ایران خوشتون میاد؟ **az ce ciz-e irān xošetun miād?** 4 همه چیز: غذاهاش، منظره‌هاش، مردمش. **hame ciz: qazāhāš, manzarehāš, mardomeš.** 5 سرگرمی‌هاتون چیه؟ **sargarmihātun cie?** 6 عکّاسی، نقّاشی، گوش دادن به موسیقی، ورزش. **akkāsi, naqqāši, guš dādan be musiqi, varzeš.** سرگرمی‌های شما چیه؟ **sargarmihā-ye šomā cie?** 7 رشتهٔ مورد علاقه‌تون چیه؟ **rešte-ye moured-e alāqatun cie?** 8 هنرهای زیبا. مال شما چیه؟ **honarhā-ye zibā. māl-e šomā cie?** 9 هنرپیشهٔ / خوانندهٔ مورد علاقه‌تون کیه؟ **honarpiše-ye/xānande-ye moured-e alāqatun kie?** 10 اگه پسر خوبی باشی، میبرمت سینما. **age pesar-e xubi bāši, mibaramet sinemā.** 11 اگه پول داشته باشم، این تابستون میرم ایران. **age pul dāšte bāšam, in tābestun miram irān.**

Comprehension

1 He lives in London because Ali says he wants to *come* to London where they could meet. 2 Going to the theatre. 3 He wants to visit London if the weather is good. 4 He is inviting Peter to go with them if he has the time. 5 By going to the theatre together, they will be able (a) to meet and chat; and (b) to see a good play.

Lesson 12

Exercise 1

1 If my father was/were here, it would be better. 2 If I were in your place/shoes, I wouldn't do that/it. 3 If I had his/her address, I would give it to you. 4 If you need me, press this button. 5 If I knew Persian well, I would speak with my mother-in-law in Persian. 6 If he should ring, I would/will give him your message. 7 If he rings, I will give him your message.

Exercise 2

1 اومد **umad** 2 کرد **kard** 3 دیدی **didi** 4 میکردید **mikardid**

Exercise 3

1d If you had eaten that rotten sandwich, you would have become ill.
2c If you had told my father about the subject, I would have been upset.
3e If we had left home later, we would not have arrived (there) in time.
4b If you had come five minutes earlier, you would have seen my brother.
5a If you had not married me, I would have committed suicide.

Exercise 4

1 اگه جای من بودید، چکار میکردید؟ **age jā-ye man budid, cekār mikardid?** 2 اگه پدرم اینجا بود، عصبانی میشد. **age pedaram injā bud, asabāni mišod.** 3 اگه خیلی پول داشتم، دور دنیا سفر میکردم. **age xeili pul dāštam, dour-e donyā safar mikardam.** 4 اگه ریشتو میتراشیدی، نمیشناختمت. **age rišet-o mitarāšidi, nemiš(e)nāxtamet.** 5 اگه آنتی‌بیوتیکو نمیخوردم، بهتر نمیشدم. **age āntibiutik-o nemixordam, behtar nemišodam.** 6 ببخشید آقا، قیمت این قالیچه / قالی / قوطی خاویار چنده؟ **bebaxšid āqā, qeimat-e in qālice/qāli/quti-e**

xāviār cande? 7 این ماشین دو میلیون تومن نمیارزه؟ **in māšin do milyun toman nemiarze?** 8 .میارزه، امّا برای من گرونه **miarze, ammā barāye man gerune.** 9 اگه میلیونر بودی، چکار میکردی؟ **age milyuner budi, cekār mikardi?** 10 یک بیمارستان برای بچّههای مریض میساختم. **yek bimārestān barāye baccehā-ye mariz misāxtam.**

Exercise 5

۱۵ تا تخم مرغ؛ ۱ کیلو گوجه فرنگی؛ ۲ کیلو خیار؛ نیم کیلو پنیر؛
۲ تا هندوانه (هندونه)؛ ۳ تا / عدد نان (نون)

punzdah tā toxm-e morq; yek kilu gouje-farangi; do kilu xiār; nim kilu panir; do tā hendevāne (*col* hendune); se tā/adad nān (*col* nun)

Exercise 6

1 تخم مرغها / نونها دونهیی چنده؟ **toxm-e morqhā/nunhā duneyi cande?** گوجهفرنگیها / خیارها / پنیر / هندونهها کیلویی چنده؟ **gouje-farangihā/xiārhā/panir/hendunehā kiluyi cande?** 2 پونزده تا تخم مرغ، دو تا هندونه و سه تا نون لطف کنید. **punzdah tā toxm-e morq, do tā hendune va se tā nun lotf konid.** یک کیلو گوجه فرنگی، دو کیلو خیار و نیم کیلو هم پنیر بدید، لطفاً. **yek kilu gouje-farangi, do kilu xiār va nim kilu ham panir bedid, lotfan.**

Exercise 7

1 He is offering it as a gift. He's being polite. 2 نه، متشکّرم. **na mot(a)šakkeram.** No, thank you.

Exercise 8

1 Sir, how much are these oranges per kilo? 2 Sir, do you sell these chickens by kilo or number? 3 Please give me five kilos of rice and two chickens. 4 How much did it come to in total? 5 Be my guest, it's not worth a mention.

Exercise 9

1 خب چقدر شد؟ **xob ceqadr šod?** 2 بفرمایید، قابلی نداره. **befarmāyid, qābeli nadāre.** 3 خواهش میکنم، چند شد؟ **xāheš**

mikonam, cand šod? 4 .پنج هزار تومن **panj hezār toman.** 5 .بفرمایید **befarmāyid.** 6 .یک اسکناس دویست تومنی **yek eskenās-e devist tomani.** 7 .یک سکّهٔ ده ریالی **yek sekke-ye dah riāli.** 8 ؟شکر و لطف میکنید **šekar-o lotf mikonid?**

Comprehension

1 Masoud is shy; Ahmad is outspoken/assertive. 2 Because he was taking back something he had bought and he needed Ahmad's help. 3 The shop owner would probably have refused to take back the overcoat. 4 Masoud says: 'The colour of the overcoat is too bright for my father'. The shop owner replies: 'Never mind; it makes him look younger'. He is made speechless when Ahmad tells him: 'My friend's father doesn't like this colour. Would you have imposed this overcoat on your father?'

Lesson 13

Exercise 1

1 ؟تو سالن میشه سیگار کشید **tu sālon miše sigār kešid?** 2 ؟دارو میشه با پست فرستاد **dāru miše bā post ferestād?** 3 ؟اونجا / اینجا میشه ماشینو پارک کرد **unjā/injā miše māšin-o pārk kard?**

Exercise 2

1c; 2a; 3e; 4b; 5d

Exercise 3

1 .باید با اونها میرفتم **bāyad bā unhā miraftam.** 2 .اون ساندویچو نباید میخورد **un sāndevic-o nabāyad mixord.** 3 .باید چلوکباب خورده باشید **bāyad celo(u)-kabāb xorde bāšid.** 4 ؟برای این نامه چقدر تمبر لازمه **barāye in nāme ceqadr tambr lāzeme?** 5 ؟توی تئاتر میشه ساندویچ / نوشیدنی برد **tu-ye te`ātr miše sāndevic/nušidani bord?** 6 ؟توی هواپیما میشه سیگار کشید **tu-ye havāpeimā miše sigār kešid?** 7 ؟این بسته‌رو میشه با پست سفارشی فرستاد **in basta-ro miše bā post-e sefāreši ferestād?** 8 ؟کجا میتونم چند تا فتوکپی بگیرم **kojā mitunam cand tā fotokopi begiram?** 9 ؟کجا میتونم فکس / ایمیل بفرستم **kojā mitunam faks/imeil bef(e)restam?**

Exercise 4

1e; 2c; 3a; 4f; 5d; 6b

Exercise 5

1 خورده شدن **xorde šodan** 2 بسته شدن **baste šodan** 3 دیده شدن **dide šodan** 4 شنیده شدن **šenide šodan** 5 گفته شدن **gofte šodan**

Exercise 6

1 I'm sorry, your voice can't be heard. 2 Your head is not seen in the picture. 3 The chicken has not been cooked well.

Exercise 7

1 مارتین لوتر کینگ در سال هزار و نهصد و شصت و هشت کشته شد. **mārtin luter king dar sāl-e hezār o nohsad o šast o hašt košte šod.** 2 گوشت خوب پخته نشده. **gušt xub poxte našode.** 3 یک دفعه در بسته شد. **yek daf`e dar baste šod.** 4 ساندویچ من کجاست؟ **sāndevic-e man kojāst?** ببخشید، خورده شد! **bebaxšid, xorde šod!** 5 ببخشید، این چک امضا نشده. **bebaxšid, in cek emzā našode.**

Comprehension

1 He wants to change £1,000 into Iranian currency, rials. 2 He has to sell at yesterday's rate because today's rate will not be announced until 11 a.m., and he's in a hurry.

Lesson 14

Exercise 1

1 خوشحالی **xošhāli** 2 شادی **šādi** 3 حسودی **hasudi** 4 پررویی **por-ruyi** 5 خستگی **xastegi** 6 آوارگی **āvāregi** 7 بارونی بودن **bāruni budan**

Exercise 2

1b; 2d; 3f; 4a; 5c; 6e

Exercise 3

1 وقتی میرم تو پارک، خیلی عطسه میکنم. **vaqti miram tu pārk, xeili atse mikonam.** 2 وقتی با جاروبرقی کار میکنم، خیلی سرفه میکنم. **vaqti bā jārubarqi kār mikonam, xeili sorfe mikonam.** 3 شب‌ها، دماغم/بینیم کیپ میشه. نمیتونم نفس بکشم. نمیذاره بخوابم. **šabhā, damāqam/binim kip miše. nemitunam nafas bekešam. nemizāre bexābam.** 4 در طول شب، باید چندین بار برم توالت. **dar tul-e šab, bāyad candin bār beram tuālet.**

Exercise 4

1 احمد گفت (که) خسته‌ام. **ahmad goft (ke) xast(e)am.** 2 برادرم گفت (که) ماشینمو فروختم. **barādaram goft (ke) māšinam-o foruxtam.** 3 حسن گفت (که) نمیدونم تلویزیون چشه. **hasan goft (ke) nemidunam televizion cešе.** 4 مهمونها گفتند (که) ما گرسنه‌ایم. **mehmunhā goftand (ke) mā gorosneim.** 5 (او) پرسید (که) ساعت چنده؟ **(u) porsid (ke) sā`at cande.**

Exercise 5

1d; 2a; 3b; 4c

Exercise 6

1 ببخشید، برای دندوندرد/کمردرد چی دارید؟ **bebaxšid, barāye dandundard/kamardard ci dārid?** 2 از این خمیردندونها کدوم بهتره؟ **az in xamirdandunhā kodum behtare?** 3 چته؟ **cete?** 4 مثل اینکه سرما خورده‌ام. **mesl-e inke sarmā xord(e)am.** 5 گفت (که) قطار ساعت نه را از دست داده‌ام. **goft (ke) qatār-e sā`at-e noh rā az dast dād(e)am.** 6 پرسید شما متأهّلید؟ **porsid šomā mota`ahhelid?** 7 تو چی گفتی؟ **to ci gofti?** 8 بهش گفتم نامزد دارم. **beheš goftam nāmzad dāram.**

Comprehension

1 B apologises for being late and for not phoning to say that he would be late. 2 Ahmad was supposed to give B a lift. 3 He phoned two hours ago to say he had sold the car and that he could not come without a car as he was very tired. 4 He has a temperature. His body aches all over. The pain is so severe he cannot sleep. 5 When B realises that A is not allergic to penicillin, he says: 'You're lucky!'. This suggests that B is allergic to it, and wishes he wasn't.

Lesson 15

Exercise 1

1 اولین روز سال **avvalin ruz-e sāl** 2 آخرین روز سال **āxarin ruz-e sāl** 3 دوّمین هفتهٔ سال **dovvomin hafte-ye sāl** 4 سوّمین ماه سال **sevvomin māh-e sāl** 5 چهارمین فصل سال **c(ah)āromin fasl-e sāl**

Exercise 2

1 Sohrab Hashemi 2 A friend 3 Merry Christmas and Happy New Year

Exercise 3

sohrāb-e aziz سهراب عزیز
kerismas va sāl-e nou mobārak! کریسمس و سال نو مبارک!
dust-e to . . . دوست تو . . .

Exercise 4

1 عزیزم، این (هدیه) قابل تو نیست. سالگرد ازدواجمون مبارک. **azizam, in (hedye) qābel-e to nist. sālgard-e ezdevājemun mobārak.** 2 صاحبش قابله. خیلی زحمت کشیدی. **sāhebeš qābele. xeili zahmat kešidi.** 3 تولّدتون مبارک. **tavallodetun mobārak.** 4 منزل نو مبارک. **manzel-e nou mobārak.** 5 دهمین سالگرد ازدواجتان را به شما تبریک میگویم. **dahomin sālgard-e ezdevājetān rā be šomā tabrik miguyam.** 6 خوبند، سلام میرسونند. **xuband, salām miresunand.** 7 به پدر (و) مادرت سلام برسون **be pedar (o) mādaret salām beresun.** 8 جات خالی، مهمونی خیلی خوش گذشت. **jāt xāli, mehmuni xeili xoš gozašt.**

Exercise 5

1 ایستاده‌اند **istād(e)and** 2 خوابیده‌اند **xābid(e)and** 3 پوشیده **pušide** 4 دراز کشیده‌ام **derāz kešid(e)am**

Exercise 6

1 اونها کنار پنجره ایستاده بودند. **unhā kenār-e panjare istāde budand.** 2 بچّه‌ها خوابیده بودند. **baccehā xābide budand.** 3 بهترین لباسشو پوشیده بود. **behtarin lebāseš-o pušide bud.**

4 روی تخت دراز کشیده بودم. **ru-ye taxt derāz keside budam.**

Exercise 7

1 Do you feel like going to a concert tonight? 2 No, I'm not in the mood (for a concert) tonight. Leave it for tomorrow night. 3 Are you in the mood for a swim this afternoon?

Exercise 8

1 دیروز رفتم دیدنش. **diruz raftam didanes.** 2 دیشب اومد دیدنم. **disab umad didanam.** 3 امشب میرم دیدنشون. **emsab miram didanesun.**

Exercise 9

1 رو تخت دراز کشیده و تلویزیون نگاه میکنه. **ru taxt derāz keside o televizion negāh mikone.** 2 من بهترین لباسمو پوشیده‌ام. تو چی پوشیده‌ای؟ **man behtarin lebāsam-o pusid(e)am. to ci pusid(e)i?** 3 لطفا ساکت باشید. بچّه‌ها خوابیده‌اند. **lotfan sāket bāsid. baccehā xābid(e)and.** 4 کنار بخاری ایستاده‌اند و شیر کاکائو میخورند. **kenār-e boxāri istād(e)and o sir kākā`o mixorand.** 5 برادرم داره اخبارو میبینه و مادرم کنارش نشسته. **barādaram dāre axbār-o mibine va mādaram kenāres nesaste.** 6 آخر هفتهٔ گذشته دوست ایرانیم اومد دیدنم. **āxar-e hafte-ye gozaste dust-e irānim umad didanam.** 7 دیروز رفتم دیدن عموم. **diruz raftam didan-e amum.** 8 امشب حالشو داری بریم تئاتر؟ **emsab hāles-o dāri berim te`ātr?** 9 امشب برنامه‌یی داری؟ **emsab barnāmeyi dāri?** 10 کی و کجا همدیگه‌رو ببینیم؟ **kei va kojā hamdiga-ro bebinim?**

Comprehension

1 Informal. Zahra does not use a title with Marjan's name, and she uses تو **to** 'you' (*inf*). 2 For the birthday present she had sent. 3 Marjan could not come to her birthday party. 4 She says جایت خالی بود **jāyat xāli bud** 'wish you had been there'. 5 She's married and has a young daughter. 6 On her wedding anniversary. 7 Her husband, Parviz, and her daughter, Sudabeh. 8 Parviz was lying on the bed and listening to music. Sudabeh was standing by the desk and watching her mother. 9 On her 'beautiful handwriting'.

Lesson 16

Exercise 1

1 خب، فرمایشی ندارید؟ **xob, farmāyes̄i nadārid?** 2 خب، فرمایشی ندارید؟ **xob, farmāyes̄i nadārid?** 3 عرضی ندارم. **arzi nadāram.**

Exercise 2

1 As far as we are concerned, our seats are good. 2 As far as money is concerned, it's no problem. 3 As for me, I know nothing about car mechanics.

Exercise 3

1 فروردین، اردیبهشت، خرداد **farvardin, ordibehes̄t, xordād.** 2 تیر، مرداد، شهریور **tir, mordād, s̄ahrivar.** 3 دی، بهمن، اسفند **dei, bahman, esfand.** 4 مهر **mehr.**

Exercise 4

1 ببخشید، شرکت کورش؟ **bebaxs̄id, s̄erkat-e kuros̄?** بله، بفرمایید. **bale, befarmāyid.** 2 از کجا تلفن میکنید؟ **az kojā telefon mikonid?** از ایران تلفن میکنم. **az irān telefon mikonam.** 3 من که از کامپیوتر هیچّی نمیدونم. **man ke az kāmpiuter hicci nemidunam.** 4 هفتهٔ/ تابستون/ بهار آینده میبینمت. **hafte-ye/ tābestun-e/bahār-e āyande mibinamet.** 5 زمستون آینده میرم ایران برای اسکی. **zemestun-e āyande miram irān barāye eski.** 6 پاییز گذشته دوست ایرانیم اومد لندن. **pāyiz-e gozas̄te dust-e irānim umad landan.** 7 مایل بودم باهاتون ملاقات کنم. **māyel budam bāhātun molāqāt konam.** کی؟ **kei?**
هرچه زودتر بهتر. **harce zudtar behtar.**
امروز بعد از ظهر چطوره؟ **emruz ba`d az zohr ceto(u)re?**
عالیه. چه ساعتی؟ **ālie. ce sā`ati?**
سهٔ بعد از ظهر خوبه؟ **se-ye ba`d az zohr xube?**
خوبه. پس ساعت سه میبینمتون. **xube. pas sā`at-e se mibinametun.**

Exercise 5

1 ببخشید، شما انگلیسی بلدید؟ **bebaxs̄id, s̄omā engelisi baladid?** 2 این جمله‌رو نمیفهمم. میتونید ترجمه‌اش کنید، لطفاً؟ **in jomla-ro nemifahmam. mitunid tarjom(e)as̄ konid, lotfan?**

Exercise 6

1 I can play tennis well. 2 Can you play the violin? 3 My brother can swim. 4 We can speak Persian well. 5 Can you drive? 6 I can't ride a horse. 7 He doesn't know anything about car mechanics.

Exercise 7

1d; 2c; 3e; 4g; 5b; 6f; 7a

Exercise 8

1 This is where J says he also knows 'a bit of Persian'. 2 The interviewer is complimenting J on his command of Persian. 3 J is applying for a translator's job but asks the interviewer to translate a sentence on the form. 4 He says it is easier for him to translate from English (his mother tongue) into Persian (a foreign language for him). 5 'Particularly if a dictionary is not available.'

Exercise 9

1 شما اسپانیولی بلدید؟ šomā espānioli baladid? نه، فرانسه بلدم. na, farānse baladam. 2 پیانو بلده؟ piāno balade? بله، پیانیست خوبیه. bale, piānist-e xubie. 3 موتور(سیکلت)سواری بلدید؟ motor(siklet)-savāri baladid? نه، امّا دوچرخه سواری بلدم. na, ammā docarxe-savāri baladam. 4 این جمله‌رو میتونید برام به انگلیسی/ فارسی ترجمه کنید، لطفاً؟ in jomla-ro mitunid barām be engelisi/ fārsi tarjome konid, lotfan? 5 چند وقته اینجا ایستاده‌اید؟ cand vaqte injā istād(e)id? 6 چند وقته اینجا نشسته‌اید؟ cand vaqte injā nešast(e)id? 7 چند وقته منتظرید؟ cand vaqte montazerid? 8 چند وقته انگلیسی میخونید؟ cand vaqte engelisi mixunid? 9 چند وقته تو انگلیس زندگی میکنید؟ cand vaqte tu engelis zendegi mikonid?

Comprehension

1 Sunday, 15th Aban 1379 (Iranian calendar). 2 It was written the following day. 3 He is inviting J to go to the firm on Saturday 28th Aban 1379, at 8:30 a.m. This is because the director wants to talk to him about the details of the job, salary and other conditions of employment. 4 If the proposed time is unsuitable, he can change it. 5 By phoning the

company's secretary. 6 He is asked to fill in a form and send it to the company by 25th Aban 1379.

Answers to the reading exercise matching the English–Persian equivalents on pp. 20–1

اَتُم ...	59	ذات ...	4	نه ...	64	ظُلم ...	20
اَغلَب ...	60	رَأس ...	63	ویزا ...	46	طوطی ...	15
اِمضاء ...	21	رَئیس ...	25	هال ...	55	ژِست ...	12
اِیدز ...	50	سایز ...	36	یارد ...	10	زیر ...	11
بَچّه ...	69	سُس ...	5	تِهران ...	29		
بُطری ...	51	سوء ...	68	نُه ...	30		
بَعد ...	18	سُؤال ...	53	عَکس ...	26		
بَنا ...	61	سِرویس ...	14	لامپ ...	34		
بَنّا ...	22	شاه ...	35	مُبل ...	33		
پاپ ...	49	صُبح ...	67	مَگَس ...	44		
پاسپورت ...	58	صَد ...	43	حَریص ...	38		
تابِع ...	40	صَغیر ...	13	مَریض ...	39		
تقریباً ...	42	فیوز ...	66	حَریف ...	32		
تیغ ...	41	فَقیر ...	28	ریش ...	19		
تَصمیم ...	52	قاشُق ...	56	آسفالت ...	27		
ثُلث ...	23	کیلو ...	47	لَذیذ ...	17		
جَذب ...	48	گاز ...	31	میخ ...	3		
چِک ...	57	ماسْک ...	9	سَخت ...	1		
حاجی ...	37	مَأمور ...	70	مَثَلاً ...	2		
حِفظ ...	16	مُؤمِن ...	45	خوب ...	6		
دارائی ...	62	مَسئول ...	54	پَنج ...	8		
دارایی ...	24	مَظلوم ...	65	ضامِن ...	7		

Reference grammar

This grammar summary is not exhaustive. To economise on space, grammar sections given in the lessons have not been reproduced here, but are cross-referenced.

1 Grammar of the sound
2 Grammar of the syllable
3 Grammar of the word
4 Grammar of the phrase
5 Grammar of the sentence
6 Grammar of communication

1 Grammar of the sound

The sounds of Persian are explained on pp. 6–19.

2 Grammar of the syllable

The syllable structure in Persian is: C+V+C+C (where C = consonant, V = vowel). This means that a single vowel may carry only one consonant before it, and a maximum of two consonants after it. Examples:

sag 'dog'; **sang** 'stone'; **bast** 'He'/'she closed'

In theory, this should not present the native-English speaker with much difficulty because the English syllable structure allows a far greater number of consonants before and after a single vowel: C+C+C+V+C+C+C+C (e.g. the word 'strengths'). However, the two languages differ in the way they distribute consonants within the syllable. For instance, **t** and **h** occur in both languages. While Persian allows the final cluster **t+h**, English does not allow this. Examples in Persian:

sath 'surface', **fath** 'conquest'

3 Grammar of the word

Word stress

Persian words having more than two syllables are mostly stressed on the last syllable. Here are some of the exceptions where the first syllable carries the stress:

ولی **vali** but; امّا **ammā** but; بلکه **balke** rather; چرا **cerā** why;
اگر / اگه **agar/age** (*col*) if; مگر / مگه **magar/mage** (*col*) except, but;
هروقت **har-vaqt** whenever; هرچند **har-cand** although;
هرکس **har-kas** whoever; زیرا **zirā** because (*lit*);
هیچ‌کس **hic-kas** nobody; هیچ‌وقت **hic-vaqt** never

Prefixes and suffixes

Some common prefixes attached to کار **kār** 'work':

همکار **hamkār** workmate, colleague
بیکار **bikār** workless, jobless, unemployed
پرکار **porkār** workaholic, hard-working
کم‌کار **kamkār** workshy

Some of the different roles played by the suffix ی **-i** are shown in the following examples. Note the stress pattern.

مرد / مردی **mard/mardi** man/a man
مرد / مردی **mard/mardi** man/manhood
خوب / خوبی **xub/xubi** good/goodness
ابر / ابری **abr/abri** cloud/cloudy
تلفن / تلفنی **telefon/telefoni** telephone/telephonic; by telephone
خوردن / خوردنی **xordan/xordani** eating/edible

We add the suffix نده **-ande** to the present stem of the verb to produce a noun of the agent or an adjective:

دیدن (بین) **didan (bin)** to see/view
بیننده **binande** viewer, onlooker
زدن (زن) **zadan (zan)** to hit
زننده **zanande** gaudy, repulsive, shocking
خسته کردن (کن) **xaste kardan (kon)** to tire; to bore

خسته کننده **xaste konande** tiring; boring

The present stem can act as a suffix to produce nouns or adjectives:

دروغ **doruq** a lie
گفتن (گو) **goftan (gu)** to tell
دروغگو **doruqgu** liar; dishonest

For possessive endings/suffixes, see pp. 34–5.

Nouns

Plural markers are described at pp. 42–3.

After a number, or چند (تا) **cand (tā)** 'how many', 'a few', a noun comes in a singular form:

پنج کتاب **panj ketāb** five books (*lit* book)
چند (تا) کتاب؟ **cand (tā) ketāb?** How many books? (*lit* book)

Pronouns

Subject pronouns are dealt with at pp. 25–6.

The possessive endings introduced at pp. 34–5 may also be used as objects after verbs or prepositions (see p. 132). Examples:

دیدمش. **didameš.** I saw him/her/it.
بهش گفتم. **beheš goftam.** I told him/her.
دو پوند ازم قرض گرفت. **do pond azam qarz gereft.**
He borrowed two pounds from me.

Definite article for the object

When the object is known to both the speaker and the listener, the speaker uses the word را **rā** after the object. It can be placed after a name, a noun or a pronoun:

احمد را دیدم. **ahmad rā didam.** I saw Ahmad.
معلّم را دیدم. **mo`allem rā didam.** I saw the teacher.
او را دیدم. **u rā didam.** I saw him/her.

(See pp. 69–71.)

Adjectives and adverbs

Most adjectives may also be used as adverbs:

احمد خوانندهٔ خوبیه. **ahmad xānande-ye xubie.**
Ahmad is a good singer.

خوب میخونه. **xub mixune.**
He sings well.

To produce a comparative form, we add the suffix تر **-tar**:

تهران از مشهد بزرگتر است. **tehrān az mas̄had bozorgtar ast.**
Tehran is larger than Mashad.

To produce a superlative form, we add the suffix ترین **-tarin**:

تهران بزرگترین شهر ایران است. **tehrān bozorgtarin s̄ahr-e irān ast.**
Tehran is the largest city of/in Iran.

Irregular forms

These include:

خوب **xub** good, well; بهتر **behtar** better; بهترین **behtarin** best

Note: Simple and comparative adjectives follow the noun; superlative adjectives precede the noun.

Prepositions

Some prepositions are formed by adding the **ezāfe** (a linking sound **-e**, or **-ye** after a vowel) to a noun or an adverb (see section 4 below for more on **ezāfe**).

داخل **dāxel** interior
داخل سینما **dāxel-e sinemā** in/inside the cinema
پشت **pos̄t** back
پشت سینما **pos̄t-e sinemā** behind the cinema
رو **ru** face; surface
روی میز **ru-ye miz** on the table

4 Grammar of the phrase

ezāfe

This is an **-e** sound which we use to link a noun (or a noun phrase) to the following word(s). If the word immediately before the **ezāfe** ends in a vowel, we use **-ye** instead. The use of **ezāfe** after a noun often signals to the listener that he/she is about to be given further information about what has just been conveyed. This information may indicate ownership, origin, description, name, and so on.

تلفن جک **telefon-e jak** Jack's telephone
فیلم ایرانی **film-e irāni** Iranian film
فیلم خوب **film-e xub** good film
فیلم تایتنیک **film-e taitanik** the film *Titanic*
خانهٔ بزرگ **xāne-ye bozorg** big house
خانهٔ بزرگ ما **xāne-ye bozorg-e mā** our big house

The **ezāfe** is used in various prepositional phrases:

از طرف **az taraf-e** on behalf of
از طریق **az tariq-e** by way of, via
به وسیلهٔ **be vasile-ye** by means of
در طرف چپ **dar taraf-e cap-e** on/to the left of

(See also pp. 33–4.)

5 Grammar of the sentence

Word order – statement

Subject + adverbs of time, manner, place + verb

من به مدرسه میرم. **man be madrese miram.**
I go to school.

من هر روز به مدرسه میرم. **man har ruz be madrese miram.**
I go to school every day.

من هر روز با اتوبوس به مدرسه میرم.
man har ruz bā otobus be madrese miram.
I go to school by bus every day.

Word order – question

Structurally, questions are similar to statements. Their main difference is in intonation.

شما ایرانی هستید. **šomā irāni hastid.** (\falling tone)
You are Iranian.

شما ایرانی هستید؟ **šomā irāni hastid?** (/rising tone)
Are you Iranian?

شما کی هستید؟ **šomā ki hastid?** (\falling tone)
Who are you?

شما کجا هستید؟ **šomā kojā hastid?** (\falling tone)
Where are you?

Intonation

You will note from the above examples that statements, as well as questions that begin with a question word (e.g. 'who', 'where', etc.) have a falling tone. 'Yes-no' questions normally have a rising tone. This is similar to English. However, in Persian, the question word normally carries the sentence stress, while in English it is the verb that is stressed:

کجا بودی؟ **kojā budi?**
Where were you? *or* Where have you been?

A stressed question word in English would make the sentence rather aggressive. The Persian sentence is neutral.
(See also p. 36.)

Verb – infinitive

Present and past stems

All Persian infinitives end with these two sounds **-an**, e.g. خوردن **xordan** 'to eat', دیدن **didan** 'to see'. Persian verbs have two stems (or roots): present stem and past stem, used for present and past tenses, respectively. The past stem is regularly obtainable from the infinitive by omitting the last two sounds **-an**. Thus, the past stems of the above verbs are خورد **xord** and دید **did**, respectively. The present stem is irregular. Therefore, with every new verb introduced, its present stem is placed in round brackets after it:

خوردن (خور) **xordan (xor)** to eat
دیدن (بین) **didan (bin)** to see

Some verbs, such as those given above, are written and pronounced in colloquial Persian as they are in literary Persian (i.e. newsreaders' style). Some verbs may be colloquialised. This may affect only the present stem (A), only the infinitive (B), or both (C):

(A) گفتن (گو) **goftan (gu)** to tell; to say (*lit*)
گفتن (گ) **goftan (g)** to tell; to say (*col*)
(B) آمدن (ا) **āmadan (ā)** to come (*lit*)
اومدن (ا) **umadan (ā)** to come (*col*)
(C) ماندن (مان) **māndan (mān)** to stay (*lit*)
موندن (مون) **mundan (mun)** to stay (*col*)

To help the learner with written Persian (which mostly uses the literary style) both forms are provided in the **Glossaries** at the end of the book. Only note that the literary present stem appears in square brackets after the colloquial. Example:

گفتن (گ) [گو] **goftan (g) [gu]** to tell; to say

Infinitive used as a gerund

The gerund is a verbal-noun form, e.g. 'eating'. 'To eat' and 'eating' are represented by the same form in Persian:

خوردن **xordan** to eat; eating

ناهار ساندویچ خوردم.
nāhār sāndevic xordam. I ate a sandwich for lunch.

سرگرمی من خوردن است!
sargarmi-e man xordan ast! My hobby is eating!

Tenses

Compared to English, Persian uses far fewer tense forms to refer to acts or facts of past, present and future. Here's the list using my favourite verb خوردن (خور) **xordan (xor)** 'to eat':

میخورم **mixoram** I eat (present simple)

دارم میخورم **dāram mixoram** I am eating (present continuous)
داشتم میخوردم **dāštam mixordam** I was eating (past continuous)
خورده‌ام **xordeam** I have eaten (present perfect)
خورده بودم **xorde budam** I had eaten (past perfect)
خوردم **xordam** I ate (past simple)
خواهم خورد **xāham xord** I shall eat (future simple)

The last form is used mostly in literary Persian. The remaining forms are used, with the help of adverbials, to convey the meanings expressed in English by no fewer than twelve different tense forms.

Subjunctive

When two verbs go together, the second verb takes a simple subjunctive form:

Prefix بـ **be-** + present stem of verb + personal ending

Thus:

دونستن (دونـ) **dunestan (dun)** to know
میدونم. **midunam.** I know.
ممکنه بدونم. **momkene bedunam.** I may know.
شاید بدونم. **šāyad bedunam.** I might know.
باید بدونم. **bāyad bedunam.** I must/should know.
میخوام بدونم. **mixām bedunam.** I want to know.
میخواستم بدونم. **mixāstam bedunam.** I wanted to know.

When the second verb relates to past act or fact, it takes a perfect subjunctive form:

Past stem of verb + ه **-e** + باشـ **bāš** + personal ending

Thus:

دیدن **didan** to see
من او را دیده‌ام. **man u rā dideam.** I have seen him.
شاید او را دیده باشم. **šāyad u rā dide bāšam.**
I might have seen him.
باید او را دیده باشم. **bāyad u rā dide bāšam.** I must have seen him.

Passive voice

To turn an active verb into a passive form, we add the suffix ه **-e** to its past stem followed by the verb (شـ) شدن **šodan (š)** 'to become'.

پختن **poxtan** to cook →
پخته شدن (شـ) **poxte šodan** (š) to be cooked
دیدن **didan** to see →
دیده شدن (شـ) **dide šodan** (š) to be seen
فروختن **foruxtan** to sell →
فروخته شدن **foruxte šodan** to be sold

Intransitive, transitive, causative

When added to the present stem of a verb, the suffix اندن **-āndan** (*col* **-undan**) turns an intransitive or transitive verb into causative:

خوابیدن (خوابـ) **xābidan (xāb)** to sleep
خواباندن (خوابانـ) **xābāndan (xābān)** to cause . . . to sleep
خندیدن (خند) **xandidan (xand)** to laugh
خنداندن (خندانـ) **xandāndan (xandān)** to cause . . . to laugh
خوردن (خور) **xordan (xor)** to eat
خوراندن (خورانـ) **xorāndan (xorān)** to cause . . . to eat

Conditionals

Type 1

اگه آنتی‌بیوتیکو بخوری، خوب میشی.
age āntibiutik-o boxori, xub miši.
If you take the antibiotic, you'll get well.

Type 2

اگه پول داشتم، یک ماشین نو میخریدم.
age pul dāštam, yek māšin-e nou mixaridam.
If I had money, I would buy a new car.

اگه جای من بودی، چکار میکردی؟
age jā-ye man budi, cekār mikardi?
If you were in my place, what would you do?

اگه فارسی میدونستم، میفهمیدم چی میگه.
age fārsi midunestam, mifahmidam ci mige.
If I knew Persian, I would understand what he says/said.

Type 3

اگه تو تلفن نمیکردی، من تلفن میکردم.
age to telefon nemikardi, man telefon mikardam.
If you hadn't phoned (me), I would have phoned (you).

Expressing a wish

(ای) کاش میدونستم. **(ei) kāš midunestam.**
I wish I knew. (But I don't.)

(ای) کاش شام نخورده بودم. **(ei) kāš šām naxorde budam.**
I wish I hadn't eaten dinner. (But I did.)

Imperative

Add the prefix بـ **be-** to the present stem.
Verb needed: نشستن (شینـ) **nešastan (šin)** 'to sit down'.

بشین. **bešin.** Sit down. (*inf*)
بشینید. **bešinid.** Sit down. (*f*)

6 Grammar of communication

The 'tut'

The 'tut' is used in both English and Persian with different meanings. The English 'tut' often expresses exasperation, while its Persian 'counterpart' signals a negative reply, complementing or even replacing the word **na** No!
(See also 'Introduction' on page 1.)

Persian–English glossary

The present stem/root of Persian verbs is irregular. Thus, the present stem of each verb is given in round brackets where the verb is introduced. To make life even easier, the present stem of most common verbs is also given as separate entries in the Persian–English glossary. This will be helpful when you meet a verb which is either new or has slipped your memory. All you need to do is to remove the prefixes and suffixes from the verb, and the verb root emerges. You can now look it up in the Persian–English glossary.

For those who do not wish to learn the Persian script (yet!) here is an indication of the order in which Persian words are arranged in the Persian–English glossary.

ā, a/e/o, u, i

b, p, t, j, c, h, x, d, z, r, z, ĝ, s, s̄, s, t, z,

ā, a/e/o, u, i, q, f, q, k, g, l, m, n, v, h, y

Note: This is just a rough guide as the position of each word is dictated by its Persian spelling. A stroke (/) shows some of the 'vulnerable' boundaries. A more reliable guide would be the alphabet itself (see pp. 7–8).

The verbal element of some compound verbs are more active than others. To economise in space, the present stem of such verbs is not given under each entry. For the present stem of such verbs, look under a separate entry in the Persian–English glossary where the verbal element appears on its own. As an example, for the present stem of سرما خوردن **sarmā xordan** 'to catch a cold', look under خوردن (خور) **xordan (xor)** in the Persian–English glossary.

آب **āb** water, juice
آبی **ābi** blue
آپارتمان **āpārtemān** apartment, flat
آتش **āteš** fire
آتش‌نشانی **āteš-nešāni** fire brigade
آخر **āxar** end; last
آخرین **āxarin** last
آخه **āxe** well, you see
آدرس **ādres** address
آره **āre** yeah
آژانس **āĝāns** agency
آسم **āsm** asthma
آسون **āsun** *col* for آسان **āsān** easy
آشپزی **āšpazi** cooking
آشنا **āš(e)nā** familiar
آفتاب **āftāb** sun(shine)
آفتابی **āftābi** sunny
آقا **āqā** gentleman, sir
آقای **āqā-ye** Mr
آلمانی **ālmāni** German
آمپول **āmpul** injection
آمدن (ا) **āmadan (ā)** to come
آمریکا **āmrikā** America
آمریکایی **āmrikāyi** American
آن **ān** that, it
آنتی‌بیوتیک **āntibiutik** antibiotic
آنها **ānhā** they
آواره **āvāre** homeless
آوردن (ار) **āvordan (ār)** *col* for آوردن **āvardan**
آوردن (اور) **āvardan (āvar)** to bring
آها **āhā** Ah, Aha, Oh
آهسته **āheste** slow(ly)
آینده **āyande** next
ا **ā** *ps* for آمدن **āmadan**
ابر **abr** cloud
ابری **abri** cloudy
اپراتور **operātor** operator

اتاق **otāq** room
اتوبوس **otobus** bus
اتومبیل **otomobil** automobile, car
اتّفاق **ettefāq** happening
اتّفاق افتادن (افت) **ettefāq oftādan (oft)** to happen
اجاره **ejāre** rent
اجاره‌یی **ejāreyi** rented
اجازه **ejāze** permission
اخبار **axbār** news *pl*
اداره **edāre** the office
ار **ār** *ps* for آوردن **āvordan**
ارادتمند **erādatmand** sincerely (yours)
ارز **arz** *ps* for ارزیدن **arzidan**
ارزون **arzun** *col* for ارزان **arzān** cheap
ارزیدن (ارز) **arzidan (arz)** to be worth
ارسال کردن **ersāl kardan** to send
از **az** than, from, of, with
ازدواج **ezdevāj** marriage, wedding
ازدواج کردن **ezdevāj kardan** to marry
اسب سواری **asb savāri** horse riding
استخدام **estexdām** employment
استرالیا **osterāliā** Australia
استرالیایی **osterāliāyi** Australian
استفراغ **estefrāq** vomiting
اسکاتلند **eskātland** Scotland
اسکاتلندی **eskātlandi** Scottish
اسم **esm** name
اسهال **eshāl** diarrhoea
اشکال **eškāl** problem
اصفهان **esfahān** Esfahan
اصلاً **aslan** at all

اضافه **ezāfe** additional
اطّلاع دادن **ettelā` dādan** to inform
اعلام شدن **e`lām šodan** to be announced
اغلب **aqlab** often
افتادن (افتـ) **oftādan** to fall
اگر **agar** if
اگه **age** *col* for اگر **agar**
الآن **al(`)ān** right now
الو **alou** hello (telephone)
امروز **emruz** today
امشب **emšab** tonight
امضا شدن **emzā šodan** to be signed
امضا کردن **emzā kardan** to sign
امضا(ء) **emzā(`)** signature
امید **omid** hope
امیدوار **omidvār** hopeful
امّا **ammā** but
انتشارات **entešārāt** publications; publishers
انداختن (انداز) **andāxtan (andāz)** to put in; to throw
انگلستان **engelestān** England, Britain
انگلیس **engelis** England, Britain
انگلیسی **engelisi** English (language); British
او **u** he, she
اومدن (ا) **umadan (ā)** *col* for آمدن **āmadan** to come
اون **un** *col* for آن **ān** and او **u**
اونها **un(h)ā** *col* for آنها **ānhā** they
اونوقت **unvaqt** *col* for آنوقت **ānvaqt** then
اوّل **avval** first
اوّلین **avvalin** first
اهل **ahl(-e)** a native (of)
ایتالیا **itāliā** Italy
ایران **irān** Iran
ایرانی **irāni** Iranian
ایستـ **ist** *ps* for ایستادن **istādan**
ایستادن (ایستـ) **istādan (ist)** to stand up
ایستگاه **istgāh** station
ایشون **išun** *col* for ایشان **išān** he, she *(pol)*
این **in** this
این اطراف **in atrāf** around here
این هم **in ham** here's
اینجا **injā** here, this place
اینکه **inke** the fact that
با **bā** with, by
با این حساب **bā in hesāb** given the situation
با ... ملاقات کردن **bā . . . molāqāt kardan** to meet (with) . . .
با هم **bā ham** together
بابا **bābā** dad
بابا بزرگ **bābā bozorg** grandad
باجه **bāje** counter
بار **bār** time(s)
باران **bārān** rain
بارون **bārun** *col* for باران **bārān**
بارونی **bāruni** *col* for بارانی **bārāni** rainy
باز **bāz** open
باز کردن **bāz kardan** to open
باز هم **bāz ham** again
بازرگانی **bāzargāni** commercial, commerce
بازی **bāzi** game
بازی کردن **bāzi kardan** to play
باشه **bāše** *col* for باشد **bāšad** OK, let it be

باشـ **bāš** subjunctive stem for بودن **budan**
باقلا پلو **bāq(e)lā polou** steamed rice with broad beans
بالا **bālā** up, upstairs
بالاخره **belaxare** at last
بالای **bālā-ye** above, over
بالعکس **bel`aks** vice versa
باید **bāyad** must, should
ببخشید **bebaxšid** excuse (me), sorry
ببر **bebar** take
ببینم **bebinam** (for me) to see
بپیچید **bepicid** (you) turn
بجای **bejā-ye** instead of
بچّه **bacce** child
بخشـ **baxš** *ps* for بخشیدن **baxšidan**
بخشیدن (بخشـ) **baxšidan (baxš)** to forgive
بخوابم **bexābam** (for me) to sleep
بخونید **bexunid** *col* for بخوانید **bexānid** (you) read
بخیر **bexeir** may it be good
بد **bad** bad
بدتر **badtar** worse
بدترین **badtarin** worst
بدن **badan** body
بدون **bedun-e** without
بذارید **bezārid** *col* for بگذارید **begozārid** (you) put
بر **bar** *ps* for بردن **bordan**
برات **barāt** *col* for برایت **barāyat** for you *inf*
براتون **barātun** *col* for برایتان **barāyetān** for you
برادر **barādar** brother
برام **barām** *col* for برایم **barāyam** for me
برای **barāye** for
برداشتن (دار) **bar dāštan (dār)** to take, to pick up
بردن (بر) **bordan (bar)** to take, to move
برف **barf** snow
برق **barq** electricity
برقی **barqi** electric(al)
برکت **bar(a)kat** blessing
بر گشتن (گرد) **bar gaštan (gard)** to return
برنامه **barnāme** plan
برنج **berenj** (uncooked) rice
بزرگ **bozorg** big, large
بزرگسال **bozorgsāl** adult
بستن (بند) **bastan (band)** to close
بستنی **bastani** ice cream
بسته **baste** parcel; closed
بشمرید **beš(o)morid** count
بشه **beše** (if) it becomes
بشینم **bešinam** *col* for بنشینم **benešinam** (for me to) sit
بعد **ba`d** then, afterwards
بعد از **ba`d az** after
بعد از ظهر **ba`d az zohr** afternoon
بعداً **ba`dan** later
بعضی **ba`zi** some
بعضی از **ba`zi az** some of
بعضی وقت‌ها **ba`zi vaqthā** sometimes
بفرمایید **befarmāyid** here you are; please go ahead
بقیّه **baqiye** the rest
بگم **begam** *col* for بگویم **beguyam** (for me)

to say
بگید **begid** *col* for بگویید **beguyid** (you) say
بلافاصله **belāfāsele** immediately
بلد **balad** able to do . . .
بلند **boland** tall, long; loud
بلند شدن **boland šodan** to get up
بله **bale** yes
بلیت **belit** ticket
بند **band** *ps* for بستن **bastan**
بو **bu** smell
بود **bud** was; there was/were
بودن (هست/ باش) **budan (hast/bāš)** to be
بور **bur** blond(e)
بوس **bus** *ps* for بوسیدن **busidan**
بوسیدن (بوس) **busidan (bus)** to kiss
بوق آزاد **buq-e āzād** dialling tone
به **be** to; in
به به! **bah bah!** Wow! How lovely!
به سختی **be saxti** with difficulty
به موقع **be mouqe`** in time
به ندرت **be nodrat** rarely
بهتر **behtar** better
بهترین **behtarin** best
بهتون **behetun** to you
بهش **beheš** to him/her/it
بیاره **biāre** *col* for بیاورد **biāvarad** (so he can) bring
بیخوابی **bixābi** sleeplessness
بیرون **birun** out
بیرون **birun-e** outside of
بیست و یکم **bist o yekom** twenty first
بیشتر **bištar** more
بیمار **bimār** patient
بینی **bini** nose
بین **bin** *ps* for دیدن **didan**
پارتی **pārti** party
پارسال **pārsāl** last year
پارکینگ **pārking** car park
پالتو **pālto(u)** overcoat
پایین **pāyin** down, downstairs
پایین **pāyin-e** below
پختن (پز) **poxtan (paz)** to cook
پخته شدن **poxte šodan** to be cooked
پدر **pedar** father
پذیرایی **pazirāyi** reception
پر **por** full
پر از **por az** full of
پرتقال **porteqāl** orange(s)
پررو **por-ru** cheeky
پرس **pors** *ps* for پرسیدن **porsidan**
پرسیدن (پرس) **porsidan (pors)** to ask (a question)
پرکردن **por kardan** to fill
پریز **periz** socket; power point
پز **paz** *ps* for پختن **poxtan**
پس **pas** then, in that case
پس بردن **pas bordan** to take back (*ST* bought)
پست **post** post, mail
پستخونه **postxune** *col* for پستخانه **postxāne** post office
پستی **posti** postal
پسر **pesar** son, boy
پس گرفتن **pas gereftan** to take back (*ST* sold)
پشت **pošt** back

پشت **post-e** behind
پلاک **pelāk** (house) number
پلیس **polis** police
پلیسی **polisi** related to police; detective
پمپ بنزین **pomp-e benzin** petrol/gas station
پنج **panj** five
پنجره **panjare** *col* **panjere** window
پنج‌شنبه **panj-šanbe** Thursday
پنیر **panir** cheese
پنی‌سیلین **penisilin** penicillin
پوست **pust** skin
پوستر **poster** poster
پوشـ **puš** *ps* for پوشیدن **pušidan**
پوشیدن (پوشـ) **pušidan (puš)** to wear
پول **pul** money
پوند **pond** pound sterling
پهلوی **pahlu-ye** next to
پهلویی **pahluyi** next door
پیاده **piāde** on foot
پیاده شدن **piāde šodan** to get off (a vehicle)
پیانو **piāno** piano
پیتزا فروشی **pitzā foruši** pizza shop
پیچـ **pic** *ps* for پیچیدن **picidan**
پیچیدن (پیچـ) **picidan (pic)** to turn, swerve
پیدا کردن **peidā kardan** to find
پیرهن **pirhan** *col* for پیراهن **pirāhan** shirt
پیش **piš** last, ago
پیش‌بینی **pišbini** forecast
پیش‌غذا **piš-qazā** starter
پیشکش **piškeš** a gift
پیشنهاد **pišnahād** proposal
پیشنهاد کردن **pišnahād kardan** to suggest
پیشنهادی **pišnahādi** proposed
پیغام **peiqām** message
پیوست **peivast** enclosed, attached
تئاتر **te`ātr** theatre
تأخیر **ta`xir** delay
تا **tā** so that
تا **tā** up to; until; also used with numbers as a classifier
تاریخ **tārix** date
تازه **tāze** fresh
تاس **tās** bald
تب **tab** fever
تبدیل کردن **tabdil kardan** to convert
تبریک **tabrik** congratulations
تپلی **topoli** plump
تحمیل کردن **tahmil kardan** to impose
تخت **taxt** bed
تخم مرغ **toxm-e morq** hen's egg
ترازو **tarāzu** scale
تراشیدن (تراشـ) **tarāšidan (tarāš)** to shave
ترافیک **terāfik** traffic
ترجمه **tarjome** translation
ترجمه کردن **tarjome kardan** to translate
ترجیح دادن **tarjih dādan** to prefer
ترجیحاً **tarjihan** preferably
ترکیدن (ترکـ) **tarakidan (tarak)** to burst
تشکّر **tašakkor** thanking
تشنگی **tešnegi** thirst
تشنه **tešne** thirsty
تصادف **tasādof** accident
تصمیم **tasmim** decision
تعارف **ta`ārof** *col* **tārof** polite verbal ritual
تعارف کردن **ta`ārof kardan** to

engage in a polite verbal ritual; to stand on ceremony

تعطیل **ta`til** closed; holiday

تعطیلات **ta`tilāt** holidays

تقویم **taqvim** diary, calendar

تکمه **tokme** button

تلفن **telefon** telephone

تلفن کردن **telefon kardan** to phone

تلویزیون **televizion** television

تماس گرفتن **tamās gereftan** to contact

تماشا **tamāšā** watching

تماشا کردن **tamāšā kardan** to watch

تمام **tamām** finished; whole

تمبر **tambr** stamp

تموم **tamum** *col* for تمام **tamām**

تنبل **tanbal** lazy

تنها **tanhā** alone

تنیس **tenis** tennis

تو **to** you *inf*

توالت **tuālet** toilet

توانـ **tavān** *ps* for توانستن **tavānestan**

توانستن (توانـ) **tavānestan (tavān)** to be able

توضیح **touzih** explanation

تولّد **tavallod** birth(day)

تومن **toman** *col* for تومان **tumān** tuman, Iranian currency = 10 rials

تونـ **tun** *ps* for تونستن **tunestan**

تونستن (تونـ) **tunestan (tun)** *col* for توانستن **tavānestan**

تو(ی) **tu(-ye)** *col* in, at

تهران **tehrān** Tehran

تهرانی **tehrāni** from Tehran

تیر **tir** arrow

جا **jā** place, seat

جان **jān** *col* جون **jun** dear

جثّه **josse** build *n*

جدا **jodā** separate

جدّاً **jeddan** seriously; really

جزئیّات **joz`iyāt** details

جشن **jašn** celebration

جلو **jelo(u)** front

جلوی **jelo-ye** in front of

جمعاً **jam`an** in total

جمعه **jom`e** Friday

جمله **jomle** sentence

جناب **jenāb-e** honorific title for men

جنوب **jonub** south

جواب **javāb** answer, reply

جوان **javān** young

جوجه **juje** (spring) chicken

جور **jur** kind, sort

جوگندمی **jougandomi** grey (hair)

جوون **javun** *col* for جوان **javān**

جیب‌بر **jib-bor** pickpocket

چارشونه **cāršune** broad-shouldered

چایی / چای **cāyi/cai** tea

چپ **cap** left

چرا **cerā** why; yes (to a negative question)

چراغ **cerāq** a light

چرک کردن **cerk kardan** to have an infection

چشم **cašm** by all means; *col* **cešm** eye

چطور **ceto(u)r** how; how about

چطور شد **ceto(u)r šod** how

come
چطور مگه؟ **ceto(u)r mage?** What about it?
چقدر **ceqadr** how much
چک **cek** cheque, check
چکار **cekār** what (activity)
چلوکباب برگ **celo(u)-kabāb-e barg** rice and grilled meat
چمدون **camedun** *col* for چمدان **camedān** suitcase
چند **cand** what; how much/many
چند تا **cand tā** a few (of them); how many
چند وقت **cand vaqt** how long
چه **ce** *col* چی **ci** what
چون **con** because
چونه زدن **cune zadan** *col* for چانه زدن **cāne zadan** to haggle
چهار راه **c(ah)ār rāh** cross-roads
چهارشنبه **c(ah)ār-šanbe** Wednesday
چی **ci** *col* for چه **ce** what
چیز **ciz** thing
چیه **cie** what's
حاضر **hāzer** ready
حافظ **hāfez** protector
حال **hāl** health; mood
حالا **hālā** now
حالتون **hāletun** *col* for حالتان **hāletān** your health
حتماً **hatman** certainly
حتّی **hattā** even
حدس زدن **hads zadan** to guess
حدود **hodud-e** about, approximately
حدّ اقلّ **hadd-e aqall** at least
حدّ اکثر **hadd-e aksar** at most; at the latest
حرف **harf** word, speech
حرف زدن **harf zadan** to talk
حرکت کردن **harkat kardan** to set off; to depart
حساب **hesāb** account
حسّاسیّت **hassāsiyat** allergy
حسّ کردن **hess kardan** to feel
حسود **hasud** jealous
حقوق **hoquq** salary
حموم **hamum** *col* for حمّام **hammām** bathroom
حواله **havāle** order
حیاط **hayāt** courtyard
حیف **heif** what a pity
خارجی **xāreji** foreigner
خاصّ **xāss** special
خاله **xāle** maternal aunt
خالی **xāli** vacant, empty
خاموش **xāmuš** switched off
خانم **xānom** lady; wife
خانه **xāne** house, home
خانواده **xānevāde** family
خب **xob** OK (then)
خجالتی **xejālati** shy
خدا **xodā** God
خدمت **xedmat** service
خر **xar** *ps* for خریدن **xaridan**
خراب **xarāb** out of order
خراب کردن **xarāb kardan** to break
خرد **xord** *col* **xurd** small
خرید **xarid** shopping
خریدن (خر) **xaridan (xar)** to buy
خسته **xaste** tired
خشک **xošk** dry
خطر **xatar** danger
خطرناک **xatarnāk** dangerous
خوا **xā** *col ps* for خواستن **xāstan**
خواب **xāb** sleep; asleep

خوابیدن (خوابـ) **xābidan (xāb)** to sleep

خواستن (خوا) [خواهـ] **xāstan (xā)[xāh]** to want, to ask

خوانـ **xān** *ps* for خواندن **xāndan**

خواندن (خوانـ) **xāndan (xān)** to read, reading; to study

خواننده **xānande** singer

خواهـ **xāh** *ps* for خواستن **xāstan**

خواهر **xāhar** sister

خواهش **xāheš** a request

خواهش کردن **xāheš kardan** to request

خوب **xub** good, fine, well

خود **xod** own, self

خودکشی **xodkoši** suicide

خوراکی **xorāki** food (general)

خوردن (خور) **xordan (xor)** to eat; to drink (*col*)

خورش **xoreš** a stew

خوش اومدید **xoš umadid** welcome (to a place)

خوش بگذره **xoš begzare** have a nice time

خوش به حالت **xoš be hālet** lucky you

خوش گذشت **xoš gozašt** had a nice time

خوشبختانه **xošbaxtāne** fortunately

خوشحال **xoshāl** happy, glad

خوشمزه **xošmaze** tasty

خوشوقت **xošvaqt** pleased

خونـ **xun** *ps* for خوندن **xundan**

خوندن (خونـ) **xundan (xun)** *col* for خواندن **xāndan**

خونه **xune** *col* for خانه **xāne**

خیابان **xiābān** street

خیابون **xiābun** *col* for خیابان **xiābān**

خیار **xiār** cucumber

خیلی **xeili** very (much/many)

دائم **dā`em** constantly

داخل **dāxel-e** inside

داداش **dādāš** brother *inf*

دادم **dādam** I gave

دادن (د) [دهـ] **dādan (d)[dah/deh]** to give

دار **dār** *ps* for داشتن **dāštan**

دارد **dārad** *col* داره **dāre** he/she/it has

دارو **dāru** medicine

دارید **dārid** you have

داشتن (دار / داشته باشـ) **dāštan (dār/dāšte bāš)** to have

داشته باشـ **dāšte bāš** *sub* stem for داشتن **dāštan**

دانـ **dān** *ps* for دانستن **dānestan**

دانستن (دانـ) **dānestan (dān)** to know

دانشگاه **dānešgāh** university

دایی **dāyi** maternal uncle

دختر **doxtar** girl, daughter

در **dar** in

در **dar** door

دراز کشیدن **derāz kešidan** to lie down

درب **darb** door /

در بارهٔ **dar bāre-ye** about, concerning

درجه **daraje** degree, class

درد **dard** pain, ache

درد کردن **dard kardan** to ache

درد گرفتن **dard gereftan** to begin to ache

درس **dars** lesson

درست **dorost** correct(ly); right

درست کردن **dorost kardan** to fix; to make

در ضمن **dar zemn** incidentally

دزد **dozd** thief, burglar

دست **dast** hand

دستخطّ **dastxatt** handwriting

دسترس **dastras** access

دستشویی **dastšuyi** toilet; washbasin

دسر **deser** dessert

دعوا **da`vā** a fight

دعوت **da`vat** invitation

دعوت شدن **da`vat šodan** to be invited

دعوت کردن **da`vat kardan** to invite

دفتر **daftar** book; office

دفعه **daf`e** time(s)

دقیقه **daqiqe** minute

دل **del** stomach; heart

دلار **dolār** dollar

دلیل **dalil** reason

دنبال ... گشتن **donbāl-e . . . gaštan** to look for . . .

دنیا **donyā** world

دو **do** two

دوا **davā** medicine *col*

دوازده **davāzdah** twelve

دوباره **dobāre** again

دوچرخه سواری **docarxe savāri** cycling

دوخوابه **do-xābe** two-bedroomed

دوربین **durbin** camera

دوست **dust** friend

دوست داشتن **dust dāštan** to like; to love

دوش **duš** shower

دوشنبه **do-šanbe** Monday

دوغ **duq** yoghurt drink

دوم **dovvom** second

دوّمی **dovvomi** the second one

دونـ **dun** *ps* for دونستن **dunestan**

دونستن (دونـ) **dunestan (dun)** *col* for دانستن **dānestan**

دو نفره **do nafare** suitable for two people

دونه **dune** *col* for دانه **dāne** number

دونه‌یی **duneyi** by number

دونه‌یی **duneyi** each

دهان **dahān** mouth

دیدار **didār** visiting

دیدن (بینـ) **didan (bin)** to see; seeing

دیده شدن **dide šodan** to be seen

دیر **dir** late

دیروز **diruz** yesterday

دیشب **dišab** last night

دیگر **digar** else; other; any more

دیگه **dige** *col* for دیگر **digar**

ذار **zār** *col ps* for گذاشتن **gozāštan**

ر **r** *col ps* for رفتن **raftan**

را **rā** definite article placed after a direct object

راحت **rāhat** easy, comfortable

رادیو **rādio** radio

راست **rāst** right

راستش **rāsteš** to be honest

راستی **rāsti** by the way

راضی **rāzi** satisfied, happy

رانـ **rān** *ps* for راندن **rāndan**

راندن (رانـ) **rāndan (rān)** to drive

رانندگی **rānandegi** driving
راه **rāh** way; route; distance
راه رفتن **rāh raftan** to walk; to move
راهنما **rāhnamā** indicator
راهنمایی **rāhnamāyi** advice, guidance
ربع **rob`** quarter
رزرو کردن **rezerv kardan** to book
رژیم **reĝim** regime; diet
رسانـ **resān** *ps* for رساندن **resāndan**
رساندن (رسانـ) **resāndan (resān)** to convey
رستوران **resturān** restaurant
رسونـ **resun** *ps* for رسوندن **resundan**
رسوندن (رسونـ) **resundan (resun)** *col* for رساندن **resāndan**
رسید **resid** receipt
رسیدن (رسـ) **residan (res)** to reach, arrive
رفتن (ر)[رو] **raftan (r)[rav]** to go
رنگ **rang** colour
رو **-ro** *col* for را **rā**
رو **ru** face
رو به **ru be** facing
رو(ی) **ru(-ye)** on
روبروی **ruberu-ye** opposite
روز **ruz** day
روزنامه **ruznāme** newspaper
روسری **rusari** headscarf
روشن **rouŝan** light, bright; switched on
رونـ **run** *ps* for روندن **rundan**
روندن (رونـ) **rundan (run)** *col* for راندن **rāndan**
روی هم **ru-ye ham** in total
ریاضی **riāzi** maths
ریال **riāl** Iranian currency (10 rials = 1 tuman)
ریختن (ریز) **rixtan (riz)** to pour
ریز **riz** *ps* for ریختن **rixtan**
ریش **riŝ** beard
ریش‌تراش **riŝ-tarāŝ** shaver
زبان **zabān** language
زبان مادری **zabān-e mādari** mother tongue
زحمت **zahmat** trouble, inconvenience
زحمت کشیدن **zahmat keŝidan** to take trouble
زدن (زنـ) **zadan (zan)** to hit; to play (music)
زرنگ **zerang** clever
زمستان **zemestān** winter
زمستون **zemestun** *col* for زمستان **zemestān**
زمستونی **zemestuni** suitable for winter
زنـ **zan** *ps* for زدن **zadan**
زن **zan** woman
زندگی کردن **zendegi kardan** to live
زنگ زدن **zang zadan** to phone
زود **zud** early, soon, quick(ly)
زیاد **ziād** much, many
زیبا **zibā** beautiful
زیباتر **zibātar** more beautiful
زیباترین **zibātarin** most beautiful
زیبایی **zibāyi** beauty
زیر **zir-e** under, below
ژاپن **ĝāpon** Japan
ژاپنی **ĝāponi** Japanese
ژاکت **ĝāket** cardigan
سؤال **so`āl** question
ساخت **sāxt-e** made in

ساعت **sā`at** time, hour, clock, watch
ساک **sāk** holdall
ساکت **sāket** quiet, silent
سال **sāl** year
سالاد **sālād** salad
سالگرد **sālgard** anniversary
ساندویچ **sāndevic** sandwich
سایر **sāyer-e** other
سبزی **sabzi** fresh herbs
سبیل **sebil** moustache
ستاره **setāre** star
سخت **saxt** difficult, hard
سختی **saxti** difficulty, hardship
سر **sar** head
سر **sar-e** at; on
سرد **sard** cold *a*
سردرد **sar-dard** headache
سرعت **sor`at** speed
سرفه کردن **sorfe kardan** to cough
سرگرمی **sargarmi** hobby
سرما **sarmā** cold *n*
سرما خوردن **sarmā xordan** to catch (*lit* eat) a cold
سرمه‌یی **sormeyi** navy blue
سعی کردن **sa`y kardan** to try
سفارت **sefārat** embassy
سفارش دادن **sefāreš dādan** to place an order
سفارشی **sefāreši** registered (mail)
سفر **safar** journey, trip
سفید **sefid** white
سلام **salām** hello, regards
سنگین **sangin** heavy
سوپ **sup** soup
سوپرمارکت **supermārket** supermarket
سوّم **sevvom** third
سوهان **suhān** a sweet

سه **se** three
سه‌شنبه **sešanbe** Tuesday
سیب **sib** apple
سینما **sinemā** cinema
سینه **sine** chest
شـ **š** *col ps* for شدن **šodan**
شاد **šad** joyful
شام **šām** dinner
شامل **šāmel-e** inclusive of
شاید **šāyad** might; perhaps
شب **šab** evening, night
شدن (شـ) [شو] **šodan (š)[šav/šou]** to become; to be possible
شدّت **šeddat** severity
شدید **šadid** severe
شرایط **šarāyet** conditions
شربت **šarbat** syrup
شرق **šarq** east
شرکت **šerkat** company
شرکت کردن **šerkat kardan** to attend
شرمنده **šarmande** ashamed; embarrassed
شروع **šoru`** beginning
شروع شدن **šoru` šodan** (for *ST*) to begin
شروع کردن **šoru` kardan** to begin (*ST*)
ششم **šešom** sixth
شکستن (شکن) **šekastan (šekan)** to break
شکل **šekl** shape
شلوار **šalvār** trousers
شما **šomā** you *f*
شماره **šomāre** number
شمال **šomāl** north
شمردن (شمر) **šomordan (šomor)** to count
شمرده **šomorde** clear(ly)
شمرده شدن **šomorde šodan** to be

counted
شمرون **šemrun** *col* for شمیران **šemirān** Shemiran (a place)
شنا **šenā** swimming
شنبه **šanbe** Saturday
شنو **šenav/šenou** *ps* for شنیدن **šenidan**
شنیدن (شنو) **šenidan (šenav/ šenou)** to hear
شو **šav/šou** *ps* for شدن **šodan**
شوهر **šouhar** husband
شهر **šahr** city, town
شیر **šir** tap; milk
شیرین **širin** sweet
شیرینی **širini** sweetness; a sweet; pastry
شین **šin** *col ps* for نشستن **nešastan**
صاحب **sāheb** owner
صبح **sob(h)** morning
صبحانه **sobhāne** breakfast
صبحونه **sobhune** *col* for صبحانه **sobhāne**
صبر **sabr** patience
صبر کردن **sabr kardan** to wait
صبور **sabur** patient
صحبت **sohbat** speech, conversation
صحبت کردن **sohbat kardan** to speak
صدا **sedā** sound, voice, noise
صدا کردن **sedā kardan** to call
صفر **sefr** zero
صندوق **sanduq** trunk, box
صندوق عقب **sanduq(-e) aqab** rear trunk, car boot
صورت **surat** face; list
صورت‌حساب **surat-hesāb** bill
طبقه **tabaqe** floor, storey
طرف **taraf** side
طرفدار **tarafdār** supporter
طوسی **tusi** grey (colour)
ظرف **zarf** container, dish
ظرف **zarf-e** within
ظهر **zohr** noon
عادی **ādi** ordinary, normal
عالی **āli** excellent
عجب **ajab** surprise
عجله **ajale** haste; hurry
عذر **ozr** forgiveness
عرض **arz** something (humbly) said to others
عرض کردن **arz kardan** humbly to say (to others)
عزیز **aziz** dear
عصبانی **asabāni** angry
عصر **asr** late afternoon
عضلات **azolāt** muscles
عضو **ozv** member
عطسه کردن **atse kardan** to sneeze
عقب **aqab** rear
عکّاسی **akkāsi** photography
عکس **aks** picture, photo
علاقه **alāqe** interest
عمده **omde** main
عمو **amu** paternal uncle
عمومی **omumi** public
عمّه **amme** paternal aunt
عوض کردن **avaz kardan** to change
عیب **eib** problem; defect
عینک **einak** glasses, spectacles
غذا **qazā** food, dish, meal
غرب **qarb** west
غم **qam** anxiety, sadness
غیر ممکن **qeir-e momken** impossible
فارسی **fārsi** Farsi, Persian
فاسد **fāsed** (of food) off; rotten

فرانسه **farānse** France; French (language)
فرانسوی **farānsavi** French (person)
فرانک فرانسه **ferānk-e farānse** French franc
فردا **fardā** tomorrow
فرستـ **ferest** *ps* for فرستادن **ferestādan**
فرستادن (فرستـ) **ferestādan (ferest)** to send
فرق **farq** difference
فرم **form** form
فرما **farmā** *ps* for فرمودن **farmudan**
فرمایش **farmāyeš** business (*lit* commanding)
فرمودن (فرما) **farmudan (farmā)** to command; to say (used for others); also replaces کردن **kardan** in compound verbs for politeness
فروختن (فروشـ) **foruxtan (foruš)** to sell
فرودگاه **forudgāh** airport
فروردین **farvardin** Farvardin (1st month in Iranian calendar)
فروش **foruš** selling
فروشنده **forušande** seller
فرهنگ لغت **farhang-e loqat** dictionary
فریزر **ferizer** freezer
فسنجان **fesenjān** a stew
فسنجون **fesenjun** *col* for فسنجان **fesenjān**
فشار دادن **fešār dādan** to press
فعلا **fe(`)lan** for now
فقط **faqat** only
فکر **fekr** thought; idea
فکر کردن **fekr kardan** to think
فکس **faks** fax
فورا **fouran** at once
فوق **fouq** above mentioned
فهمـ **fahm** *ps* for فهمیدن **fahmidan**
فهمیدن (فهمـ) **fahmidan (fahm)** to understand
فیلم **film** film
قابل **qābel** worthy
قابلی نداره **qābeli nadāre** it is not worthy (of you)
قاشق **qāšoq** spoon(ful)
قبل از **qabl az** before
قبلا **qablan** previously
قبول کردن **qabul kardan** to accept
قدم زدن **qadam zadan** to walk, walking
قدّ **qadd** height
قرار **qarār** arrangement; appointment
قراره **qarāre** it's (been) arranged
قربان **qorbān** sir
قربانت **qorbānet** cheerio (*lit* your sacrifice)
قرص **qors** tablet, pill
قرمه‌سبزی **qorme-sabzi** a stew
قشنگ **qašang** nice, pretty
قصد **qasd** intention
قطار **qatār** train
قطع شدن **qat` šodan** to be disconnected
قطع کردن **qat` kardan** to interrupt
قفل **qofl** lock
قلمی **qalami** slim
قهوه **qahve** coffee
قهوه‌یی **qahveyi** brown
قیمت **qeimat** price
قیمه‌بادنجان **qeime-bādenjān** a

stew with aubergines
کاپشن **kāpšan** bomber jacket
کار **kār** job, work, business
کار کردن **kār kardan** to work
کارت اعتباری **kārt-e e`tebāri** credit card
کارمند **kārmand** (civil) servant
کافی **kāfi** enough
کامپیوتر **kāmpiuter** computer
کاناپه **kānāpe** sofa, settee
کانادا **kānādā** Canada
کانادایی **kānādāyi** Canadian
کباب **kabāb** kebab
کت **kot** jacket, coat
کتاب **ketāb** book
کتابخونه **ketābxune** *col* for کتابخانه **ketābxāne** library
کثیف **kasif** dirty
کجا **kojā** where
کجاست **kojāst** where's
کجایی **kojāyi** where from
کد **kod** code
کدام **kodām** which
کدوم **kodum** *col* for کدام **kodām**
کردن (کنـ) **kardan (kon)** to do, make (mostly in compound verbs)
کرم **kerem** cream
کریسمس **kerismas** Christmas
کس **kas** person
کسی **kasi** someone
کشتن (کشـ) **koštan (koš)** to kill
کشته شدن **košte šodan** to be killed
کشیدن (کشـ) **kešidan (keš)** to pull, draw, smoke
کفش **kafš** shoe(s)
کلاس **kelās** class(room)
کلاه **kolāh** hat
کلفت **koloft** thick
کم **kam** little
کم اشتها **kam eštehā** with little appetite
کمبود **kambud** shortage
کمتر **kamtar** less
کمر درد **kamar dard** backache
کمرو **kamru** shy, bashful
کمک **komak** help
کمی **kami** a little
کنـ **kon** *ps* for کردن **kardan**
کنار **kenār-e** by; near
کنسرت **konsert** concert
که **ke** that, which, who
کو **ku** Where is it? (*col*)
کوتاه **kutāh** short
کوچک **kucek** young; small
کوچکتر **kucektar** younger; smaller
کوچه **kuce** lane; side road
کی **kei** when, what time
کی **ki** who
کیف **kif** briefcase, bag
کیک **keik** cake
کیلو **kilu** kilo
کیلویی **kiluyi** by kilo, weight
کیلویی **kiluyi** per kilo
گـ **g** *col ps* for گفتن **goftan**
گاز **gāz** gas
گاهی **gāhi** occasionally
گذاشتن (ذار) [گذار] **gozāštan (zār)[gozār]** to put; to leave; to let/allow
گذرنامه **gozarnāme** passport
گذشته **gozašte** last; past
گرد **gard** *ps* for گشتن **gaštan**
گرد **gerd** round

گرد و خاک **gard o xāk** dust
گردش **gardeš** tour, stroll
گرسنگی **gorosnegi** hunger
گرسنه **gorosne** hungry
گرفتن (گیر) **gereftan (gir)** to take; to catch; to get
گرفته **gerefte** blocked
گرم **garm** warm
گرون **gerun** *col* for گران **gerān** expensive
گز **gaz** a sweet
گشتن (گرد) **gaštan (gard)** to turn; to go around
گفتن (گـ) [گو] **goftan (g)[gu]** to tell, to say
گلابی **golābi** pear
گلو **galu** throat
گلو درد **galu dard** sore throat
گم کردن **gom kardan** to lose
گو **gu** *ps* for گفتن **goftan**
گوش **guš** ear
گوش دادن **guš dādan** to listen, listening
گوش کردن **guš kardan** to listen, listening
گوشی **guši** receiver
گیر **gir** *ps* for گرفتن **gereftan**
لازم **lāzem** necessary
لازم داشتن **lāzem dāštan** to need
لاغر **lāqar** slim; thin
لباس **lebās** clothes
لحظه **lahze** moment
لذا **lezā** therefore
لطف **lotf** kindness
لطف کردن **lotf kardan** to give kindly; to do a favour
لطفاً **lotfan** please
لندن **landan** London
لوازم **lavāzem** appliances
لوله **lule** pipe

ما **mā** we
مادر **mādar** mother
مادر شوهر **mādar šouhar** mother-in-law (husband's mother)
مارک آلمان **mārk-e ālmān** German mark
ماشین **māšin** car; machine
مال **māl** property, belonging
مانـ **mān** *ps* for ماندن **māndan**
ماندن (مانـ) **māndan (man)** to stay
ماه **māh** month
ماهی **māhi** fish
ماهی **māhi** per month
مایل **māyel** inclined, interested
مبارک **mobārak** (may it be) blessed, happy
متأسّفانه **mota\`assefāne** unfortunately
متأهّل **mota\`ahhel** married
مترجم **motarjem** interpreter, translator
مترو **metro** metro
متشکّر **mot(a)šakker** grateful
متوسّط **motavasset** average, medium
مثل **mesl-e** like; similar to
مثل اینکه **mesl-e inke** it seems
مجبور **majbur** forced
مجلّه **majalle** magazine
محلّ **mahall** place
محلّه **mahalle** area, neighbourhood
مخالف **moxālef** opposed
مخصوصاً **maxsusan** particularly
مداد **medād** pencil
مدرسه **madrese** school
مدیر **modir** manager,

مکانیکی **mekāniki** car mechanics

مکیدن (مک) **makidan (mak)** to suck

مکیدنی **makidani** suckable

مگر **magar** but (indicating surprise)

مگه **mage** *col* for مگر **magar**

ملافه **malāfe** sheet (bedding)

ملاقات **molāqāt** meeting

ملاقات کردن **molāqāt kardan** to meet

ملّی **melli** national

ملّیت **melliyat** nationality

ممکن **momken** possible

ممکنه **momkene** it's possible; may(be)

ممنون **mamnun** grateful

من **man** I

مناسب **monāseb** suitable

منتظر **montazer** waiting

منزل **manzel** home

منشی **monši** secretary

منظره **manzare** view, scenery

مو **mu** hair

مورد علاقه **mo(u)red-e alāqe** favourite

موزه **muze** museum

موسیقی **musiqi** music

موضوع **mouzu`** subject, matter

موفّق **mo(v)affaq** successful

مونـ **mun** *ps* for موندن **mundan**

موندن (مونـ) **mundan (mun)** *col* for ماندن **māndan**

مهمون **mehmun** *col* for مهمان **mehmān** guest

director, principal

مذاکره کردن **mozākere kardan** to negotiate

مراجعه کردن **morāje`e kardan** to refer

مرد **mard** man

مردان **mardān** men *l*

مردن (میر) **mordan (mir)** to die

مردها **mardhā** men

مرسی **mersi** thanks

مرطوب **martub** humid

مرکز **markaz** centre

مریض **mariz** ill, sick

مزاحم **mozāhem** nuisance

مسئله **mas`ale** issue, problem

مسافر **mosāfer** passenger

مسافرت **mosāferat** travelling, holiday

مستقیم **mostaqim** straight

مسکّن **mosakken** pain-killer

مسلمان **mosalmān** *col* مسلمون **mosalmun** a Muslim

مسنّ **mosenn** elderly

مشتری **moštari** customer

مشخّص **mošaxxas** particular, known

مشخّصات **mošaxxasāt** distinctive features

مشکل **moškel** problem; difficult(y)

مشکی **meški** black

مصاحبه **mosāhebe** interview

معذرت **ma`zerat** pardon, forgiveness

معلّم **mo`allem** teacher

معمولاً **ma`mulan** usually

مقطوع **maqtu`** fixed

مکاتبات **mokātebāt** correspondence

مکانیک **mekānik** mechanics

مهمونی **mehmuni** *col* for مهمانی **mehmāni** party
مهندس **mohandes** engineer
میاد **miād** *col* for میآید **miāyad** he/she comes
میارزه **miarze** it's worth
میام **miām** *col* for میآیم **miāyam** I come
میاند **miānd** *col* for میآیند **miāyand** they come
میای **miai** *col* for میآیی **miāyi** you *inf* come
میاید **miaid** *col* for میآیید **miāyid** you come
میایم **miaim** *col* for میآییم **miāyim** we come
میخواد **mixād** *col* for میخواهد **mixāhad** he/she wants
میخوام **mixām** *col* for میخواهم **mixāham** I want
میخواند **mixānd** *col* for میخواهند **mixāhand** they want
میخوای **mixai** *col* for میخواهی **mixāhi** you *inf* want
میخواید **mixaid** *col* for میخواهید **mixāhid** you want
میخوایم **mixaim** *col* for میخواهیم **mixāhim** we want
میدان **meidān** *col* **meidun** square; circus
میز **miz** desk, table
میزان **mizān** rate, size
میشه **miše** *col* for میشود **mišavad** it is possible; it becomes
میگم **migam** *col* for میگویم **miguyam** I say, tell
میل **meil** inclination
میل دارید **meil dārid** would you like
میوه **mive** fruit
ناپدید شدن **nāpadid šodan** to disappear
ناراحت **nārāhat** upset, offended
نامه **nāme** letter
نان **nān** *col* نون **nun** bread
نانوایی **nānvāyi** *col* نونوایی **nunvāyi** bakery
ناهار **nāhār** lunch
ناهارخوری **nāhārxori** dining-room
نباید **nabāyad** must not
نبش **nabš** corner
نبود **nabud** was not; there was/were not
نتیجه **natije** result
نرخ **nerx** rate (currency)
نزدیک **nazdik** near (not far)
نزدیک **nazdik-e** near (close to)
نزدیکی‌ها **nazdikihā** the nearby area
نشان **nešān** target
نشان دادن **nešān dādan** to show
نشستن (شینـ) [نشینـ] **nešastan (šin)[nešin]** to sit down
نشه **naše** *col* for نشود **našavad** (if) it doesn't become
نشون دادن **nešun dādan** *col* for نشان دادن **nešān dādan**
نشینـ **nešin** *ps* for نشستن

nešastan

نظر **nazar** view, opinion

نفر **nafar** person

نفس **nafas** breath

نفس کشیدن **nafas kešidan** to breathe

نقد **naqd** (in) cash

نقّاشی **naqqāši** painting

نگاه کردن **negāh kardan** to look

نگران **negarān** worried

نگرانی **negarāni** worry

نگه دارید **negah dārid** stop; hold

نگه داشتن **negah dāštan** to stop; to hold

نمایشنامه **namāyešnāme** play (drama)

نمیشه **nemiše** *col* for نمیشود **nemišavad** it's not possible; it does not become

نو **nou** new

نوار **navār** tape

نوشابه **nušābe** a cold (fizzy) drink

نوشتن (نویس) **neveštan (nevis)** to write

نوشیدنی **nušidani** a drink

نوع **nou`** kind, type, sort

نون **nun** *col* for نان **nān**

نویس **nevis** *ps* for نوشتن **neveštan**

نه **na** no

نه بابا **na bābā** Oh no

نیست **nist** he/she/it is not; there is/are not

نیستم **nistam** I am not

نیستند **nistand** they are not

نیستی **nisti** you are not *inf*

نیستید **nistid** you are not

نیستیم **nistim** we are not

نیم **nim** half

و **o** *col* for و **va** and

و **-o** *col* for را **rā** definite article placed after a direct object

و **va** and

واقعاً **vāqe`an** truly

والله **vāllā** well, to be honest, *lit* by God

وان **vān** bath tub

ورزش **varzeš** sport

وضع **vaz`** situation

وقت **vaqt** time

وقتی **vaqti** when

وکیل **vakil** lawyer

ولی **vali** but

ویدیو / ویدئو **vidio/vide`o** video

ویولن **violon** violin

هتل **hotel** hotel

هدیه **hedye** present, gift

هر **har** every, each, any

هر دو **har do** both

هر روز **har ruz** every day

هرچه زودتر **harce zudtar** as soon as possible

هرچه زودتر بهتر **harce zudtar behtar** the sooner the better

هست **hast** *ps* for بودن **budan**

هست **hast** there is/are

هفته **hafte** week

هفته‌یی **hafteyi** per week, a week

هم **ham** too, also

همانجا **hamānjā** right there

همدیگر **hamdigar** each other

همدیگه **hamdige** *col* for همدیگر **hamdigar**

همراه **hamrāh** companion; accompanying

همسایه **hamsāye** neighbour

همکار **hamkār** colleague

همکاری **hamkāri** cooperation
همگانی **hamegāni** public
همون **hamun** *col* for همان **hamān** that same one
همونجا **hamunjā** *col* for همانجا **hamānjā**
همه **hame** all
همیشه **hamiše** always
همین **hamin** (this) same
همینجا **haminjā** right here
همینطور **haminto(u)r** (in the) same way
هنوز **hanuz** yet, still
هوا **havā** weather
هول **houl** panicky; nervous
هیچ جا **hic-jā** nowhere; anywhere
هیچ چیز **hic-ciz** nothing, anything
هیچ کار **hic-kār** nothing/ anything (done)
هیچ کدام **hic-kodām** neither
هیچ کدوم **hic-kodum** *col* for هیچ کدام **hic-kodām**
هیچ کس **hic-kas** nobody; not anyone
هیچوقت **hic-vaqt** never; ever
هیچی **hicci** *col* for هیچ چیز **hic-ciz**
یا **yā** either; or
یاد **yād** memory
یاد . . . کردن **yād-e . . . kardan** to remember . . .
یبوست **yobusat** constipation
یخچال **yaxcāl** refrigerator
یعنی **ya`ni** that is to say; you mean; it means
یک **yek** one
یک‌دفعه **yek-daf`e** suddenly
یک‌شنبه **yek-šanbe** Sunday
ین ژاپن **yen-e ĝāpon** Japanese yen

English–Persian glossary

Verbs are given in infinitive forms. Thus, e.g., for 'eat' look under 'to eat'. For reasons of space, the present stem of those verbs that also appear in the Persian–English glossary has not been given here.

a **yek** یک
a bit **(yek) kami** (یک) کمی
a few **cand tā** چند تا
a little **kami** کمی
a lot **ziād** زیاد
a lot of **te`dād-e ziādi** تعداد زیادی
about (approximately) **hodud-e; taqriban** حدود ؛ تقریباً
about (concerning) **dar bāre-ye; rāje` be** در بارهٔ؛ راجع به
above **bālā** بالا
accident **tasādof** تصادف
actor **honarpiše; bāzigar** هنرپیشه ؛ بازیگر
address **ādres** آدرس
aeroplane **havāpeimā** هواپیما
after **ba`d az** بعد از
afternoon **ba`d az zohr** بعد از ظهر
ago **piš** پیش
all **hame** همه
ambulance **āmbulāns** آمبولانس
America **āmrikā** آمریکا
angry with . . . **az . . . asabāni** از . . . عصبانی
anniversary **sālgard** سالگرد
antibiotic **āntibiutik** آنتی‌بیوتیک
any **har** هر
area **mahalle** محلّه
around here **in atrāf** این اطراف
around (the world) **dour-e** دور
as for me **man ke** من که
as soon as possible **harce zudtar** هرچه زودتر
asleep **xāb** خواب
at **dar** در
aunt (maternal) **xāle** خاله
aunt (paternal) **amme** عمّه
Australian **osterāliāyi** استرالیایی
autumn **pāyiz** پاییز
backache **kamardard** کمردرد
bad **bad** بد
bathroom **hammām** حمّام
col **hamum** حموم
be my guest **befarmāyid** بفرمایید
be quiet **sāket bāšid** ساکت باشید
bear with me a few moments **cand lahze sabr konid** چند لحظه صبر کنید
beard **riš** ریش

beautiful **zibā** زیبا
because **con** چون
bed **taxt;** تخت ؛
taxtexāb تختخواب
bedroom **otāq-e xāb** اتاق خواب
before **qabl az** قبل از
behind **pošt-e** پشت
below **pāyin-e** پایین
beside **pahlu-ye** پهلوی
best **behtarin** بهترین
better **behtar** بهتر
big **bozorg** بزرگ
bill **surat-hesāb** صورتحساب
birth(day) **tavallod** تولّد
black **meški; siāh** مشکی ؛ سیاه
blond **bur** بور
book **ketāb** کتاب
boss **ra`is** رئیس
both **har do** هر دو
both X and Y
ham X (va) ham Y هم X (و) هم Y
boy **pesar** پسر
bread **nān** نان
col **nun** نون
breakfast **sobhāne** صبحانه
col **sob(h)une** صبحونه
broad-shouldered
cahār-šāne چهارشانه
col **cāršune** چارشونه
broken **xarāb;** خراب ؛
šekaste شکسته
brother **barādar** برادر
burgled **dozd zade** دزد زده
business **kār** کار
but **ammā; vali** امّا ؛ ولی
by (before) **tā** تا
by (means of) **bā;** با ؛
be vasile-ye به وسیلهٔ
by (near) **kenār-e** کنار
by all means **cašm** چشم
cake **keik** کیک
can (*see* 'to be able')

can *n* **quti** قوطی
car **māšin;** ماشین ؛
otomobil اتومبیل
car key **su`ic-e** سوئیچ
(māšin) (ماشین)
carpet **qāli; farš** قالی ؛ فرش
caviar **xāviār** خاویار
central Tehran
markaz-e tehrān مرکز تهران
centre **markaz** مرکز
certainly **hatman** حتماً
chair **sandali** صندلی
cheekiness **por-ruyi** پررویی
cheese **panir** پنیر
cheque **cek** چک
child **bacce** بچّه
Chinese food
qazā-ye cini غذای چینی
cinema **sinemā** سینما
city **šahr** شهر
class **kelās** کلاس
close *a* **nazdik** نزدیک
coffee **qahve** قهوه
coin **sekke** سکّه
cold *a* **sard** سرد
cold *n* **sarmā** سرما
computer **kāmpiuter** کامپیوتر
concert **konsert** کنسرت
country **kešvar** کشور
cucumber **xiār** خیار
dad **bābā** بابا
date **tārix** تاریخ
day **ruz** روز
degree **daraje** درجه
delay **ta`xir** تأخیر
diary **taqvim** تقویم
dinner **šām** شام
doctor **doktor** دکتر
door **dar** در
drink *n* **nušidani** نوشیدنی
driving licence
gavāhi-nāme; گواهی‌نامه ؛

tasdiq تصدیق
during **dar moddat-e;** در مدّت ؛
dar tul-e در طول
e-mail **imeil** ایمیل
egg **toxm-e morq** تخم مرغ
either X or Y
yā X yā Y یا X یا Y
embassy **sefārat** سفارت
engaged: I'm engaged
nāmzad dāram نامزد دارم
England **engelestān;** انگلستان ؛
engelis انگلیس
English **engelisi** انگلیسی
enjoy the party **pārti** پارتی خوش
xoš begzare بگذره
evening **šab** شب
ever **hic-vaqt** هیچوقت
every **har** هر
everything **hame ciz** همه چیز
exactly **daqiqan;** دقیقاً ؛
dorost درست
excellent **āli** عالی
excuse me **bebaxšid** ببخشید
exhibition **namāyešgāh** نمایشگاه
expensive **gerān** گران
col **gerun** گرون
eye **cešm** چشم
face **surat; ru** صورت ؛ رو
family **xānevāde** خانواده
fat **cāq** چاق
father **pedar** پدر
favourite
moured-e alāqe مورد علاقه
fax **faks; fāks** فکس ؛ فاکس
few **kam** کم
film **film** فیلم
finally **belaxare** بالاخره
fine **xub** خوب
fine arts
honarhā-ye zibā هنرهای زیبا
fire **āteš** *col* **ātiš** آتش
fire (heater) **boxāri** بخاری
first **avval** اوّل
five-star hotel
hotel-e panj-setāre هتل پنج‌ستاره
flat **āpārtemān** آپارتمان
floor **tabaqe** طبقه
food **qazā; xorāki** غذا ؛ خوراکی
for **barāye** برای
fourth **c(ah)ārom** چهارم
French
farānse (language); فرانسه ؛
farānsavi (native) فرانسوی
Friday **jom`e** جمعه
fridge **yaxcāl** یخچال
friend **dust** دوست
from **az** از
fruit **mive** میوه
garden **hayāt** حیاط
gentleman **āqā** آقا
gentlemen **āqāyān** آقایان
German **ālmāni** آلمانی
gift **hedye** هدیه
glad **xoshāl** خوشحال
go ahead **befarmāyid** بفرمایید
going **raftan** رفتن
good **xub** خوب
grey **xākestari;** خاکستری ؛
tusi; طوسی ؛
jougandomi (of hair) جوگندمی
guest **mehmān** مهمان
col **mehmun** مهمون
had a pleasant time
xoš gozašt خوش گذشت
hair **mu** مو
half **nim** نیم
half past six **šeš o nim** شش و نیم
hall **sālon; hāl** سالن ؛ هال
happy **xoshāl** خوشحال
happy with . . .
az . . . rāzi از . . . راضی
happy birthday
tavallodet
mobārak *inf* تولّدت مبارک

Happy New Year
sāl-e nou mobārak سال نو مبارک
have a nice weekend
āxar-e hafte xoš begzare آخر هفته خوش بگذره
he/she **u** او
col **un** اون
pol **išun** ایشون
headache **sar-dard** سردرد
height **qadd** قدّ
hello **salām** سلام
her car **māšinaš** ماشینش
col **māšineš**
here **injā** اینجا
himself **xodaš** خودش
col **xodeš**
his car **māšinaš** ماشینش
col **māšineš**
hobby **sargarmi** سرگرمی
home **manzel;** منزل؛
xāne خانه
col **xune** خونه
homelessness **āvāregi** آوارگی
hoovering
jāru(b) kardan جارو(ب) کردن
hospital **bimārestān** بیمارستان
hot chocolate
šir-kākā`o شیرکاکائو
hotel **hotel** هتل
hour **sā`at** ساعت
house **xāne** خانه
col **xune** خونه
house to rent
xāne-ye ejāre-yi خانهٔ اجاره‌یی
how **ceto(u)r** چطور
how long?
cand vaqt? چند وقت؟
how many?
cand tā? چند تا؟
how much?
ceqadr? چقدر؟
How about X?
X ceto(u)r? X چطور؟
How come?
ceto(u)r šod? چطور شد؟
How far is it?
ceqadr rāhe? چقدر راهه؟
husband **šouhar** شوهر
ice cream **bastani** بستنی
if **agar** اگر
col **age** اگه
in **dar** در
col **tu(-ye)** تو(ی)
in front of **jelo(-ye)** جلو(ی)
income **darāmad** درآمد
into **be** به
it **ān** آن
col **un** اون
it seems **mesl-e inke** مثل اینکه
I **man** من
I insist
xāheš mikonam خواهش میکنم
Iranian **irāni** ایرانی
it's not worth mentioning
qābeli nadāre قابلی نداره
it's snowing
barf miād برف میاد
Italian **itāliāyi** ایتالیایی
jealousy **hasudi** حسودی
job **kār** کار
journey **safar** سفر
joy **šādi** شادی
kilo **kilu** کیلو
kind *a* **mehrbān** مهربان
col **mehrabun** مهربون
kind *n* **nou`; jur** نوع؛ جور
kitchen **āšpazxāne** آشپزخانه
col **āšpazxune** آشپزخونه
ladies **xānomhā** خانم‌ها
col **xānum(h)ā**
lady **xānom** خانم
col **xānum**
large **bozorg** بزرگ

larger **bozorgtar** بزرگتر
last month **māh-e piš/gozašte** ماه پیش / گذشته
last time **āxarin bār** آخرین بار
last year **pārsāl** پارسال
letter **nāme** نامه
library **ketābxāne** کتابخانه
col **ketābxune** کتابخونه
light *n* **cerāq** چراغ
lighter **fandak** فندک
like (similar to) **mesl-e** مثل
listening **guš dādan/kardan** گوش دادن / کردن
little **kam** کم
located in **vāqe` dar** واقع در
London **landan** لندن
Londoner **landani** لندنی
long **boland** بلند
lunch **nāhār** ناهار
madam **xānom** خانم
col **xānum**
man **mard** مرد
manager **modir** مدیر
marriage **ezdevāj** ازدواج
married **mota`ahhel** متأهّل
may **momken ast** ممکن است
col **momkene** ممکنه
(*lit* it's possible)
meal **qazā** غذا
meat **gušt** گوشت
medicine **dāru** دارو
col **davā** دوا
medium (size) **motavasset** متوسّط
meeting **molāqāt;** ملاقات ؛
jalese (board) جلسه
member **ozv** عضو
message **peiqām** پیغام
Middle East **xāvar-e miāne** خاور میانه
might **šāyad** (perhaps) شاید

milk **šir** شیر
millionaire **milyuner** میلیونر
mine **māl-e man** مال من
minute **daqiqe** دقیقه
mirror **aine** آینه
Monday **došanbe** دوشنبه
money **pul** پول
month **māh** ماه
morning **sobh** صبح
mother **mādar** مادر
Mr **āqā-ye** آقای
Ms **xānom-e** خانم
col **xānum-e**
much **ziād** زیاد
mum **māmān** مامان
museum **muze** موزه
music **musiqi** موسیقی
must **bāyad** باید
my car **māšinam** ماشینم
myself **xodam** خودم
name **esm; nām** *l* اسم ؛ نام
nationality **melliyat** ملّیّت
near (to) **nazdik(-e)** نزدیک
nearest **nazdiktarin** نزدیکترین
neighbour **hamsāye** همسایه
neither X nor Y **na X (va) na Y** نه X (و) نه Y
never **hic-vaqt** هیچوقت
new **tāze; jadid** تازه ؛ جدید
news **xabar** *sing* خبر
axbār *pl* اخبار
newspaper **ruznāme** روزنامه
next **ba`d; āyande** بعد ؛ آینده
next time **daf`e-ye ba`d** دفعهٔ بعد
next to **pahlu(-ye)** پهلو(ی)
nice **qašang** قشنگ
night **šab** شب
ninth **nohom;** نهم ؛
nohomin (before a noun) نهمین
no **na** نه

no idea! **nemidunam** نمیدونم
noon **zohr** ظهر
normally **ma`mulan** معمولاً
nose **bini** بینی
col **damāq** دماغ
not much! **na ziād** نه زیاد
note (money) **eskenās** اسکناس
nothing **hic-ciz** هیچ‌چیز
col **hicci** هیچی
now **hālā** حالا
number **šomāre** شماره
occasionally **gāhi** گاهی
off (food) **fāsed** فاسد
office **edāre; daftar** اداره ؛ دفتر
often **aqlab** اغلب
oh **āhā** آها
OK **bāše** باشه
old (people) **pir** پیر
(more *pol*) **mosenn** مسنّ
old (things) **kohne** کهنه
on **ru(-ye)** رو(ی)
on fire **āteš gerefte** آتش گرفته
open **bāz** باز
opinion **nazar; aqide** نظر ؛ عقیده
opposite *p* **ruberu-ye** روبروی
our car **māšinemān** ماشینمان
col **māšinemun** ماشینمون
out **birun** بیرون
outside the cinema
birun-e sinemā; بیرون سینما ؛
jelo-ye sinemā جلوی سینما
painting **naqqāši** نقّاشی
parcel **baste** بسته
parents **vāledein** والدین
col **pedar (o) mādar** پدر (و) مادر
Parisian **pārisi** پاریسی
park **pārk** پارک
particulars
mošaxxasāt مشخّصات
party **pārti; mehmuni** پارتی ؛ مهمونی
past **gozašte** گذشته
patience **sabr** صبر

pear-shaped
golābi-šekl گلابی‌شکل
pen **qalam** قلم
people **mardom** مردم
perhaps **šāyad** شاید
per month **māhi** ماهی
Persian **fārsi** فارسی
petrol station
pomp-e benzin پمپ بنزین
phone book
daftar-e telefon دفتر تلفن
photocopy **fotokopi** فتوکپی
photography **akkāsi** عکّاسی
pianist **piānist** پیانیست
piano **piāno** پیانو
piece **tekke** تکّه
col **tikke**
place **jā/mahall** جا / محلّ
plan **barnāme** برنامه
please **lotfan** لطفاً
pleased **xošvaqt** خوشوقت
pleasure = you're welcome
xāheš mikonam خواهش میکنم
plump **topoli** تپلی
police station
kalāntari کلانتری
pool **estaxr** استخر
possible **momken** ممکن
post **post** پست
post office **postxāne** پستخانه
col **postxune** پستخونه
preferably **tarjihan** ترجیحاً
present, gift **hedye** هدیه
president
ra`is jomhur رئیس جمهور
pretty **xošgel;** خوشگل ؛
qašang قشنگ
price **qeimat** قیمت
prime minister
noxost vazir نخست وزیر
problem **moškel** مشکل

purse **kif-e pul** کیف پول
quarter **rob`** ربع
question **so`āl** سؤال
radio **rādio** رادیو
railway station
istgāh-e qatār ایستگاه قطار
raininess (the fact that it's rainy/raining)
bāruni budan بارونی بودن
rarely **be nodrat** به ندرت
regards **salām** سلام
registered mail
post-e sefāreši پست سفارشی
reliable
qābel-e etminān قابل اطمینان
rent **ejāre** اجاره
riding a bicycle
docarxe-savāri دوچرخه‌سواری
riding a motorbike
motor-savāri موتورسواری
right now **alān** الآن
road **jādde; xiābān** جادّه؛ خیابان
room **otāq** اتاق
rug **qālice** قالیچه
salt **namak** نمک
sandwich **sāndevic** ساندویچ
Saturday **šanbe** شنبه
scenery **manzare** منظره
seat **jā** جا
second **dovvom;** دوّم؛
dovvomin (before a noun) دوّمین
sentence **jomle** جمله
separate **jodā** جدا
seventieth **haftādom;** هفتادم؛
haftādomin (before a noun) هفتادمین
several **candin** چندین
she/he **u** او
col **un** اون
pol **išun** ایشون
shop **maqāze** مغازه
shopping centre
markaz-e xarid مرکز خرید
short **kutāh** کوتاه
should **bāyad** باید
shower **duš** دوش
sick **mariz** مریض
singer **xānande** خواننده
single **mojarrad** مجرّد
single room
otāq-e yek-nafare اتاق یک‌نفره
sir **āqā** آقا
sister **xāhar** خواهر
sitting (down)
nešaste نشسته
skiing **eski** اسکی
slim **lāqar** لاغر
small **kucek** کوچک
smaller **kucektar** کوچکتر
some **ba`zi;** بعضی؛
cand tā; kami چند تا؛ کمی
some of **ba`zi az** بعضی از
someone **kasi** کسی
something **cizi** چیزی
sometimes
ba`zi vaqthā بعضی وقت‌ها
son **pesar** پسر
soon **zud** زود
sorry! **bebaxšid** ببخشید
Spanish **espānioli;** اسپانیولی؛
espāniāyi اسپانیایی
sport **varzeš** ورزش
spring **bahār** بهار
stamp (post) **tambr** تمبر
station **istgāh** ایستگاه
street **xiābān** خیابان
col **xiābun** خیابون
subject **mouzu`** موضوع
suddenly **nāgahān** ناگهان
col **ye(k) daf(`)e** یک دفعه
summer **tābestān** تابستان
col **tābestun** تابستون
Sunday **yekšanbe** یک‌شنبه

Sunday best
behtarin lebās بهترین لباس
supermarket
supermārket سوپرمارکت
swimming **šenā** شنا
table **miz** میز
tablet **qors** قرص
tall **boland** بلند
tea **cai** *col* **cāyi** چای ؛ چایی
Tehran **tehrān** تهران
col **te(h)run**
telecom centre
markaz-e telefon مرکز تلفن
telephone **telefon** تلفن
television **televizion** تلویزیون
than **az** از
thank you
mot(a)šakkeram متشکّرم
thanks **mersi; mamnun** مرسی ؛ ممنون
that *con* **ke** که
that *dem* **ān** *col* **un** آن ؛ اون
their car **māšinešān** ماشینشان
col **māšinešun** ماشینشون
then (afterwards) **ba`d** بعد
then (if that's the case) **pas** پس
there **ānjā** *col* **unjā** آنجا ؛ اونجا
there is/are **hast** هست
they **ānhā** آنها
col **un(h)ā** اونها
third **sevvom;** سوّم ؛
sevvomin (before a noun) سوّمین
this **in** این
this way (i.e. follow me) **az in taraf** از این طرف
Thursday **panjšanbe** پنجشنبه
time **vaqt** وقت
time(s) **bār/daf`e** بار / دفعه
tired **xaste** خسته
to **be** به
to arrive **residan** رسیدن

to ask **xāheš kardan** خواهش کردن
to ask (a question)
porsidan پرسیدن
to be **budan** بودن
to be able **tavānestan** توانستن
col **tunestan** تونستن
to be born
be donyā āmadan به دنیا آمدن
to be closed
baste šodan بسته شدن
to be cooked
poxte šodan پخته شدن
to be eaten
xorde šodan خورده شدن
to be heard
šenide šodan شنیده شدن
to be killed
košte šodan کشته شدن
to be said **gofte šodan** گفته شدن
to be seen **dide šodan** دیده شدن
to be signed
emzā(`) šodan امضا(ء) شدن
to be told **gofte šodan** گفته شدن
to book
rezerv kardan رزرو کردن
to bother
zahmat dādan زحمت دادن
to breathe
nafas kešidan نفس کشیدن
to bring **āvardan** آوردن
col **āvordan**
to build **sāxtan (sāz)** ساختن (ساز)
to buy **xaridan** خریدن
to call **sedā kardan** صدا کردن
to close **bastan** بستن
to collapse
qaš kardan غش کردن
to come **āmadan** آمدن
col **umadan** اومدن
to come to see . . .
be didan-e . . . āmadan به دیدن . . . آمدن

to congratulate *SO* on *ST* **ST rā be SO tabrik goftan** ST را به SO تبریک گفتن
to cough **sorfe kardan** سرفه کردن
to do **anjām dādan; kardan** انجام دادن؛ کردن
to drink **nušidan (nuš)** نوشیدن (نوش‍)
col **xordan** خوردن
to drive **rāndan** راندن
col **rundan** روندن
to eat **xordan** خوردن
to explain **touzih dādan** توضیح دادن
to feel like doing . . . **hāl-e . . . rā dāštan** حال . . . را داشتن
to get blocked (e.g. a pipe) **gereftan** گرفتن
to get (to become) **šodan** شدن
to get (to obtain) **gereftan** گرفتن
to get well/better **xub/behtar šodan** خوب / بهتر شدن
to give **dādan** دادن
to go **raftan** رفتن
to go to see . . . **be didan-e . . . raftan** به دیدن . . . رفتن
to happen **ettefāq oftādan** اتّفاق افتادن
to have **dāštan** داشتن
to hear **šenidan** شنیدن
to help **komak kardan** کمک کردن
to include . . . **šāmel-e . . . šodan** شامل . . . شدن
to interrupt **qat\` kardan** قطع کردن
to invite **da\`vat kardan** دعوت کردن
to know **dānestan** دانستن
col **dunestan** دونستن
to learn **yād gereftan; xāndan** یاد گرفتن؛ خواندن
to leave **tark kardan** ترک کردن
to let/allow **ejāze dādan; gozāštan** اجازه دادن؛ گذاشتن
to lie (down) **derāz kešidan** دراز کشیدن
to like **dust dāštan** دوست داشتن
to listen **guš kardan/ dādan** گوش کردن / دادن
to live **zendegi kardan** زندگی کردن
to look **negāh kardan** نگاه کردن
to look for . . . **donbāl-e . . . gaštan** دنبال . . . گشتن
to lose (*op* to find) **gom kardan** گم کردن
to make (to fix) **dorost kardan** درست کردن
to meet **molāqāt kardan** ملاقات کردن
to meet *SO* (for the first time) **bā *SO* āš(e)nā šodan** با SO آشنا شدن
to miss (a train) **az dast dādan** از دست دادن
to need *SO* **bā *SO* kār dāštan** با SO کار داشتن
to need *ST* ***ST* lāzem dāštan** ST لازم داشتن
to open **bāz kardan** باز کردن
to park **pārk kardan** پارک کردن
to pass **dādan** دادن
to phone . . . **be . . . telefon kardan** به . . . تلفن کردن
to pick up **bar dāštan** برداشتن
to play (game) **bāzi kardan** بازی کردن

to play the piano
piāno zadan پیانو زدن
to read **xāndan** خواندن
col **xundan** خوندن
to recognise **šenāxtan** شناختن
(šenās) (شناس)
to remember X
yād-e X kardan یاد X کردن
to rent **ejāre kardan** اجاره کردن
to return **bar gaštan** برگشتن
to say **goftan** گفتن
to see **didan** دیدن
to sell **foruxtan** فروختن
to send **ferestādan** فرستادن
to shave (beard) **(riš)** (ریش)
tarāšidan تراشیدن
to sit down **nešastan** نشستن
to sleep **xābidan** خوابیدن
to smoke (cigarette) (سیگار)
(sigār) kešidan کشیدن
to sneeze **atse kardan** عطسه کردن
to speak
sohbat kardan صحبت کردن
to speak up
bolandtar sohbat kardan بلندتر صحبت کردن
to stand (up) **istādan** ایستادن
to stay **māndan** ماندن
col **mundan** موندن
to take (*SO/ST* to a place) **bordan** بردن
to take (medicine)
xordan خوردن
to take (photocopies)
gereftan گرفتن
to take (pick up)
bar dāštan برداشتن
to telephone (see 'to phone')
to tell **goftan** گفتن
to think **fekr kardan** فکر کردن
to translate
tarjome kardan ترجمه کردن
to travel **safar kardan** سفر کردن
to turn off
xāmuš kardan خاموش کردن
to turn on
roušan kardan روشن کردن
to visit Iran **az irān** از ایران
didan kardan دیدن کردن
to wake up
bidār šodan بیدار شدن
to walk **piāde raftan;** پیاده رفتن؛
qadam zadan قدم زدن
to want **xāstan** خواستن
to watch
tamāšā kardan تماشا کردن
to wear (put on)
pušidan پوشیدن
to work **kār kardan** کار کردن
to write **neveštan** نوشتن
today **emruz** امروز
together **bā ham** با هم
toilet **tuālet** توالت
tomato **gouje farangi** گوجه فرنگی
tomorrow **fardā** فردا
tonight **emšab** امشب
too **ham** هم
toothache
dandān-dard دندان‌درد
col **dandun-dard** دندون‌درد
toothpaste
xamir-dandān خمیردندان
col **xamir-dandun** خمیردندون
train **qatār** قطار
Tuesday **sešanbe** سه‌شنبه
tuman **tumān** تومان
col **toman** تومن
twenty first
bist o yekom; بیست و یکم
bist o yekomin بیست و یکمین
(before a noun)
uncle (maternal) **dāyi** دایی
uncle (paternal) **amu** عمو

under **zir-e** زیر
university **dānešgāh** دانشگاه
upset **nārāhat** ناراحت
very **xeili** خیلی
very much **xeili ziād** خیلی زیاد
waiting for
montazer-e منتظر
walking **piāde-ravi** پیاده‌روی
watch *n* **sā`at** ساعت
water **āb** آب
watermelon
hendevāne هندوانه
col **hendune** هندونه
way **rāh** راه
we **mā** ما
weather **havā** هوا
wedding **ezdevāj; arusi** ازدواج؛ عروسی
Wednesday
c(ah)āršanbe چهارشنبه
week **hafte** هفته
weekend **āxar-e hafte** آخر هفته
well **xub** خوب
what **ce** چه
col **ci** چی
what a surprise!
ce ajab چه عجب
what's **cie** چیه
when *con* **vaqti (ke)** وقتی (که)
when (question word)
kei کی
where **kojā** کجا
which (conjunction) **ke** که
which (question word)
kodām کدام
col **kodum** کدوم
which of **kodāmyek az,** کدامیک از
col **kodumyeki az** کدومیکی از
who **ki** کی
who's speaking
jenāb(e`)āli جنابعالی
whose car **māšin-e ki** ماشین کی
why **cerā** چرا
wife **xānom** خانم
col **xānum**
window **panjare** پنجره
col **panjere**
winter **zemestān** زمستان
col **zemestun** زمستون
with **bā** با
word **kaleme** کلمه
col **kalame**
work **kār** کار
working **kār kardan** کار کردن
world **donyā** دنیا
worth **bā arzeš** با ارزش
wow! **bah bah** به به
writing **neveštan** نوشتن
year **sāl** سال
yes **bale** بله
yesterday **diruz** دیروز
you *f* **šomā** شما
you *inf* **to** تو
young **javān** جوان
col **javun; kucek** جوون؛ کوچک
younger **javāntar;** جوانتر؛
kucektar کوچکتر
youngest **javāntarin;** جوانترین؛
kucektarin کوچکترین
yours **māl-e šomā** مال شما
yourself **xodetān** خودتان
col **xodetun** خودتون
zero **sefr** صفر

Index